WINDOWS ON INTERESTING TIMES

MICHAEL JANSEN

RIMAL BOOKS

First published in 2018
Rimal Books,
Cyprus
www.rimalbooks.com

ISBN 978-9963-715-20-6

Cover artwork by Nabil Anani
Cover design by Ali Shawwa

For Godfrey and Marya,

my fellow travellers,

and the people met on this long journey

CREDITS

Descriptive entries *in* the book are adapted from my dispatches published in *The Irish Times* which sent me on many news-worthy missions. Some of the other reportage is based on articles in *Middle East International* and columns in *The Deccan Herald* (Bengaluru), *The Gulf Today* (Sharjah) and *The Jordan Times* (Amman). My description of the Hajj, the Muslim pilgrimage, is condensed from, my lengthy article carried by *Aramco World* inNovember 1974.

I kept this book under wraps while writing but, once an early draft was completed, Xanthi Kollitsis read the text and encouraged me to persevere. Stalwart old friend Liza Seymour slaved with me, chapter by chapter, with restructuring and revisions. My past publisher Roger van Zwanenberg, appointed himself my agent and worked out ways to promote the book. Lamia Gailani Werr, correctly called the book a "story of stories." Charles Glass, toted a bulky printout around till he had time to read it and provided a helpful assessment. Janice Terry went through the revised text and made useful comments. My present publisher Nora Shawwa, chased away my doubts about trying to tackle the last turbulent 50 years in the Middle East in an experimental, impressionist form. Fadia and Ali Shawwa worked diligently to turn a computer scriptinto a book.

CONTENTS

PREFACTORY NOTE

This book is not a history of the past half-century of the Middle East, not a memoire, not an autobiography. *Windows on Interesting Times* is just what the title says: windows. Windows meant to illuminate the times. Windows opened by journalism. Windows with datelines providing whereabouts for eyewitness accounts of seminal or dramatic events.

The book is not a chronological account of people and events but an impressionist literary experiment, as one reader suggested, or "a story of stories," as another proposed. Stories gliding along streams of thought rather than daily entries in a journal or systematic press coverage. Stories of people and happenings in my region over the past half-century.

When a stream of thought starts to flow, it finds its own course among impressions and recollections, it zig-zags, goes backward and forward, up and down, gathering force until the mind forms pictures of people, events and happenings, relevant or irrelevant. When the stream roils over the rocks of reality, preconceived images are shattered, evocative sounds are overborne by the rumble of thunder, and familiar smells are spirited away by winds. This book is meant to be a fresh look at the events of the past 50 years.

My windows are solid objects with shutters, frames and glass as well as electronic computer windows utilising the ether of the internet to conjure up information, ideas, and impressions. Chapter headings – liberation, incarceration, and sanctuary – matter.

Since I am the teller of the stories, my background and baggage shape what I have seen and heard and influence my judgement and vision. Consequently, I have tried to merge a few formative aspects of my personal story with the stories I report. No journalist is detached or neutral.

We all are subjective in our own distinct ways. Therefore, it is imperative to make a statement of interest before beginning the story of stories.

The book's title was inspired by the Chinese curse, "May you live in interesting times."

The flags are very noisy today.

They were woken up very early in the morning and they're nervous,

they were roused up hurry-scurry from their basement

and they're nervous

Otherwise I don't believe they fail to approve of the celebration.

Freedom is fine, freedom is first,

But sometimes it has a slavery for you,

it has a slavery for you!

Costas Montis
Anthology of Cypriot Poetry by Costas Montis and Andreas Christophides
Translated from the Greek by Amy Mims. Nicosia, 1974

Al-Mutanabbi, the great 10th century Arab poet, summed up the current Arab situation in a few lines:

They entered Time

Still at prime,

And were well pleased,

We find Time

Foully diseased

Muhammad's People, Eric Schroider, collected and translated: Portland, Maine

1

LIBERATION

Cairo, January 28th, 2011

Horses harnessed to gharries stomp nervously beneath the October 6th bridge flyover. Drivers are in a clutch, smoking. The roar from Tahrir Square rises and falls punctuated by the metallic report of weapons. Above our heads voices of watchers assembled on the terrace of the Ramses Hilton. Conor and I hurry into the lobby and hurtle up the stairs to take up positions behind dusty, prickly bushes planted in troughs along the terrace wall. To the left, a tight phalanx of protesters marches toward Abdel Moneim Riyad Square at the entrance to Tahrir. Black helmeted, black clad and body armoured riot police fire clouds of tear gas, birdshot, beating back rank after rank. Wedges of demonstrators thrust forward in relays and are repulsed.

To the right, men, women and children are trapped on October 6th bridge and, further down the river, they are caught on Qasr al-Nil bridge that opens onto Tahrir. Men on October 6th form lines to perform the *asr* (afternoon) prayer, bowing and standing, devout, peaceful, in the afternoon's golden light. A pause in the battle for Tahrir. The ancient Nile, its gun-metal grey surface ruffled by a gentle breeze.

On the western bank, police mow down the throng on October 6th with powerful jets of water from cannon-mounted armoured vehicles.

Lines of marchers emerge from the eastern riverside corniche as well as the streets behind the hotel. Disciplined. Solid ranks. Unarmed. Determined to reach Tahrir despite gas, rubber bullets and deadly birdshot. Thousands upon thousands of Egyptians. In the stare of my mind's eye their advance winds down to slow motion, the scene is enveloped in silence. The sky veiled by clouds of gas and smoke. I see only the colossal clash of two titan teams. Locked in a deadly game, protesters in faded motley, police in black, buttons and shoulder stars gleam silver. A roar from Tahrir breaks through the deafness of my concentration.

My nasal passages, eyes and skin burn from scentless, colourless gas, driving me into the lounge. Conor is the last to retreat. The lobby doors are locked. The security man says we can leave once the situation calms. We wait. Eyes tearing, skin tingling. Impatient. Blind to what is happening. Outside at last. The thrust of the protesters and parry of the police is suspended for a moment. The horses have fled with their open carriages and the street is empty. Conor and I flag down a lone rattletrap black and white taxi. I get in. He stays on; I have to file a story. "*Al funduk Marriott, minfudlak.*" ("To the Marriott hotel, please.") Five minutes later we cross the Nile on Boulaq bridge. The driver charges the fare registered on the meter.

Cairo, July 21st, 1961

I boarded the train for Cairo at Rafah in the Gaza Strip before dawn. At el-Arish, three Egyptian army officers a bit older than I entered the carriage. They introduced themselves, but their names are long forgotten. One spoke good English, the other two smiled stiffly. It was a long, hot haul along the Sinai coast. Fine grit entered through the loosely-framed windows and settled on my arms, in my cropped hair. The officers treated me to bright pink sparkling drinks and cheese sandwiches with sharp vinegar crinkle-cut carrot and cucumber pickles that set my teeth on edge. We crossed into Egypt "proper" at Qantara and turned south to Ismailiya, passing through verdant farmland, rushing towns and villages, until we reached Cairo's Ramses station. Beside the cream building with its blue mosaic decorative trim stood a gigantic granite Ramses, stiff arms at his sides, on his head the double crown of Upper and Lower Egypt. The youngest, shy, silent officer was ordered by the English-speaker to see me safely to my hotel.

Hassan, a Palestinian friend in Beirut, had booked me into a small pension run by countrymen in the area dubbed "Downtown." I had a clean room with a bed and basin, a narrow green-shuttered window. The toilets and showers were separate, to my dismay. But affordable at one Egyptian pound a night. Hassan, who was also visiting Cairo, called and carried me off to the Gezira club, the former playground of British colonial masters taken over by Egypt's independence elite. We sat in stands and watched competitive clay pigeon shooting. As the traps released their pottery disks with a clack and hiss, Hassan and his friends expressed outrage over the latest nationalisations declared by the government of president Gamal Abdel Nasser. At the end of the sward of dusty, faded grass just out of range of the guns, an elderly Egyptian in shabby *dishdasha* and turban collected yellow shards in a basket.

At Giza as dark descended we listened to the hollow booming recorded voice narrating Egyptian history while beams of light played on the stepped sides of the pyramids and illuminated the Sphinx, its nose said to have been shot off by a cannonball fired by Napoleon's soldiers at the end of the 18th century although earlier travellers had drawn the face without his nose.

Bay City, 1946

I climbed on a chair to reach a child's reader on the third shelf in the bookcase and hurried to my room where I sat on the floor and opened the stiff green cover. On page after page there were a few disappointing illustrations in black and grey interspersed with words lined up in sentences corralled into daunting paragraphs. I worked out a word, letter by letter, then another. Recognised phrases and grasped entire sentences. My understanding seized upon paragraphs and climaxed with an entire story.

A story about St. Louis, a crusading king of France who landed his troops at Damietta on the Egyptian coast in 1249 and force-marched his soldiers towards Cairo until they joined battle in the Nile Delta with Egyptian troops. St. Louis' army was defeated. He was captured and ransomed but died in Tunis twenty years later at the outset of yet another crusade.

After my triumph with St. Louis, I sulked when presented with *Dick and Jane* at school and grew restive in class.

Cairo, January 29th, 2011

The city comes to life slowly, wearied by three days of mass protests in Tahrir Square.

The few shops and cafes are late opening in the mainly residential district of Zamalek on the northern end of Gezira Island at the centre of the sluggish Nile. A small boy holds out a bunch of fresh mint as Conor and I walk towards October 6th bridge. Armed police block vehicular traffic but ignore the few pedestrians seeking to cross. Tahrir is empty, dozing in the warm rays of the sun, awaiting the uprising's "Day of Wrath" to come.

We stride through the square, heading north-east through nearly deserted streets, past mosques and shuttered shops. The faithful had attended the midday service and departed. A pretty, young woman hails us in fluent English from the open window of a battered blue car. "You know, you shouldn't be out in the streets. There is trouble today. Where are you going?"

"Zamalek," Conor replies. "Get in, I'll give you a ride. I'm going to Zamalek as well."

When she drops us off, I ask her where she is headed. "Tahrir Square," the battleground between the people and regime. "I'm meeting four friends and we'll join the protests. There were more of us, but we couldn't work out where to meet since mobile phones and the internet are down."

"Why are you protesting?" I ask, angling for a quote. "I've lived my whole life under Mubarak," she explains. Egypt's president for 30 years. As she drives off, Conor says, "Did you notice, her eyeshadow matches her shirt?"

We recross the Nile on Boulaq bridge and walk along the corniche toward Tahrir. Tanks are drawn up in front of the pot-bellied beige building housing Egyptian television, riot police have formed a cordon to prevent protesters from mounting an attempt to take control: Hosni Mubarak is still in charge. Regimes rise and fall over control of television and radio stations.

In the alley next to the building, plain clothes security men carrying wooden staves leer at passers-by. A youth breaks from their custody, runs across the street, and plunges down the riverbank but is caught by a fleet footed policeman and dragged back into the alley. We walk on, drawn by a roar from Tahrir.

Cairo, November 25th, 2010

The City of the Dead was still asleep. Unpaved Imam al-Assi Street deserted. The doors and gates of the house tombs and grand mausoleums were firmly closed. Some doors were padlocked, others bricked up. Marble plaques affixed to the wall gave the names and dates of the deceased who inhabit the tombs; squatters, sometimes family members claiming to be caretakers, do not identify themselves. An empty bus careened by. A woman in a blue caftan appeared at the door of a house flanked by two stunted trees. A widow from Upper Egypt, Raya, one of, perhaps, half a million squatters, had lived here for 30 years. Further down the street, an elderly man sat reading the Quran at the gate of a tomb house where his son's body lay. Men were at work, children at school, and women busy with their chores within the walls of these small compounds. Only the dead were granted repose.

Wooden frames for armchairs stacked outside a workshop, a satellite dish perched on the room of a mausoleum, laundry drying in an alcove, and chicken scratching in an alleyway were proofs of life in this vast cemetery, dating to the Muslim conquest of Egypt in 642 AD. At the end of the street, limp vegetables and bruised fruit were displayed in plastic bins at fly-blown shops. The living denizens of the City of the Dead could not afford fresh produce or the rent of flats in the poor quarters of greater Cairo.

Between elections, politicians forgot about the trials and tribulations of the families dwelling here but were eager to court voters once campaigning began. The square was bedecked with posters and banners advertising candidates standing in the parliamentary election.

At a table on the side of the road sat two men eager for a chat. They introduced themselves as Sayyed Muhammad Abdel 'Al and his uncle Hag Subhi Abdel 'Al. As the waiter set out small glasses of sugary tea before us, Sayyed said they were the "guardians of the quarter." They turned out to be "guardians" serving Mubarak's ruling National Democratic Party (NDP). While the Hag bubbled smoke through his water pipe, Sayyed said, "Voters won't be paid by candidates. The Watani [NDP] is strong here. We are for president

Hosni Mubarak. We love Hosni Mubarak." What about Gamal, his son and reputed successor? I asked. "No," the men replied in unison. "Only Hosni Mubarak!"

But backing Mubarak did not mean they supported the government and ruling party uncritically. The issue stirring people was "privatisation," notably the sale of the government hospital to a private concern. "The people here don't have money for treatment," Sayyed complained. "They also sold Imam Shafei girls' school. People are very angry." Sayyed issued an invitation to return in the evening to attend election rallies.

At dusk, the City of the Dead had come to life. Cafes were packed with men. Repairmen tinkered with car engines and motorbikes on the roadside. People strolled in the streets, comfortable in the company of ghosts of their forebearers. Sayyed and the Hag waited at the cafe where we had met in the morning. In their beat-up old car, we charged into the night in search of the campaign convoy of Nasser Shurbagi, an independent seeking one of the elected assembly seats. We tracked him down in the jammed streets and bright lights of the vibrant quarter lying beneath the massive walls of the Citadel, fortified in the 12th century by Salah ed-Din, the sultan of Egypt who defeated the Crusaders at the Battle of Hittin in Palestine on July 4th, 1187.

"Nasser Shurbagi for people's assembly, Nasser Shurbaggi," proclaimed an amplifier mounted on the back of a lorry. Drummers on the lorry struck their instruments between announcements. A smiling man with a gleaming bald pate surrounded by a fringe of dark hair, Shurbaggi paused his convoy to shake hands with a knot of potential voters. He pledged to repair roads, ensure the living are not evicted from the City of the Dead, and return the hospital to the public sector. As he sped away in his battered orange car, a youth snapped, "Bullshit!"

Most of the living in the City of the Dead had not registered and were wary of police stations where voting cards were issued. The dead were expected to cast proxy ballots that boosted the margin of the NDP.

Low turnout, clashes, and allegations of vote rigging and ballot stuffing characterised polling day. Candidates, party monitors, and voters were denied entry to voting stations in constituencies where the opposition had done well in the 2005 assembly election. Around 5,200 candidates stood for the 508 elected seats, 1,100 fielded by parties, 780 of them by the NDP. The majority of the 4,100 independents were also from the NDP. The party was determined to secure a solid majority ahead of the 2011 presidential poll. Mubarak was the sole candidate. Of the 40 million Egyptians eligible to vote, only 10 percent were said to have cast ballots in the assembly election. This was the last under Mubarak.

Cairo, July 1961

A servant in caftan and cap opened the door of the grand villa on Mohamed Mazhar, a street of splendid Italianate mansions built in Zamalek by political figures and merchants who made fortunes during the British protectorate. I was led through spacious high-ceilinged rooms shuttered against the afternoon heat and glare, the furniture robed in dust sheets as if the owner had gone on a long holiday.

Sitt Leila Doss received me on the veranda overlooking the choppy brown Nile. Tea was served, my delicate porcelain cup and saucer consigned to an untrustworthy spindly-legged table. Constantine had given me her phone number and said she could brief me about the advances women were making in this deeply conservative country. She spoke of her work providing care for tubercular children and described how society had changed since the 1920s and 30s when she grew up.

"The *niqab* and veil are disappearing, women are playing a more active role. But educated, privileged women only."

She dispatched me to a village in the countryside to see how the government was reaching out to the *fellaheen*, providing them with seed and advice to increase yields. At the junction of four irrigation channels stood a whitewashed walled compound surrounded by eucalyptus trees. A combined centre, the earthen floor of the courtyard scored by a broom's stiff straws, housed an agricultural extension office, school and tidy clinic where a nurse was weighing babies and prescribing for peasant children.

I flew back to Gaza in the cockpit of a white UN Hercules piloted by two cheerful Canadians.

Below us unfolded the majestic Nile, its tentacles fanning out in the Delta, plots of farmland defined by irrigation canals, villages shadowed by cloud, beige silt staining the edge of the cobalt Mediterranean, the estuaries along the coast of Sinai, the desert, el-Arish and, finally, Rafah, divided between Egypt and Gaza.

Cairo, overnight, January 28th, 2011

Police withdraw from the streets, leaving Egyptians prey to thugs and criminals released from prisons by Mubarak loyalists eager to punish the people for deserting him.

Isolde, Tom, Conor and I wait impatiently in front of the television set in the family room of the Irish residence for Mubarak to deliver an address to the nation. Congo squeezes past our knees, wagging his substantial rump and tail, threatening to sweep our wine glasses from the low table. Mubarak appears just after midnight, dismisses the cabinet and appoints intelligence chief Omar Suleiman vice-president. Oblivious to the blaze engulfing the headquarters of the ruling National Democratic Party, Mubarak does not resign.

Conor leashes Congo and walks me back to the Marriott along July 26th avenue, ignoring the curfew. I enter the hotel compound through the back gate, cross the parking lot. The hotel's automatic door opens-sesame and I flop my bag onto the conveyor belt of the scanner, collect the bag, nod to the men on duty. I pass Roy's Country Kitchen and the Casino, hurry to the Gezira tower through the garden, past empty tables and chairs outside the palace where chic Cairo lunches and takes tea.

Cairo, July 2013

Leila, "Lili" Doss had moved from her elegant Nile side mansion, sold long ago, to an eighth-floor flat in a dull brown building among heavily guarded embassies in Garden City next to Tahrir. From where she had descended four times in her wheelchair to take part in the uprising, becoming Egypt's oldest revolutionary. "People are so happy to see me. They kiss my hand and bring their kids to take photos with me... we had to get rid of Mubarak and his group because they went beyond belief in making money. People grew poorer and poorer. The nation told the government to resign. It was amazing."

Born in 1916, Lili's life spanned three Egyptian revolutions: 1919 against the British, 1952 against the king, and 2011-13 against autocracy. Her revolutionary career began early. She revolted against her conservative father, Coptic Christian monarchy-era minister Tewfik Pasha Doss who laid the cornerstone of the Qasr al-Nil bridge, a main gateway to Tahrir. At five Lili donned her brother's trousers, so she could climb trees in the mansion's garden. As an eligible young woman, she refused marriage, even to the Ethiopian crown prince. Her father, who did not believe girls should go to university, told her to take up charity work. Lili became a founder of

Tahseen al-Seha, established in 1936 to provide medical treatment for poor children.

Lili repeatedly challenged successive regimes. During president Gamal Abdel Nasser's time she was banned from travelling abroad. His successor, Anwar Sadat awarded her a medal for 25 years service; she sold it and gave the proceeds to the children's hospital near the pyramids. Lili fought Mubarak's wife, Suzanne, who wanted to turn the hospital into a museum. "Over my dead body," Lili said. "At 65, I retired, made my GCE, and got my BA and MA" at the American University in Cairo. By that time, her father was not around to disapprove.

Cairo, Early 1965

We crossed Boulaq bridge and turned into the drive of the Omar Khayyam hotel in the early evening as the stars were just beginning to spark in the darkening sky. Up the wide palace stair to reception where we checked in and received a key to our chalet. The clerk smiled. "Welcome to Egypt."

Ma remarked, "look, there are so many carpets that they overlap." Baluch prayer rugs, Anatolian and Persian carpets, the edge of one upon the other formed ridges with tangled fringe.

We followed the porter along the hall, down the back steps and into the garden. Our wooden chalet was chilly, the porter switched on the air conditioner to heat the simply furnished room with attached bath perfumed with kerosene poured down the toilet to disinfect and deodorise.

After dinner in a gracious but cold garden-level room in the palace, we went to the bar and ordered apricot brandies to warm ourselves. Ma's flecked hazel eyes shone with wonder in the soft light. The bar was constructed of highly polished wood inlaid with patterns in mother-of-pearl and woods of different types and colours. The walls were cloaked in a dull, dark green silk. Ma was wearing a sleeveless green suede dress over a cream long-sleeved silk shirt, a warm shawl wrapped round her shoulders. Her hair twisted on top of her head. Wide, ribbed silver bracelets heavy on her wrists.

The next morning, we took a taxi to the pyramids, Ma in high brown boots, wrapped in a red and grey checked coat, headscarfed against the wind. Fortunately, I was in jacket and trousers.

Once we had arrived at the plateau of Giza, she decided I should climb Khufu's Great Pyramid, locked hand-to-wrist to a tall guide in *galabiya* and woollen scarf wrapped round his head.

The stone blocks formed thigh-high steps, some crumbling, others uneven. My guide, in rubber flip-flops, knew the route well and placed his feet precisely on the blocks. "Follow me, follow me," he urged in English as he hauled me up the face of the pyramid. "Hold on, hold on." He did not pause a moment but dragged me, block-by-block to the top, where we stopped to peer at Ma, small and alone on the desert, and inspect initials carved by predecessors on the flat surface of the summit, before we hurried down, block-by-block, the muscles in my calves shivering, my ankles buckling. "Seven and a half minutes," stated Ma when we joined her. The guide, who claimed his best time was four minutes, was quite pleased with a twenty-dollar tip.

Cairo, January 29th-February 11th, 2011

Lines of departing tourists form at the reception desks in the Marriott-Omar Khayyam hotel, luggage is piled high on trolleys next to the information desk. Special flights organised by national carriers are ferrying them out of Egypt. Banks and ATMs are shut down but credit cards still work at check out.

The sky is overcast, the air soft and humid. On the eastern bank of the Nile, the gutted multi-storey building that housed Mubarak's National Democratic Party continues to smoulder.

On an attached billboard the smiling faces of two young Egyptians are untouched by the blaze and thick black smoke.

After a taxi-borne hunt for the *AFP* office, I transmit two articles using the agency's satellite, aware that I must find an alternative to both this connection and Isolde's diplomatic internet link, excluded from the communications blockade. The solution is simple: my colleagues and I print and fax our copy from the Marriott, forcing our email-dependent newspapers to unearth obsolete machines until mobile phones and the internet are reactivated.

Thousands of Egyptians of all classes and ages converge on Qasr al-Nil bridge, walking under the gaze of the statue of Khedive Ismail Pasha, the 19th century ruler who built the modern city centre. They walk between the pairs of massive bronze lions sitting on pedestals flanking the bridge at either end. Egyptians carry flags, banners and placards bearing one word, "*Erhal*," "Leave." They glance round for black clad riot police and *baltagiya*, plain-clothes thugs. Egyptians freely walk to Tahrir. Walk between the guardian lions, boys sitting at their feet. At the makeshift barricade slung across the entrance to the square, men and women pause separately at checkpoints for bag searches by polite volunteers. Fathers with small children on their shoulders, women in headscarves and bare heads mingle with youths in t-shirts chanting, "*Al-sh'ab yurid isqat al-nizam.*" "The People want the fall of the regime."

"*Thawra, thawra*!" "Revolution, revolution!" responds the throng. "We will leave this square when Mubarak leaves Egypt," asserts Ahmad, a lad in a knitted cap. Young men gather round to put across their points of view. Ahmad commands, "Write, write what we say, tell the world that we want democracy and freedom. No more corruption. No more Mubarak."

Karin, a German colleague, arrives from Damascus and joins me in the 20-minute walk from the hotel to Tahrir. We become students in running seminars we dub "Revolution 101," surrounded by professor protesters urging us to report their views. A Nubian taxi driver who needs money for this wife's diabetes medication and son's education. A Tahrir-soiled man who claims Mubarak has stolen $70 billion. When asked where he has learned this, the man replies, "*The Guardian*," although he speaks no English. University students who spend nights and days in Tahrir to maintain the popular occupation; but go home to shower and shave every morning.

Helicopters fly overhead, a tank slaloms through Tahrir, cheered by protesters as they part to make way for the creaking behemoth. The people of Tahrir, Tahriris, believe the army – which has stayed out of the fray – is on their side against Mubarak, his security men, and *baltagiya*. A thin youngster in a red shirt proffers a casing from a live round, a man holds out a handful of shotgun shells. "You see, this one is from *Amreeka*," he cries, holding up the green shell to display its brass butt: "USA."

Men sporting Salafi beards without moustaches and beards in the Muslim Brotherhood fashion; *niqabis* and *hijabis*, curly-haired women in jeans and jumpers, young, old and middle-aged, everyone and anyone is here. Here in Tahrir, liberation time.

The smash against the sky of jet fighters drowns out Tahrir's voices as hundreds of senior judges protest the withdrawal of the police and call for investigations into shootings of unarmed demonstrators. Ghada Shahbender of the Egyptian Organisation for Human Rights says the death toll is 100 in Cairo, 30 in Alexandria and 60 in Suez.

The four o'clock curfew is ignored. People are on the streets at all hours of the day and night. Neighbourhood watch volunteers armed with staves and walking sticks deploy along July 26th to fend off crooks and *baltagiya*. A man in a brown leather jacket accompanied by a large Alsatian offers to escort me to the residence. Conor, who has joined the watch, boasts, "We've got Molotov cocktails as well as broomsticks."

The army rings Tahrir with armoured troop carriers, scout cars, and main battle tanks painted in the beige camouflage of the desert and out of sync with the urban landscape. Cuts access with coils of razor wire. Soldiers become gatekeepers to the square, examining identity cards without recording names.

Kites in the colours of the Egyptian flag dip and soar over Qasr al-Nil. Vendors sell flags, green, black and red Mad Hatter toppers, and t-shirts. Youths offer to paint cheeks with tiny Egyptian flags. You'd think Egyptians had been preparing for a revolution for months and years instead of having an uprising sprung upon them. Organiser Sherif says when the Facebook call went out for demonstrations on the 25th, "We expected 50 at one place, 150 here." Fifty thousand came.

Boys wheel bicycles, handlebars hung with plastic sacks filled with takeaway cartons of foul and spaghetti to feed the throng. Others carry bags of round loaves and hand out bottled water. Portraits of martyrs are mounted on makeshift stands at the eastern end of the square. Activists display drawings of Tahrir and, kneeling on the ground on sheets of card, make posters calling for Mubarak's ouster. Queues near Hardee's fast food form at the main stage where volunteers man the audio system which blasts impromptu speeches throughout the day. Egyptians are free to have their say.

Restaurants and shops on the square are closed, some shuttered, others not. None have been breached, not a window is cracked. At a field hospital in a tent on the traffic circle, a graphic designer calling himself Horus after the ancient Egyptian god, remarks, "This is the first time in 30 years we are proud to be Egyptians. We had become numb, we are surprised to take things into our own hands."

As we walk toward Qasr al-Nil, a young man in a blue jersey calls out to Karin and me, "Thank you for coming," as if we had been attending a tea party rather than a revolution.

Organisers call for a "million-man march" from Tahrir to the presidential palace at Heliopolis but the way is blocked by the army. Mubarak appears again on television, this time at eleven at night, to announce he will not run again for the presidency. Tahrir hisses and boos in disbelief.

Mubarak's supporters gather on the corniche in front of the television building. One man carries a bouquet of flags on sticks and hands them out to all comers: impressed civil servants and workers from factories belonging to loyalists, unshaven hard men from internal security and policemen out of uniform. Karin and I hasten to reach the safety of Tahrir.

The army loosens its grip on Tahrir to allow camels and horses to be ridden into the square by Mubarak's men wielding whips and clubs. They are driven back by protesters bearing shields of corrugated plastic and armed with paving stones torn from the street. The clash is dubbed, "The Battle of the Camel," after a landmark engagement in Islamic history. The next morning, there are neat piles of rough paving stones set out at strategic locations around the square. Sentries beat a tattoo on hollow lamp posts whenever regime thugs approach. Men arm themselves with lengths of blue aluminium piping from the construction site in front of the museum. Protesters angry that troops and tanks did not halt the invaders no longer chant, "The people and the army one hand."

All the approaches to Tahrir are dangerous except Qasr al-Nil. Plain-clothes security men, *baltagiya* and agents provocateurs lurk on Talaat Harb and Muhammad Mahmoud streets, wait for activists and journalists. A French television crew is abducted and held at a police station for hours. Karin and I are stopped by two well-dressed burly types within sight of Talaat Harb Square. When they demand to search Karin's bag, she thrusts her camera to the bottom under a scarf and pulls out her tape recorder. A young Egyptian standing nearby sizes up the situation and intervenes. "Don't talk to them and come with me." He leads us to the square where we catch a battered black and white taxi and drive through the laundry-festooned sandy back alleys of Boulaq before crossing the bridge to Zamalek. Our abductor introduces himself as Hussein and gives us his email before we three alight near the Diwan bookshop.

Egyptians bound for Tahrir flow along the crooked streets and broad avenues of Zamalek to Qasr al-Nil bridge and stand cheerfully in lines stretching from one pair of lions to the other. Little boys armed with flags climb over the beasts. Gone are the piles of paving stones, staves and shields defenders used to maintain the revolution's hold on the square. In a flip-flop, soldiers in helmets and flak jackets are on hand to protect protesters from invaders. Vice-president Omar Suleiman calls for parents to tell their children to go home but their parents and grandparents are also in the square, celebrating liberation.

A man given the microphone on the main stage mourns 300 martyrs. Isolde, elegant in pant suit and silk scarf, comes to Tahrir to listen to what people have to say. Christians provide protection by surrounding ranks of Muslim men performing daily prayers. A Coptic priest preaches to a mainly Muslim congregation. We all sing *Biladi*, Egypt's national anthem. Mira a student holds up a placard bearing the mock-up of an identity card: "Name: Citizen; Religion: Egyptian; Place of Birth: Tahrir Square; Occupation: Revolutionary."

Soldiers manning the barricades at Tahrir's entrance tell Karin and me we need Egyptian press cards to enter the square. A call to the press office gains us entry. Just inside Tahrir are two lines of men holding drums and tambourines. "Wait, wait," cries the conductor. "Out, out, Omar," they chant as they beat the drums and shake the tambourines while we pass. General Hassan al-Roueini, commander of the Cairo garrison, enters the square surrounded by armed soldiers and climbs onto the stage. "All your demands will be met today," he announces and is paraded on the shoulders of cheering youngsters.

Mubarak again appears on late television and again declares he will stay on until a presidential election is held in September. Tahrir erupts in fury. At dusk on Friday 11th, a pale, strained Suleiman, an army officer standing to one side, announces Mubarak "has decided to leave his position as president" and has appointed the military to run the country. Tahrir roars in joy, firecrackers explode, empty streets fill with cars hooting horns and flashing headlights. Egyptians dance in the streets, hug each other, cry, laugh, shout, "*Hurriyeh, hurriyeh!*" (Freedom, freedom!)

Cairo, February 12th, 2011

Egyptians are walking, walking to Tahrir. Walking across Qasr al-Nil carrying brooms and buckets, plastic bags, and tins of paint and brushes. A tow truck pulls burnt cars out of the entrance to Sadat metro station. Egyptians in surgical masks and gloves sweep up rubbish and shovel it into sacks. A well-dressed woman in knee-length leather boots, an Egyptian flag wrapped round her shoulders, wields a broom awkwardly. Grimy street children wheel barrows piled with filled bags to collection points where pick-ups carry them away. Egyptians lay flowers on plastic sheets stretched on the ground to mark where martyrs fell. Teams scrub graffiti from the statue of Abdel Moneim Riyad and the walls of buildings. Youngsters paint a sentry box outside the villa that formerly housed the foreign ministry and renew the black and white stripes on curbs. Barricades are dismantled and dragged away. Girls sweeping the street wear signs pinned to the backs of their jumpers: "Sorry for the inconvenience. We are building Egypt."

Larnaca-Ayios Dhometios, February 14th, 2011

Andreas thrust the paid parking ticket in the slot of the machine that lifts the bar to exit the airport. "My wife and I were worried about you. We watched the events in Egypt on television. When you didn't ring to tell me to come to the airport, we worried," he scolded. "I was in Egypt once. We took a ship to Alexandria and a train to Cairo. All the Egyptians we met demanded money."

He parked in front of my gate near the tall, slanting umbrella pine and lifted my wheelie out of the boot of the Mercedes. I picked up the case, slung my computer bag over my shoulder and climbed the stairs to the veranda. A note had been stuck between the *fer forgé* grille and glass of the door. "Please call." Another worrier. The entrance hall was cold, a bit damp. Pine needles from the precariously leaning tree in front of the house had blown under the door and banked against the fringe of the red and green Bedouin carpet stretched on the red tile floor. My face and shoulders were reflected in the mirror with the three-peacock wooden frame carved by a prisoner in Baakline jail but dumped in a second-hand shop in Beirut when his wife complained peacocks are unlucky. Over the door to the sitting room Maath's painting of five clown heads round a table, irreverently dubbed the "Last Supper." Over the study door a painting by a Cypriot in the manner of Van Gogh, tiny blue and gold ovals swirling in bursts. Faxes curled on the Persian kilim lying on the wood board floor, the red light of the answering machine flashed. Once the computer was switched on, I rang Mar and told her I was home, safe.

She replied in a cheerful, brisk voice. All was well with Brian and Lili. "I mentioned on Facebook that you were in Egypt and had everyone asking what you were doing. So, I posted links to your articles."

His lips pursed, hand open to emphasise a point, Godfrey peered out at me from the ceramic-framed photo on the bookshelf next to the section holding the phone and fax. He would have revelled in the Tahrir scene and captured it in words far better than I. "You did your best, leave the rest," he would have said.

I opened the doors to the side veranda to let the stale air out of the sitting room where the green and gold metal peacock stood sentinel by the smoked stone fireplace. I brought in the Christmas poinsettia and set it in the silver pot on the copper tray top of the table parked on grandma Fancher's rose, white and blue Sarouk, purchased in 1908, the year of my father's birth.

2

INCARCERATION

Bay City, 1940s

Grandma Fancher allowed only a few light pieces of furniture to sit on the Sarouk and prohibited shoes. But did not mind if I ran my model cars along the blue flower strewn roadway along the edge. The Sarouk is a well-travelled carpet. Made in Iran, purchased in Bay City, transported to Denver and back, thence to Beirut, Damascus, and finally to the 2,000-year-old Ayios Dhometios suburb-village where I live.

Grandma Fancher dwelt in a suite of rooms in her sister Minnie's handsome house with a garden. The Sarouk covered the wood floor in my grandmother's salon and three blue Chinese silk carpets were ranged round her bed next door. On her dressing table, an art deco silver-backed mirror, comb and hairbrush set depicting a woman with streaming hair. Propped up in bed in a padded jacket, she used to breakfast off a tray with legs brought in by cook. At the top right-hand side were a small flowered tea pot and matching cup and saucer. Overnight a spider-web hairnet etched a fading fine line across her forehead. Once bathed, talcum powered and dressed, she applied an electric curling iron to her wiry grey hair, kept short but not bobbed.

A small woman with deep set dark eyes, she was always elegantly attired in soft woollen dresses in dark blue or burgundy, a brooch pinned at the point of the shallow v-neck, grandma Fancher looked nothing like her tall, raw-boned, fair-skinned elder sister.

Before lunch the house was perfumed by yeasty bread rolls and roasting chicken. At the table I was bade to sit still, eat quietly, and clean my plate. I had to shoulder the honour of my side – the junior, disadvantaged side – of the family. Great aunt Minnie's side were the wealthy, senior side.

My grandmother, Ida, graduated from high school at the top of her class and wanted to go to Vassar but her father, who was prosperous enough to send her, said, "Girls don't go to college, they get married." Ida retaliated by stealing Minnie's fiancé. On Ida's bedside table there was a photo in a silver frame of tall, solemn Arthur and herself, in white, with broad-brimmed hats, during a holiday at Palm Beach.

She had always wanted to go to Hawaii. Arthur promised they would but died in Denver before he could take her. She returned to Bay City with my father and mother. To be ensnared in the net of the family, cast wide by widowed great aunt Minnie.

I credit grandma Fancher with laying the groundwork for my triumph with the story of St. Louis. Sitting in my father's flat on the wing chair, covered in golden brocade, she read to me from Grimm's and Hans Christian Andersen's fairy tales until I knew them by heart and the words had by stealth been imprinted on my subconscious. When confronted in the story about St. Louis, they fair jumped off the page.

Bay City, September 1951

The pale teacher, our first male in elementary, was new and did not know the ropes in the school, so when he read out the class roll call and a girl stood when he called, "Billie Carlisle" he was stumped. But let it pass. When a second girl rose after the name, "Michael

Fancher," he sent us both to the principal's office. The good soul led us back to the class and explained that we really did have mannish names. He should have realised, of course, that Billie can be a girl's name although with Michael he should have expected a boy. After this contretemps, he never did ask why I had been given my name.

Many people have done so but I do not really have a satisfactory explanation. Ma said, depending on her mood: "Your father didn't like girls' names."

Or, she had chosen the first name of "Michael Strange," the stage, pen, and favoured name of Blanche Oelrichs, a celebrated actress and writer (with whom my mother falsely claimed acquaintance). Blanche (Michael) was the second wife of actor John Barrymore; he was second of her three husbands. Her biography, *Who Tells Me True*, was published in 1940, the year of my birth. That may have had a bearing on my "Michael."

Or, Ma said she was an admirer of Michael Arlen's *The Green Hat*, a racy novel that was adapted for a play performed in both New York and London and for a film starring Greta Garbo and John Gilbert. Like Blanche, I feel at ease with Michael and believe it suits me although it does, from time to time, cause consternation. For some weeks after I began writing for *The Irish Times*, I was told by a diplomat that it was an "in" thing among readers at the Department of Foreign Affairs to know Michael Jansen was a woman.

Beirut, April 1965

During initial phone consultations about a job, Godfrey began to call me "Miss F." He was flat on his back in bed in his apartment during our key encounter. He had slipped a disk carrying a heavy box of groceries from car to house while visiting friends in the mountain village of Chemlan. I had been instructed to collect the key to the door under the mat, let myself in and walk round to his bedroom, where he had been confined for six months. Before the interview, the professor who had proposed me for the post of assistant editor had warned, "Jansen is a six-foot tall, bearded Sikh who eats little girls." Uncertain whether this was a joke or not, I left my large Syrian boyfriend on the mat.

Godfrey was, of course, not a tall, bearded Sikh who ate little girls for lunch, dinner or tea, but a slender man with a decided Indian, or Sub-Continental cast of face, horn-rimmed glasses, slightly wavy black hair, and a commanding way. "Go to the kitchen and fix us a couple of whiskeys," he ordered. I did as I was told, returned, sat down on the chair provided for visitors, and we began to discuss how to transform the Middle East Forum from an irregular monthly to a serious quarterly.

Work had to wait until his doctor decided if he had been cured or he needed a risky operation. I was eager to start as I needed the money and rang him from time to time to learn what was happening. Finally, he went to the hospital for tests. "They strapped me to a table, injected a dye into my spine, turned me on my head in a dark room, and took X-rays. I was there for quite a long time before Suhail came in and said, 'Your disk has healed but since the nerves are still tingling, you have to do physiotherapy.' When I asked what the colour of the dye was, he drew it out and held up the syringe. 'See, it's colourless.' The table was righted, I was freed, and I walked home." I had reservations about the business of the dye but kept quiet.

Godfrey was the perfect choice for the honorary editorship of the quarterly. He had been in and out of the region since 1948 as Indian press attaché in Cairo, Beirut and Istanbul. He had wide contacts around the region as well as deep appreciation of its economic and political workings. Although he planned to commission articles on his travels, he soon dispatched me to Cairo in search of contributors.

Cairo, Summer 1965

Armed with a list of people provided by Godfrey, I flew to Egypt and took up residence in a chalet in the garden of the Omar Khayyam. The first person I met was the editor of a major daily who without formality handed me over to Muhammad Sid Ahmad, a pale, rather shy man in spectacles who was told to arrange appointments for me. He had just joined the paper and was, then, a lowly apprentice. The figure Godfrey particularly wanted as a contributor was Kamal el-Din Rifaat, a former general who was, at the time, director of information for the ruling Arab Socialist Union. Muhammad proposed to introduce me to Egyptian intellectuals and journalists and invited me to dinner that night.

He drove tentatively through Cairo traffic to Giza and onto a narrow rough track into the desert to a restaurant with a grand view of the pyramids. "This is the first time I've come out since my curfew was lifted," he stated, explaining that he had been released from prison several months earlier. He had been a communist as a youth, converted by fellow students and teachers at the lycée. He had joined a clandestine communist cell but his father sent him abroad in the expectation that Muhammad would prefer the amusements of Paris to conspiring in Cairo.

Instead, he told me over dinner with *son et lumière* echoing and flickering in the background, he returned home and lived underground for some time in a cell led by a French woman called Odette Hazan until the members of his branch of the divided party were arrested. "Prison was a relief after being underground under her command," Muhammad said. During his first time in detention he was held until shortly after the Free Officers Movement overthrew the king in 1952, and in 1954, put Nasser in power. In 1959 Muhammad was imprisoned again in the desert with an array of communists and other dissidents and was freed in 1964. "Prison was a university. We had intellectuals who could teach many subjects. We benefitted." During this time, he and his colleagues re-examined his party's view of the revolution and gradually grew to accept Egypt's new order until, he wrote in 2002, it began to degenerate, culminating in the visit to Jerusalem by Nasser's successor Anwar Sadat in 1978.

Muhammad belonged to the Ottoman upper class that had once ruled Egypt. His father, a pasha under the king, and governor of Port Said and Suez as well as a member of parliament, did not accept his son's political calling. Muhammad later wrote, his father, fearing for his son's life, had arranged for his first stay in prison to be extended. His father died in 1955, broken-hearted over the loss of extensive landholdings in reforms instituted by Nasser's government.

Muhammad's mother, the sister of Sidki Pasha, a former prime minister, was a great lady. I met her over tea in the family flat on Ibn Zanki street in Zamalek. The sitting room was filled with elegant French furniture which former French socialist minister and deputy André Philippe had told Muhammad belonged in a museum. His bookshelves, lined with the standard simply bound communist classics, revealed prison had not dimmed his youthful commitment.

He decided we should drive to Alexandria for the meeting with Rifaat, who was on holiday with his family. I took over the wheel about half way there, turning it over to Muhammad only when we reached the coastal city where his mother, who had moved to their summer flat a few days earlier, had organised a splendid lunch of cold fresh salmon with mayonnaise. I stayed at the Palestine hotel, a beautiful villa set in a palm shaded garden on the beach.

Rifaat received us at his beach cabin and agreed to contribute an article on the "development of socialist relationships" designed to ensure Egypt reached the "take off" stage in economic development. He eventually delivered the first of two articles – on the theory of what Egypt was trying to do – but not the second, which was meant to deal with practice.

Muhammad and I toured the countryside and visited a far larger and more developed combined centre than the one I had seen during my first trip to Cairo in 1961.

During this and subsequent visits to Cairo, Muhammad took me to "Night and Day" a 24-hour cafe in the Semiramis hotel popular with intellectuals. There I met Lakhdar Brahimi, then Algeria's ambassador to Egypt, who promised to write an article on his country's independence struggle.

I was introduced to Feshawi, the most famous tea and coffee house in Khan el-Khalil, located in Cairo's central souk. Opened in 1773, Feshawi was a haunt of journalists, writers and academics, who smoked pot in their water pipes while they argued politics over tea.

Godfrey's friend Khaled Muhieddine collected me from the Omar Khayyam hotel in his black Fiat with two stars on the side, signifying that he was a member of the revolutionary Free Officers Movement. To be certain our conversation was not bugged, we talked as we walked round the Gezira club's grounds. Back at the hotel, the doorman saluted when he saw me step out of the car.

Beirut, 1965-66

Although he was meant to be honorary editor, Godfrey came regularly to the Middle East Forum office, two tiny rooms built as an afterthought on the roof of the headquarters of the Alumni Association of the American University of Beirut (AUB) next to the university hospital. Sweltering in summer and freezing in winter, we shared the space with a cheerful, solidly built young secretary called Alice who was hopeless at her job. In a range of peremptory tones, Godfrey continued to call me "Miss F," to my face and on the phone. It was a bit daunting until I realised that was his way. He did not mean to be brusque or commanding.

When summer came, Godfrey turned up in a short-sleeved "bush shirt" and Rajastani curly toed shoes embroidered in fine gold thread. Alice tittered. When he came to a party on my wide terrace, my poodle Nana jumped up and left her dusty footprints on his white achkan. He did not seem to mind. Initially jealous, Nana eventually came to like him and stayed with him over Christmas when I paid another visit to Cairo in search of contributors.

There was no thought on either side of getting together until around Easter, then there was no thought that we could be apart.

Araya, Spring 1966

Liza, two, blonde bombshell, hurtled down the stairs of Prue and Ian's house and grabbed Godfrey around the knees. "Goffey, Goffey!" bestowing on him the affectionate nickname of "Gof." Which he preferred to the name given to him by parents who had a penchant for providing names Godfrey considered uncomfortable for their five children: Albert, Eunice, Elaine, and Daphne or "D," were the other four. Two whites – Eunice and Elaine – and three browns, although the brood was only one-quarter Indian by blood. Their father belonged to the Sub-Continent's centuries-old European stock – designated "domiciled Europeans" – while their mother was Anglo-Indian, the community to which the entire family was consigned in India. Elaine migrated to Britain where she "passed" as a returned Englishwoman.

Tabarja-Antelias, April 13th, 1975

For some reason I don't recall why John and Peggy decided to have their annual Easter lunch party a week early according to the Orthodox calendar. We gathered at Tabarja under a slate grey sky. The old Lebanese house with its high-ceilinged rooms was quite bare but for the long dead stuffed baby elephant in the salon. The fare was roast lamb and rice, tinted blue, pink and yellow in line with a medieval recipe John had found in an ancient book in the British Museum. "I brought the sheep from Aleppo. It sat in the front seat of the service," John joked, his bristling moustache twitching over his small smile. The meal finished with a flourish of gorgonzola and pears and lashings of red wine. A fine rain began to fall.

We drove south to Beirut along the coastal highway as dusk set in. At Antelias our journey became stop-and-start. Checkpoints. Troops. Rough plain clothes gunmen. Godfrey switched on the car radio and caught the tail end of a bulletin. "...the toll is 30 Palestinians and at least four Christians killed, clashes have erupted in Ain el-Rummaneh..." The announcer listed hot districts as if it was a weather report.

The Ain el-Rummaneh massacre was the culmination of months of rising tension and violent incidents that coincided with strikes. The previous December, former president Camile Chamoun's trawler firm had attempted to monopolise fishing off the coast of Sidon, eliciting protests from fishermen in the south that spread to their brethren in the north. Charismatic MP Marouf Saad organised a mass demonstration in Sidon on February 26th. While marching at the front of the throng, he was shot, it was said, by an army sniper, and died just over a week later. His funeral on March 7th set Sunni Muslim Sidon and Saad's allies in the nearby Palestinian refugee camps against the Maronite-dominated establishment.

Godfrey filed his first civil war dispatch to *The Economist* as Marya's school closed down.

Beirut, February 1976

"Let's stop and see Brahim on the way into town," Godfrey said as we sped along the highway toward the city. We parked the car outside the Farid al-Atrash nightclub in Raouche and entered the lobby of the sleazy block. The concierge stopped us before we began the climb to Brahim's flat. "*Ustaz* Brahim is in AUB hospital." When? "Three days ago."

On the floor outside his room was a great bouquet of flowers. In the bed sat a man with a raw, roasted, swollen face, his hands wrapped in bandages, his body covered with a light sheet.

He croaked a greeting. "We didn't know." Godfrey explained. Marya shrank back, horrified, I said nothing. He was unrecognisable.

Someone, I cannot recall whom, told us Brahim had gone to the office of the newspaper published by the Iraqi Baath party the night the Syrians decided to strike. The editor was slain sitting at his desk after Brahim had gone to the basement to see the presses at work. He had loved the smell of printer's ink and the swish and clang of the presses.

"The Syrians rolled barrels of petrol down the ramp and into the basement. Anyone who tried to escape was shot. Brahim crouched near the floor, out of the smoke, until he dared leave," said our informant. "The flowers are from the Syrian information minister."

We drove to Beirut daily, or every other day. Brahim rallied, his inflamed face returned to its normal size and shape; his burnt body we sponged with cool water. Christianne came from Cairo. Jacqueline, his second wife, as well. He recovered his spirits but hated hospital food. I cooked creamed spinach and made fresh orange juice jelly – soft food that had some taste. Brahim strengthened and joked. He and Godfrey talked about the war. Just as he appeared to be on the mend, we found him in intensive care on machines, his breathing rasping, stentorious. Godfrey sat and held his hand until he died. The doctor said if he had not been a smoker he might have survived.

Brahim had been one of Godfrey's oldest and closest friends. They had met in Cairo during Godfrey's first posting as press attaché in independent India's first mission to Egypt. Like Muhammad Sid Ahmad, Brahim was a communist – as so many young Egyptians were at the time. An amazing man who, taught to read and write Arabic at a Quranic school, Brahim had emerged from the backstreets of Alexandria to work at its docks while he learned English word by word from a dictionary. When he was about to be detained by the pre-revolution Egyptian police in a crack down on leftists, Godfrey, then Indian press attaché in Cairo, put Brahim on a flight to India with the promise of a job in *All India Radio*'s Arabic service. Once the Egyptians realised Brahim was on the plane, an air traffic controller ordered the captain to return. He refused as he had left Egyptian air space. In India, Brahim met and married Christianne. He spent seven years in prison under the republican regime headed by Nasser, worked in the press, and then left Egypt to serve as a correspondent for a Yugoslav newspaper.

Grieving, Godfrey fled Beirut for Jerusalem. I cut almond branches from the tree in our garden in Chemlan and laid them on Brahim's coffin on the steps of the mosque in south Beirut, before Christianne took him home to be buried in Cairo, the city he had abandoned.

Beirut, March 1976

We drove to Beirut to permit Marya a few days at the Louise Wegmann college which had closed the school's campus at Bchamoun below Chemlan and moved into cramped quarters beneath the old lighthouse at the end of Hamra street in Beirut. Penny had given us the key to her parents' flat not far from the school. We bought food and candles at Smith's supermarket, made the beds with sheets and blankets we had brought with us and prepared for power cuts we did not have in Chemlan. At night we could hear looters blasting open the metal grilles of the shops below, one by one, advancing up the street until they were below the flat. Marya slept on but Godfrey and I lay awake, worrying that she would hear and take fright.

One mild night we were sitting on the balcony watching the news on the television of the family in the next door flat when an army officer entered the studio, took a chair at the table where Nicole had sat to broadcast and laid his pistol on it. Nicole was stunned silent. He introduced himself as Abdel Aziz Al-Ahdab, commander of the Beirut military garrison, and proclaimed himself temporary military governor of Lebanon. He demanded the resignation of president Suleiman Franjieh and prime minister Rashid Karami. Ahdab said he sought to prevent the disintegration of the army into sectarian factions and to rescue Lebanon from its year-long civil war. Militias were shelling Beirut, kidnapping civilians, robbing, dividing Beirut into Christian east and multi-sect west and sniping anyone who tried to cross between the sectors. The government was paralysed and could do nothing to halt the mayhem, protect the populace, or preserve the army.

Neighbours all round sat transfixed in front of their television screens, glowing softly in the dark, then one after the other cheered, celebratory gunfire erupted across Beirut, church bells rang out in support. Few slept well that night, hoping the conflict would end, and that the politicians and militias would take Ahdab seriously.

The next morning, we walked to the Radis' house in Raouche. Ma Radi was cooking as usual, Selma and Nuha were trawling Lebanese radio stations for news of the coup, of Ahdab, who had suddenly become a hero. War-weary Lebanese from all communities were phoning into the stations to voice their support and praising Ahdab for taking action to halt the war. Callers came from Sunni Sidon and Tripoli, Christian and Druze mountain villages, and both sides of the dividing line in Beirut. They gave their names, risking retribution by local militias.

Ahdab was ignored by the politicians and Syria, which supported Franjieh, he retired at 65 shortly after his aborted coup. The war had paused for a moment.

Chemlan, Spring 1976

Cyprus radio was a lifeline in a world turned upside down by war. I sat in the cool, fig-tree-shaded library of our house listening to the revolutionary songs of Mikis Theodorakis and poetic melodies of Manos Hadjidakis. Writing on a yellow legal pad a book about the Greek junta's coup followed by the Turkish invasion and occupation of northern Cyprus. Writing about our looted house not far from the municipal market in the coastal town of Kyrenia. Writing while shells roared from Ainab's 75 mm Howitzer and rushed overhead to strike a distant village on the Maronite mountain on the other side of the broad Damascus highway. Sitting outside in the garden eating strawberries with cream, Neville, a former British army officer, had warned us to take deep cover if a shell made a woo-woo sound as it would be spinning end to end and could fall at any time. The best we could do was two-roofs, the roof of the house and the floor between the sitting room and library. While I wrote, Godfrey sat in his usual place on the divan in the sitting room reading and Marya received tutorials from George or Elie in French or maths, their Kalashnikov's parked outside the back door.

Cheerful, round-faced Elie had fought in the Battle of the Hotels in December and emerged unscathed. George, tall and thin, helped Nimr in the shop beneath the platform on which the church stood. The butcher, Selim who always had a small flock of sheep grazing on the grass across from his shop, kept the village fed during those thin months. Whenever we went to Beirut, we would stop at the bakery in Aramoun and buy a stack of bread for friends in the village who refused to descend to the city, fearing sectarian checkpoints, kidnap and murder.

We gathered a stock of essentials in case we were trapped in the village: lentils, beans, flour, tinned bully beef, powdered milk, coffee and tea; charcoal for cooking when bottled gas was no longer available.

Chemlan-Beirut, June 1976

Marya refused to stay in the village with Penny and Eric who lived in Nimr's old house around the corner from us so the three of us drove to Beirut in Penny's parents' Mercedes, leant to us after we deposited our tank-like Volvo in Damascus. On the way downhill, we stopped at the petrol pump in Bchamoun to buy *mazout* to fuel the generator at *Reuters* where Godfrey filed his stories to *The Economist*. Traffic was slack along the seafront highway and in Ras Beirut. I drove the car alongside the fence of the park in Sanayeh and drew up next to the building where the agency's office was located. The moment the three of us stepped into the shelter of the entrance hall, crack-carrump, a mortar shell landed outside, its impact jarring the building to its foundations. A white-faced journalist who had taken refuge in the hall observed, "It's particularly bad this morning." Godfrey walked up the stairs to hand in his copy and deliver the *mazout*, our modest offering for telex transmission. When Godfrey returned we peered anxiously around the corner and found the car covered with lumps of earth and shredded leaves. The mortar had landed just inside the wrought iron fence of the park, spattering the area with dirt and debris, but had done no serious damage.

Shaken by the close call, I sped the car through empty streets to Nicole's building on Verdun and halted inside the parking area. We took the steps to her flat where we found her calmly preparing lunch. "What about a drink?" she asked after we told her about the mortar. "Muhammad just rang, he'll be coming soon."

Since I had forgotten something in the car, I hurried down the steps to the parking area and found Muhammad Mashnouk leaning up against the side of his car. What happened? "I left my office and locked the door when I remembered there were papers I wanted to bring with me. But when I put the key in the lock a mortar hit the room and blew the door out. If I had been inside, I would have been killed." When we reached Nicole's flat, she poured him a large brandy.

Everyone had a story. Nicole had been on the other side of the table when Ahdab mounted his popular but pointless coup. We had driven through a Lebanese Hawker-Hunter air raid on rebels along the road between the coast and Bchamoun en route to Chemlan. The gunmen, Druze in uniforms armed with rifles, waved us on.

Eric arrived at our back door one day, hands trembling, bleary-eyed, demanding a large tot of whiskey. "I was driving along the coast road when two armed men stopped me and asked to see my ID. They got into the car. The thin one in the front with me and the fat one in the back. They demanded cigarettes and money. I gave them my pack and the few pounds I had on me. 'That's all?' asked the fat one, using his Kalashnikov to prop up a piece of cloth hanging from the car's ceiling. 'Yeah.'

"They began to laugh and ordered me to stop, they handed me back my money and cigarettes and said good luck as they got out of the car. I thought I was a goner. Don't tell Penny." Eric had survived revolutions in Latin America and described to us the art of making and throwing Molotov cocktails – "if you make 'em spin from end to end, they pack a bigger punch."

Incoming mortar shells announced themselves with the tinkle of shrapnel on our red tile roof. Balu, who was outside, barked frantically until we let her into the house. The Range Rover at the British Middle East Centre for Arab Studies, commonly known as the "spy school," was said to have been buried in the garden for safekeeping while the school closed due to the escalation in fighting. Afraid of kidnap or death by bombs or bullets, Raymond, a classmate in my AUB economics course, had stopped going to work in Beirut. He was killed in his garden while watering his mint and his remains were buried in shoeboxes in the village cemetery. He was our first and only fatality while we still dwelt in the village. There were more deaths later: the blacksmith, the nurse, her husband and an old gentleman who boarded with them. An entire family who lived along the road below Chemlan was massacred.

Chemlan-Damascus, June 1976

Godfrey and I folded the Sarouk and lifted it into the boot of the Volvo, a homemade Indian flag on the radio's aerial. Grandma Fancher's blue silk carpets, a brown Turkish rug woven by Greeks before they were expelled from Turkey in 1922, and a red and black Baluch prayer rug came next. The silver packed in a suitcase and essential papers in another. Godfrey belted Marya into her child's seat in the back. The car scrambled up the rough gravel road by the house before taking the hairpin bends to the main road where we met Neville and Rosemary in their faded burgundy Peugeot.

We followed them up the nearly deserted Damascus highway, taking a detour round Syrian army lines in either Bhamdoun or Sofar before cresting the mountain and beginning the descent to the green Bekaa Valley. We paused at the border post at Masnaa as Saudi tanks rolled into Lebanon, deployed by the Arab League to dilute the mainly Syrian intervention force.

Our crossing to Syria was uneventful and the road was clear to Damascus where Neville and Rosemary went about their business while we collected Mr. Hayani at the Indian embassy and drove to his home to drop off the carpets and silver. The two men carried the Sarouk up the stairs and lifted it onto the top of Mr. Hayani's armoire then piled on the rest of the carpets. The cases of silver and documents went under his bed.

We dropped the Volvo at the garage under the British embassy where one of the drivers had promised to look after it until we decided to leave Lebanon. It was safer to deposit the car in Damascus than keep it in Chemlan where it was used by our local militia for nightly patrols to prevent outsiders from stealing it. We picnicked off bread, cheese, hummus, and fried eggplant at Mr. Hayani's farm where the peace of the Eastern Ghouta seeped into our bones before we returned with Neville and Rosemary to Chemlan and the hollow crack of shell fire from the deep throat of the Howitzer positioned on the top of the hill above Ainab. Some months after we left, Neville and Rosemary were shot dead on the doorstep of their home above Chemlan.

Chemlan-Limassol, July 9th-10th, 1976

We packed our records, clothes, china, linen, and books in 11 tin trunks used by Godfrey for moving during the days he was India's most undiplomatic diplomat. Since many of our friends had left home with only the clothes on their backs and lost everything, we had decided to be "heavy refugees." Into one trunk we put items Prue had asked us to take to Cyprus where she and her family had gone earlier in the year. When we visited their flat near Sanayeh garden to collect clothing and other things she had listed, we found the bloated body of Orlando, the marmalade cat in the sitting room. Her maid had been paid to feed the cat and clean the dusty house. D packed clothing and shoes in a trunk we had reserved for her to augment a brace of suitcases brought from her flat in Beirut to our house the evening before we were scheduled to depart.

I backed Hajji out of her garage and drove up the steep hill to the main road and turned down the steeply curving street into the overgrown garden at Ramez's handsome two-storey house at the bottom of the village. He had offered to keep an eye on the MG until we returned – we had hoped that in three months without really believing, we would be back in time for Marya to go back to school.

George and Leila were married by the village priest that afternoon. We celebrated with wine and sandwiches at the house of a high-spirited Sunni woman from the Baydoun family. She brought out her Kalashnikov and began firing until Nimr convinced her to stop. Trigger-happy vigilantes below might begin shooting back, he warned her.

Abu Hamzeh came early the next morning in Muhammad Mashnouk's car along with a hired pickup sporting a tall canvas storage space at the back – a mechanised version of a covered wagon. We lifted the trunks into the back of the pickup and slid in sideways the round antique copper tray that had served as Godfrey's dining table top for years: pre-me and after. I closed the kitchen shutter, bolted the door and turned the key in the lock of the heavy wooden front door, backing away to have a long look at the house. Chiselled white stone blocks, red tile roof, blue wooden shutters, olive trees on the upper and lower terraces, climbing roses along the white gravel path. Balu wagged her feathery tail and T.S. squalled from confinement inside a soft suitcase – holes punched so he could breathe. The key lay heavy in my hand. Refugees always keep keys close. Keys are proofs of ownership, of belonging to a home, a place. Packed in one of the trunks was the key to our house in Kyrenia, a large key with a tag bearing the name Brookings, the previous owner, written by hand. We had become double refugees.

George and Leila climbed into the pickup cab, Godfrey sat in the front of the car with Abu Hamzeh, Balu at his feet, Marya, D and I in back. The case with T.S. on my lap. Abu Hamzeh signalled us to peer over the back of the seat, lifted one trouser leg to display a small pistol, tucked into his sock, and then the other to reveal a dagger. He was ready to defend us – without Muhammad's vintage Chicago gangster-style Tommy gun.

Our village neighbours gathered at the top of the drive to say goodbye. Khalil, a small man with a long, sharp nose and thin white hair, had tears in his eyes. We were not the first to leave but the Hindi's departure was seen as the beginning of the end for Chemlan. Which it was for our Chemlan.

Soon after we had moved into our house, the first to be built within the precincts of the village for a century, Godfrey asked Khalil, a former librarian at the British Council in Beirut, how long it would take for us to gain acceptance. The house had been designed by a Beiruti friend but contracted by a villager, the stonework and iron mongering had been done by other Chamlanis, and the carpentry by Khalil's cousin. Khalil lifted an eyebrow and replied, "Well you see, Mr. Jansen, Chemlan was settled by the Hittis in the 11th century. The land, you know, belonged to the Druze. The Tabibs came in the 15th century. We Hittis still don't speak to the Tabibs." The division was formalised by a feud, he said, when a Tabib barber stabbed Khalil's father with scissors after a disagreement over some long-forgotten issue.

Our leaving heralded our belonging more than we knew. More than 30 years later George and Leila collected me from the Mayflower hotel in Beirut and drove me up to a restaurant in the town of Brummana in mainly Maronite Christian Mount Lebanon. We were joined by another couple from the Hitti side of the village, the Farajallahs. Over dinner I related to Maud what Khalil had said to Godfrey. She replied, seriously, "Oh, no, you Jansens were always more acceptable than the Tabibs."

The journey south to Tyre took us down the slope to the coast and along the shore road with pauses at one Syrian army checkpoint after another. Traffic was light as we convoyed through the banana groves on either side of the road, slalomed through Sidon and carried on to Tyre, passing one of our favourite seaside restaurants, Hassan and Hussein, where fish was always fresh and well-cooked. At the dock in Tyre we learned a freighter would be departing for Cyprus that very evening and hurried to the company's office to book passages and pay from a booklet of traveller's cheques we had brought from Cyprus on a previous visit. For several months we had been compelled to collect Godfrey's salary from our account in Nicosia because transfers to banks in Lebanon had been halted due to the civil war. The bar at the foot of the quay stocked yellow tins of Keo beer from Cyprus instead of Lebanon's Almaza and Aziza.

The vessel's cabins had all been booked so we settled for space on a hatch cover on deck, arranging our trunks to create a laager. We laid out a kilim and set the tray on top of a trunk to make a low table. A touch of home on the run from war. Dinner was a shared bottle of champagne and ghastly sandwiches of feta spread on bully beef made that morning by D when we were not looking. David Hirst of *The Guardian* – also on board – joined us in toasts to George and Leila.

A seasick Balu was partnered at the rail by an elegant Irish settler before lying down in our mini-fort between Godfrey and Marya. I partially unzipped the lid of the suitcase and pushed my hand inside through the tight opening to calm T.S. and stop him from moaning and clawing at the sides of the canvas case. He hated to be confined. But as long as the Siamese knew I was nearby he felt secure. We slept little, watching for the dawn which emerged in layers of mist and cloud, chilly and damp, off Limassol. The ship dropped anchor outside the port and waited for lighters to land us with our trunks in the harbour where an official in a perfectly creased white uniform snatched Balu's lead. "You can't bring in the dog," he declared. "But you're lucky, there's a man from the veterinary department here at this moment. He'll take the dog to the quarantine kennel in Nicosia." We kept mum about T.S. in the suitcase and T.S. did not give himself away. The official wrote down the telephone number of the kennel and led Balu away, slowly, her tail hanging low, her ears down.

At immigration we provided a financial guarantee for George and Leila: Cyprus had been swamped with cash-strapped Lebanese refugees. But another smart, white clad customs officer waved our trunks through without opening even one after I mentioned that we were not only refugees from Lebanon but also from Kyrenia. "Welcome to Cyprus," he said.

3

SANCTUARY

South Hadley, September 1958

My escape from Bay City was on a train, in Ma's company, with Mount Holyoke College as my destination. From a small town of 60,000 in Michigan to a town with a quarter of its population in Massachusetts. Ma accompanied me to my room on the ground floor of Porter Hall, an age-stained brick building with staring windows, heavy doors and rumpled linoleum floors. In my pocket was $120, my first earnings from journalism. I spent the money on a red bicycle that gave me the freedom to roam the campus and countryside, to pedal slowly up steep hills and swoop down.

I had submitted three articles to *The Bay City Times*. The topic was the "Iraqi revolution" that had overthrown the monarchy and slain young king Faisal II, his hated uncle Abd al-Ilah and Nuri al-Said. I knew nothing about Iraq's politics until the summer of 1957 when I met a group of Iraqi students at the University of Michigan where I was attending a two-week journalism seminar for high school students.

Shy, a skinny 41 kilos, hair cropped short and teeth bound with platinum bands and wires, I was dispatched along with another journalism hopeful called Kay to a foreign students' reception and told to find interesting people to interview. Kay disappeared. I froze on the edge of the gathering until a tall man with dark hair appeared.

"Can I help you?" Handsome, charming with a somewhat high-pitched voice, Sami, an Iraqi, offered to introduce me to his friends. The next day we met at the students' union where I interviewed a short, round middle-aged Iraqi called Mr. Fayyad, with Sami punctuating the start and stall conversation with cruel jests against Mr. Fayyad. I don't recall what I wrote or how it was received by the instructors at the workshop. I met Sami and his group several other times before returning to Bay City, with a small window slivered open on countries I could not even find on the map.

The window cracked a bit further over the next year as Sami, a student of ancient history at the University of Chicago who had been taking a summer course at Michigan, wrote, urging me to read the Quran – which I did – and sent me a couple of books to drag me out of the depths of my ignorance.

Following the July 14th coup in Iraq, I drove to Ann Arbor two or three times to interview Sami and other Iraqis who, I found, wholeheartedly welcomed the end of the monarchy. "Nuri al-Said had my uncle strung up on a lamppost in Hillah," Sami said during one of these sessions over sweet, milky coffee which I had previously disliked but learned to drink, associating for years its aroma with those discussions.

There were others who came to the union beside Iraqis: Hussein, a Cuban student of Arabic at Harvard, and George the Egyptian, a gentle man with a cautious smile who, as a youth, used to ride horses into the desert near the pyramids. Set to attend Harvard law that fall, George convinced me to become a Nasserite.

One chance encounter fixed my course in life. When I asked the man where he was from, he said, "Palestine." Where is that? I asked. "Next to Jordan, Lebanon, Syria." I've never heard of Palestine. "It doesn't exist. They gave my country away." But, if it doesn't exist, what kind of passport do you have? "British." I never knew his name and never saw him again.

"They gave my country away," those words have reverberated in my head these many years.

Back at home, I had to find out about Palestinians whose country had been given away. I hurried to our public library and found *They Are Human Too*, by Per Anderson, a coffee table book of photographs of Palestinian refugees.

At Mount Holyoke I majored in international relations focusing on the Middle East and travelled to Beirut as an intern at the UN Relief and Works Agency for Palestine Refugees, UNRWA, to open fresh windows on the region where I have spent my life.

Beirut, June 10th, 1961

Pumped with vaccinations for everything from typhoid and paratyphoid to yellow fever and provided by Ma with a roll of toilet paper, I arrived at Beirut's international airport on an afternoon flight, after being shunted round Europe. Unused to dealing with Middle Eastern destinations, my Bay City travel agent had put me on Trans World Airlines to London's Heathrow and Air India from there to Beirut. But there was no Air India flight to Beirut. I was rushed across the tarmac in a car by a member of the ground staff and put onto an Alitalia flight to Rome, where I was seated in first class as the plane was nearly empty. From Rome I flew to Athens where I stood outside the small airport on the dusty airfield waiting for a plane for Beirut. At the time, Greece remained largely devastated by World War II and was not the tourist hotspot it later became.

I was confused and nervous as this was my first trip outside the US. When I had failed to turn up, an UNRWA driver waited at the airport until I arrived. He whisked me to the Mayflower hotel in Hamra street and told me the UNRWA bus would pick me up at 07.30 Monday morning.

My room was on the second or third floor, very simply furnished with two beds, a chair and table. The shower was located at the centre of the ceiling of the bathroom which had a drain in the floor, but the toilet and basin got wet when I took a shower. I slept until six when I was awakened by the squawk of the horn mounted on a wheeled kerosene drum drawn by a donkey. The street was alive with commerce. Vendors pushed carts loaded with fruit and vegetables and called out their wares: eggplants, beans, potatoes, strawberries, and *akadinia*, small, oval orange fruit I had never seen before. Most shoppers were men bearing baskets, some in suits and ties attired for office, others in t-shirts or vests and pyjama bottoms. On the balcony across the street a woman in a flowered housecoat let down a basket on a string with a list of items she wanted. Still in my nightwear, I pulled my chair onto my balcony and sat down, entranced with the morning's street theatre.

Over buffet breakfast on the roof under an awning I met my first "expat:" Genevieve Maxwell, a lady of a certain age with the bounce of a teenager. Who was I, why was I in Beirut, would I like to join the Foreign International Group (FIG) she was setting up to bring young people together. "No Lebanese allowed, you know," she stated firmly. Since we were in Lebanon, I felt this was very inhospitable and was reluctant to attend the FIG's first event on the hotel roof that week. I did, bringing Saud, who had been going out with a classmate at Mount Holyoke. He and I had run into each other crossing Bliss street in front of the American University. He was in Beirut visiting his family. "He's a Saudi who goes to Amherst," I told Genevieve when I introduced them. Her ban was not on Arabs but only on Lebanese. I never went to another FIG gathering.

The hotel, at $20 a night was too expensive for me, so I had to find alternative accommodation. I think it was Genevieve who suggested I try to get into the women's hostel at the university which was what I did. During that summer I made my first lasting friends in the region. Americans were still popular, thanks to US president Dwight Eisenhower's pressure on Israel to pull its troops out of Egypt's Sinai Peninsula in 1957 following the disastrous Suez war waged on Nasser by France, Britain and Israel. American girls were considered exotic.

After a false start with an Iranian girl who spent an hour and a half primping each morning, I shared a room with Sawsan, a Syrian archaeologist. She was following a summer course but took it easy, rising late, while I had to go early to the university's Medical Gate to catch the UNRWA bus. Breakfast was often a cheese and tomato sandwich or chocolate biscuit and a cup of Nescafé with milk ordered from the UNRWA canteen.

That summer I had two lives: one touring Palestinian refugee camps to learn what sort of vocational training Palestinian girls of my age would like to have. I spoke no Arabic but went around with local staff who could translate, rode in jeeps, and walked between raw cement boxes housing refugees down hardpacked earth alleyways with canals of sewage flowing down the middle. Refugee children pressed from all sides, curious about my closely cropped head. "Jeanne D'Arc," some said, recalling billboards for the 1950s film *Saint Joan*, starring Jean Seberg. Their elders were invariably welcoming and generous, infusing their last tea leaves scraped from the bottom of a tin or emptying their sugar bowls to sweeten small cups of Turkish coffee.

Jerusalem, June 1961

Muhammad Jarallah picked me up at the airport in Amman, drove to the Automatique at the town centre where we picked up sandwiches, before setting off for the holy city. A very tall man with a broad smile and grey flecked hair and moustache; Muhammad was UNRWA's press officer in Jordan, the West Bank and East Jerusalem. As we descended from the plateau to the Jordan Valley the air blowing through the car's windows grew oppressively hot and Muhammad suggested we stop for a dip at the Dead Sea. It is the lowest spot on the face of the planet where the temperature was over 40 degrees Celsius and the flat, silver, slippery salt body of water not much cooler. We rented heavy knit bathing suits from the concessionaire and floated high on the surface, careful not to get any water in our eyes, ears or mouths.

I had booked a room in the Casa Nova, a Franciscan pilgrim hostel, in the Old City a few steps from the Church of the Holy Sepulchre. My room was small and spare. A lunch of soup and bread was served in the handsome refectory at a long table flanked by monks and guests. After the meal I walked around the Old City, peering shyly into shops selling spices, sweets, and clothing, admiring heavily embroidered traditional Palestinian dresses hanging from wires strung across metal shop doors. On that or a subsequent visit I bought an old dress in a gold satiny material embellished with Bethlehem's distinctive couching work. The elderly woman who kept the shop gave me a headdress and bracelet as present, paid six Jordanian dinars. Such a dress is worth hundreds now.

Muhammad came with a friend called Aref, a journalist, in the evening and we drove to Ramallah to meet with Elise, a secretary at UNRWA headquarters in Beirut who was to accompany me as translator on my first trips to the field. We dined beneath fairy lights at a garden restaurant on a modest meze of, perhaps, a dozen small dishes, tippling beer and arak. One of my first tastes of the potent, anise flavoured drink. When we returned to Jerusalem at midnight, the gates of the Old City were closed, and we had to wade along Khan al-Zeit street through streams of water washing the cobbled streets to the door of the Casa Nova, which was locked, and no amount of ringing could rouse the keeper.

Muhammad took me to his family house in Sheikh Jarrah where he gave me a green and white striped pyjama suit and put me up in his room while he went upstairs to sleep in his sister's chamber. I lay awake a long time fearing the disapproval of his turbaned father, a former mufti of Jerusalem who stared unblinking at me from a framed oil portrait on the wall opposite the foot of the bed.

The next morning, we breakfasted with the family's lodger, an Italian engineer who was working on the renovations at the splendid Dome of the Rock in the Haram al-Sharif, the Muslim compound on the acropolis of the Old City. "Come this afternoon, see how the work is going," he said. On the ground round the shrine were piles of beautifully painted Iranian tiles, many dating to the 16th century, that had been stripped from the walls, so they could be replaced by new tiles ordered by Jordan's king Hussein, who was custodian of the Dome of the Rock, the Aqsa Mosque, and other buildings within the compound. The engineer offered me a couple of tiles but I, like a fool, did not accept them as I was worried about the weight of my luggage on the flight home.

I toured Aqabat Jaber camp on the slopes above Jericho in the Jordan Valley, where 30,000 people dwelt. An elderly man in caftan and headdress dismissed UNRWA's plan to give girls vocational training. He had seven children, both boys and girls, all with university degrees. For Palestinians education was seen as the only route to a decent life.

Most camp residents had come here during the smouldering summer of 1948 when driven by Israel's underground army from villages north of Haifa and the towns of Ramleh and Lydda, emptied on the orders of chief operations officer of Israel's elite Palmach, Yitzhak Rabin. Ramleh's inhabitants were bussed to the Arab lines, held by Jordan's Arab Legion, while Lydda's residents were expelled in mid-July and forced to walk to Jericho where local people provided drinking water and prepared quantities of cooked food for exhausted families. Many People died on the way. Later Dyala, who was seven or eight at the time, recalled their arrival: thousands of men, women and children, footsore, dehydrated, suffering from sunstroke. They had slept in olive groves and fields on the way. Many died from dehydration and exposure.

Damascus, July 1961

My second life was with my new friends and acquaintances at the university. Sawsan introduced me to her circle, including Dyala. We went to the beach, swam, scoffed ham and cheese toasted in flat Arabic bread, drank shandies of lemonade and beer. Young men and women went out in threes or fours rather than twos, constrained by this still conservative society. We were comfortable without the challenge of one-to-one. We dressed in cotton dresses with swirling skirts and high heels that pinched our toes; the young men wore suits and ties. They invited, and they paid. We walked or rode in service taxis, shelling out 25 Lebanese piastres or a quarter of a Lira ($0.33) for a ride downtown shared by anyone else hailing the car.

One morning Sawsan and I boarded a service taxi for Damascus and swept up the broad highway snaking up Mount Lebanon through villages where Lebanese and foreigners escaped the heat and humidity of Beirut by spending summers in villas shaded by umbrella pines. We paused at the *laiterie* of retired belly dancer

Badia Masabni at the Bekaa Valley town of Chtura for sandwiches of *labneh* spread on thin rounds of mountain bread and rolled into tubes. At the border there was no fuss and bother over visas: Lebanon and Syria were – almost – one country. On the outskirts of Damascus, an oasis that claims to be the world's oldest city, we passed orchards of apricots and peaches and groves of ancient olive trees with silvery green leaves.

The city itself was very different from Beirut. Damascus was a metropolis of tree-lined avenues and handsome French colonial buildings, of fountains and parks. The sharp summer sun seemed to have bleached the colours out of the new city outside the walls, transforming it into golden beige, in contrast with Beirut's vibrant pinks, yellows, blues and greens, set against the backdrop of the turquoise Mediterranean. As we made our way to Sawsan's home in a local taxi, she remarked, "See the streets. They're much cleaner than Beirut. Even before my father was governor."

Earlier Sawsan and I had had lunch with her father, Rashad, at the Blue House near the university in Beirut. A handsome, stocky man with dark hair and moustache, he had great charm and considerable wit. As head of the Syrian state oil company he had taken his British wife to live in desolate Deir al-Zor in the east during 1939-41. He was later appointed manager of a company in Damascus, governor of Damascus province, minister of public works and telecommunications, and eventually agriculture.

The Jabri house was a modest bungalow with a garden carefully tended by Sawsan's mother, Pearl, who had met Sawsan's father in Manchester while he was studying civil engineering.

Determined to show me round town, Sawsan insisted we should lunch at a nightclub which, if I remember rightly, bore the same name, spelt differently, of Les Caves du Roy in Beirut. The place was dark, the food excellent, as is the case almost always in Damascus.

Lunch was acceptable for girls on their own, night-time excursions without escorts were not. In the afternoon, we walked around the old city and visited the dusty tomb of Salah ed-Din, the Arab commander who drove the Crusaders from Palestine during the 12th century.

That night or the next we attended a party at the very grand flat of one of Sawsan's friends. The parents had decamped for the evening, leaving us on our own. There was no alcohol, but a great deal of food laid out on a long table covered in a fine linen cloth. We listened to Arabic music and *The Green Leaves of Summer*, a ballad popular that summer which somehow had become a theme song of the Algerian liberation war. A song played over and over everywhere. The talk was political – of Nasser and the United Arab Republic merger between Syria and Egypt supported by Sawsan and her friends who either belonged to or sympathised with the Nasserite Arab Nationalist Movement which they hoped would energise and unite the Arab world against Israel and the former colonial powers that continued to intervene in Arab domestic and regional politics.

On Monday, the UNRWA office in Damascus took me to the Yarmouk camp, the largest outside Palestine, where around 17,000 refugees lived in spare one-storey breeze-blockhouses with flat roofs built by the refugees themselves along unpaved roads. The next day Sawsan came with me to the camps at Homs, where we visited the famous clock tower and I bought a postcard to send to the man due to teach Arabic at Mount Holyoke during the coming year. At Hama we lunched at a restaurant near the ancient waterwheels, the norias. Some of the surviving wheels may have been constructed during the rule of the 12th-13th century Ayyubid dynasty, founded by Salah ed-Din, although the original wheels were in use much earlier. Nasser was, by enthusiasts, compared to beloved and honoured Salah ed-Din.

South Hadley, September 28th, 1961

Television evening news reported a Syrian army coup and the country's withdrawal from the union with Egypt. Nasser had miscalculated when he accepted, reluctantly, to join with Syria, where the power of the communist party was growing, stoking fear in the country's Baath party, influential commercial class and the western powers. Nasser agreed, but on terms Syria's rulers rejected. Nevertheless, the union documents had been signed on February 22nd, 1958.

Nasser had made a number of major mistakes in his handling of the union. While he cracked down on the communists, he also dissolved Syria's political parties, and banned the army from taking part in politics. His own National Union became the sole party of both wings of the new state but the 600-member parliament was heavily weighted in Egypt's favour as it had been allocated 400 deputies as compared to 200 for much smaller Syria and he issued his nationalisation decrees without consulting Damascus.

Although the communists had been crushed in Syria and Egypt, Jordan and Lebanon viewed the union as a threat to their existence while the western powers believed the United Arab Republic and the popular Nasser, who had fought in 1948 against the creation of Israel, endangered the Jewish state. When Lebanese president Camille Chamoun attempted to amend the country's constitution to give himself a second term in office in May 1958, the country's Sunni and Druze communities revolted and appealed for help from Nasser, who was drawn into what became Lebanon's first civil war. Western concerns over his intentions were whipped up after, on July 14th, the Iraqi army overthrew the monarchy installed in by Britain in Baghdad after World War I. US president Eisenhower responded by deploying troops to Beirut to ensure there would be a peaceful handover of power although the US was in no position to keep Chamoun in office.

The crisis was resolved by UN envoys Rajeshwar Dayal and Norwegian general Odd Bull, who set up an observer mission to report on possible smuggling into Lebanon of weapons and men across the border from Syria. With the help of Godfrey, then Indian chargé d'affaires in Beirut, they cooked up a report denying UAR involvement, thereby averting a major crisis. General Fuad Chehab, a figure acceptable to Lebanon's divided communities, was elected president and took over from Chamoun on completion of his term in September.

The external adventures of the UAR plus Syrian internal pressures had led to the Syrian coup which was supported by both the Baath party and members of the country's commercial and political elite. Several weeks after the collapse of the union, I received a bitter letter from Sawsan, saying her father had been seriously involved in the dissolution of the union.

South Hadley, January 1962

Shortly after returning to college after Christmas holidays, UNRWA's education chief Dr. Van Diffelen wrote describing the crackle of gunfire on New Year's Eve during a coup mounted by junior army officers in collusion with the Syrian Social Nationalists (SSNP), the first pan-Arab political party. Founded in 1932, by Antoun Saadeh, the secular party's goal was to unite the countries of the Fertile Crescent. The officers were promptly arrested and scores of SSNP members were rounded up, putting an end to the attempt. Among the detainees were friends I had made during my summer in Beirut.

Beirut, September 10th, 1962

I returned to Beirut exactly a year after I had departed. For my Mount Holyoke graduation present I had asked for a third-class ticket on a Trans Atlantic liner and passage from its home port to Lebanon. The ship was the Queen Frederica, a Greek ship built in 1926, used for troop transport during the war, and repeatedly refitted as a passenger liner. I shared a four-bunk bed double cabin with seven other women, one an elderly Greek grandmother who took to her bed as soon as she boarded and stayed put until we reached Athens six days later. Among my roommates were a cheerful middle-aged Greek woman, Sophia, who taught me folk dancing, and a couple of other university students. At the beginning of the voyage, there were only three in the third-class dining room, where Greek food and retsina were served. The rest were or imagined themselves too ill to eat.

While standing at the rail, I was taken up by three young Italian-Americans from Chicago: Franco, Mario and a large tough man whose name I have long forgotten. Ex-jailbirds, they were being deported to Sicily before they could break the law again and end up with long prison terms. When I asked Franco why he was being exiled, he replied he had beaten up his girlfriend for going with someone else while he was inside. Franco tried to excuse himself and his friends by saying they had grown up in violent families living in violent neighbourhoods, so they always dealt violently with problems. I responded by saying that he had a choice. He did not have to remain trapped in this cycle, he could escape. But when I mentioned there was a rather threatening Greek who followed me and the women sharing my rooms in the bowel of the ship, Franco told his large com-panion, who carried a knife in his sock, to accompany us and make certain we arrived safely. When we docked at Palermo, we shook hands. Franco gave me an address. I sent him a postcard from Beirut, not expecting a reply, but he wrote back in a childish hand and ungrammatical but well-expressed English.

I arrived at Beirut port on a small Greek vessel where I was the sole passenger. Our stops at Alexandria and Limassol en route from Pireaus made me even more eager to land and I urged the mate to get us there early, so early that I missed Sawsan and UNRWA friend Constantine who had come to meet me. I hired a taxi to take me and my two trunks to the Medical Gate of the university but have no recollection of how I got the trunks down the long flight of steps to the women's hostel for graduate students. My room had a grand view of the Mediterranean, azure beneath a clear blue sky; once again, I had escaped the clutches of Bay City.

Despite the coup attempt on New Year's Eve, Lebanon was a land of hope and glory. It remained a refuge for talented or dissident Arabs from across the region, especially for next door neighbours, Palestinians driven from their homes during Israel's war of establishment and Syrians fleeing chronic political instability. My classmates were Iranians, Jordanians, Lebanese, Palestinians, Egyptians, Iraqis, Afghans, Pakistanis, Syrians, Cypriots, and the occasional American, one of whom was paid by the CIA to spy on fellow students.

I took master's degree level courses at the AUB with professors from the US, Syria, and Palestine and worked at the Economic Research Institute as the research assistant of Yusif Sayigh, a Palestinian with a Syrian passport who was preparing a book on the political and social components of economic development. As its offices were still under construction, most of the institute's personnel were temporarily parked in the cavernous entrance to West Hall and in spare rooms elsewhere. Yusif and I were dispatched to a small room in Jessup Hall which housed the political science department.

Dispersal did not dim the enthusiasm of the professors and their aides for the task of trying to record the ongoing economic "take off" of the countries of the Arab world.

There were also great expectations on the political front. Arabs were optimistic because while serving in the Senate young president John Kennedy had called for Arab self-governance and an end to meddling in Arab affairs. He was prepared to seek rapprochement with Egypt's charismatic Nasser rather than plot to overthrow him.

Beirut was a pleasure-loving city. We swam at the AUB beach and the Sporting Club in the shadow of the landmark Pigeon Rocks that rise out of the sea below Raouche and sipped negronis or Turkish coffees at the Dolce Vita across from the promenade. Cinemas showed the latest films, shops carried Chanel, Jacques Fath, Givenchy, and Mary Quant. A Tunisian friend, Rashid, managed to do the impossible: teach me to dance, mostly at Les Caves du Roy where we went when one of us had money and where Aldo, the bartender, served us strawberries with cream as well as too, too expensive champagne cocktails. He was eventually accused of being an agent for one snoopy foreign power or another, no one knew which. A confirmed spy, British-Soviet double agent Kim Philby attended the Sayighs' Christmas party a few weeks before Britain's secret service failed to kidnap him. He eventually turned up in Moscow.

Having had enough of hostel life, I moved into a two-room flat off Hamra, the main street of West Beirut, but within months abandoned it for a fourth-floor walk-up roof flat on a hill above Raouche, a flat with a slice of sea view between the Shell building and other sprouting high rises. Goats grazed on the grassy mound below my wide terrace, bells on their collars warning the old shepherd if they strayed.

August 1963

Usama met me on campus one morning to register the transfer of ownership of his 14-year-old MG-TC, called "Hajji" by mechanics at the garage where she was serviced because she made the pilgrimage so often. I had admired Hajji for months. She had been parked near the Medical Gate, abandoned. Usama, a professor of biochemistry, had decided to sell Hajji after buying a family car. As he drove to the office on the edge of Beirut where ownership would be transferred, and cars were subjected to the *mechanique*, the roadworthiness test, Usama explained the mysterious workings of the stick shift as I had been brought up with the automatic system. I watched and hoped I had absorbed the verbal lesson until we returned to town and I was plunged into action when, in midday traffic, Usama stopped in front of the building where he lived, got out with the engine running, and told me to takeover. I clambered over the gearbox and learnt the stick shift instantly. Hajji forgave grinding mistakes. As far as I know, I was the first female to drive a sports car in Beirut. Many people, however, dismissed Hajji, a beautiful British racing green, as an old car, beyond the age of admiration.

Hajji and I toured Beirut, choosing routes where buildings on either side of the street produced the most satisfyingly resonant roar. Since parking was a problem in the city centre, I rode the little red tram to shop in Souk al-Franj for cheese from Mr. Mahmoud, a small round man in a tight beige overall, who had 250 varieties in summer and 500 in winter, and warm fresh bread from the bakery just outside the souk.

Gaza, Easter 1963

Neville Kanakaratne invited me to visit Gaza for a gala event staged by UN peacekeepers, but I had no leave for the dates it was being held. So, I went for a few days over Easter vacation in mid-April, flying to Gaza, once again, on the UNRWA plane, an ancient DC3, sitting in a bucket seat and wrapped in a blanket to keep out the cold as the aircraft was not airtight. I booked in at Marna House, a small guest house run by Margaret Nassar, a handsome Palestinian woman with good business sense. I had resided there during my first visit to Gaza and have stayed there ever since. Marna House has always been a home away from home In Gaza for UN visitors and journalists, although now there are more up-to-date hotels along the seafront.

Dinner with the Indian contingent was a splendid affair in the Indian officers' mess with the regiment's battle honours, flags, and silver on display – gleaming candlesticks, mugs, plates and trays. Lovingly polished. Standing behind each person at the long table was a formally uniformed jawan who served food and drink.

The next morning, Neville organised for me a private acrobatic display by Indian troops. I was parked in a wicker chair on a sandy knoll on the edge of the camp, a glass of beer in my hand. On one side stood Neville, a wicked gleam in his eyes, on the other, Patrick, a portly sergeant of Irish-Indian background. On the level area below, Indian soldiers climbed a greased poll, tumbled, somersaulted, and displayed agility and expertise while I, feeling like a young Queen Victoria, sat a little embarrassed and somewhat bemused, viewing the exercises. Queens expect such treatment, mere mortals do not.

Bay City, September 18th, 1961

Television broadcast news announced the death of UN secretary general Dag Hammarskjöld and 15 aides in a plane crash flying over Northern Rhodesia en route to negotiate a ceasefire between warring parties in the Congo. My parents – wondering how I could have a connection to this event in distant Africa – stood by as I desperately rang common friends in New York, demanding. "Was Neville on the plane?" No one knew.

As Hammarskjöld's legal adviser, Neville should have been on the flight but had been left behind because he had no French, the language spoken by both parties to the conflict since the Congo had been colonised by Belgium. Neville's lack of French saved his life.

We had met at Mount Holyoke when Neville, a brilliant, articulate delegate on the Ceylon UN mission, had come to lecture on the decolonisation of Africa before the international relations club – of which I eventually became president. A small, finely boned man with thinning greying hair, a strong nose, and wide eyes framed with thick, long lashes, Neville loved coming to the women's college and staying in the dorm, surrounded by female students, many of them admiring. When I went to New York to stay with a friend who lived in a Sutton Place maid's apartment, Neville would take us out to lunch or dinner. I tasted my first Sub-Continental food at a party at the home of his Ceylonese friends: the fish pickle brought tears to my eyes but did not discourage me from developing a taste for hot, spicy *khana*.

Neville had presented me with a ticket to attend the 1960 opening of the UN General Assembly and dropped me off at the appropriate entrance to the vast hall where I suddenly found myself standing next to Fidel Castro while he greeted colleagues. My front row seat, reserved for senior officials not college students, gave me a close view of the proceedings and the leaders attending. The main address that day was given in Serbo-Croat by Yugoslav president Tito. Many delegates slipped away but I dared not.

In the spring of 1961, Neville invited me to his going away party at his flat in New York, but I was due to present a paper at a seminar presided over by the formidable Ruth Lawson, professor of international relations. After agonising over whether to give my paper or go to the party, I chose the party. Held at Neville's flat, it was a small gathering. He cooked an array of spicy dishes, learnt in self-defence while he was a student at Cambridge University. The guests were mostly female, some tearful, as Neville, who was gay, was very much loved by young women who found him a firm friend and grand escort. None of us knew that he was set to move from the delegates' lounge to the hallowed 38th-floor housing the secretary general's offices.

The morning after the party I went to the tiny UNRWA office, located in the bowels of the UN building, to see if there had been any reply to my request to serve as a summer intern in the agency's Beirut headquarters. Molly, the lady in charge, said, "You're in luck. The high commissioner's here. I'll ask if he can see you." He agreed and told me there were some in Beirut who wanted to turn me down: "A young American girl could be a problem." But John Davis had decided to accept me as the agency's first intern and first volunteer. "You'll have to come for three months. There's no point in travelling all the way to Beirut for six weeks," he said.

If I had not attended Neville's going away party, my life would have been very different. My fall-back internship application had been submitted to the office of the UN High Commissioner for Refugees in Geneva. The place was taken up by a classmate. Miss Lawson, who had fallen ill and could not preside over the seminar, was delighted with both internships which were significant additions to the programme. It was a close-run thing – that choice.

New Delhi, 1959

Following the first Lebanese civil war, Godfrey returned to New Delhi, his role in wrapping up the conflict mentioned in parliament by prime minister Jawaharlal Nehru and the Lebanese Order of the

Cedar in hand. Godfrey applied for another posting in the region but was offered, instead, Washington or Paris.

Invited for breakfast at Nehru's official residence, Godfrey arrived a few minutes late due to Delhi traffic and was shown into the dining room where the prime minister, his daughter Indira Gandhi, and Lady Edwina Mountbatten had already taken their places at the table. The bearer asked softly how many eggs Godfrey would like. "One." The three glanced at each other, discreet smiles on their lips.

Some years later, he asked Mrs. Gandhi why they had smiled and glanced at each other after he had placed his order for breakfast. She replied that they used to bet on whether a guest was a one- or two-egg person. "We were right about you."

On the issue of posting, "Mr. Nehru apologised to me," Godfrey told me, "He said he could not change the minds of the bureaucrats in South Block."

Godfrey quit the foreign service and worked briefly in Delhi for the *National Herald*, published by Indira Gandhi's husband Feroze, before taking up the post of regional correspondent for *The Statesman* of New Delhi and Calcutta, fleeing India and returning to the Beirut flat he had occupied as a diplomat, content he would no longer have to attend diplomatic receptions or wear a tie. If he had stayed on as a diplomat, we would never have met.

4

LIBERATION

India, February 1967

Godfrey was asked by *The Statesman* to return to India to cover the election for the lower house of parliament, the Lok Sabha, the fourth since independence. He was not tasked with reporting on issues but on process: conduct of the campaign, candidates, voters, local colour. The editors thought the paper's foreign correspondents could provide a fresh look at the workings of Indian democracy. He suggested I should join him after he met in Delhi with his editors who had assigned him the south – Hyderabad, Karnataka, Tamil Nadu, Kerala, and Goa. "Before we get married, you must see if you can live in India, in case I decide to go back," he reasoned.

I was granted leave from my jobs and a friend on *The Christian Science Monitor* said he would take a couple of feature articles on the election. After spending several hours people watching at Bombay's airport, I caught a flight to Hyderabad where I met Godfrey at a hotel newly opened in a small palace located in the city centre. Our bathroom was larger than the bedroom, furnished in Anglo-Indian colonial style. We ordered an expensive bottle of Chianti with dinner to celebrate our reunion.

The first leg of our tour took us from Hyderabad to Bangalore, Godfrey's home town. Forty years earlier, his aggressively Protestant father, a customs officer working on the Irrawady River in Maymyo in British-ruled Burma, had retired, packed up his family and moved to Richmond Town in Bangalore after his eldest son had married a Catholic Anglo-Burmese girl. Godfrey quoted his father as saying, "I won't live in the same country with them," a son who wed a Catholic woman. His father sold at a loss two houses he owned in Maymyo.

Godfrey, who was eight at the time of the migration, showed me Baldwin Boys' School where he had studied. "I was small and slight. When I was beaten by a teacher, my father went to the school armed with a walking stick and told the headmaster if anyone laid a finger on me, he would use it. I was never beaten again."

Godfrey's mother decided she had had enough of raising children after the eldest three had matured and departed to pay long visits to friends. Godfrey and his sister Daphne, "D," 18 months older, did not get along with their father. D took up a teaching job and moved out. Eager to learn about religions other than his father's narrow evangelical Protestantism, Godfrey read Buddhist texts, the Quran, and the Hindu Gita. "The Gita was the last straw for my father, he kicked me out of the house. I went to live with D for some time." At fifteen he went to Christian College in Madras where he received his BA in English literature. He took courses at Madras University until he secured a teaching job in a boys' school but left to volunteer for the war against Japan. On the application he was asked to list by preference branches of the services he wanted to join. He wrote, "Infantry, infantry, infantry," and was assigned to the air force as an official war correspondent.

In Bangalore we stayed in a rambling British-era bungalow with a sway-backed faded red-tile roof, a veranda with a rickety railing and a view of the dusty maidan where youths played cricket during the afternoons and stable boys exercised polo ponies in the evenings. From our base we made forays into the countryside around Mysore City, to the south, travelling with candidates from Congress and other parties. On one occasion, we drove through the dark in jeeps along rough tracks until we were met by a delegation from the village where the candidate was set to address a rally. We climbed down and walked in procession, drummers leading the way, elders armed with bright petromax lamps leading the march through fields of stubble to the panchayat hall which had been adorned with a huge portrait of slain US president John Kennedy. They had been told "an American" was coming and wanted to honour me.

For our class in domestic politics, my Mount Holyoke roommate Caroline and I had been instructed to campaign for Republican senatorial candidate Leverett Saltonstall, a "Boston Brahmin." We gathered flyers from his headquarters in Holyoke, a short bus ride from South Hadley, before going to the Democratic party offices and collecting material on presidential candidate Kennedy. Then we began knocking on doors with the aim of convincing potential voters to split their ballot between Saltonstall, a popular liberal who had served in the senate from 1945, and the handsome junior senator from the state. He had captured the imagination of the country's youth – and of many round the world. We celebrated when both "our" candidates won their races, Saltonstall easily, Kennedy narrowly.

We had also been in Washington on April 17th, 1961, a dramatic day for the new administration. As our crocodile of Mount Holyoke and Amherst students ambled past a news agent, I caught a glimpse of a bold newspaper headline proclaiming the invasion of Cuba by US-sponsored insurgents seeking to topple the Castro regime. We made our way to the White House and the office of Kennedy speechwriter and adviser Theodore Sorensen, with whom we had a longstanding appointment. He refused to comment. The next day other senior members of the cabinet tried to fob us off with, "It's a hold-over from the Eisenhower administration." But we were not mollified. Our hero had let us down. He had behaved as a typical imperial president rather than as a president prepared to break with the past.

I heard the news of Kennedy's assassination on November 22nd, 1963, on the *BBC* the next morning before going to office at the American University of Beirut. Shocked, stunned, numb, I drove through what seemed to be the hushed streets of the city, silenced by this death in far away Dallas. My colleague Mona was red-eyed. She had been in her bedroom when her mother called out, "They've killed the president!" Mona remarked, "I thought she meant our president...Not Kennedy." Despite failings and faults, Kennedy had been a president admired by the world. The last US president to win hearts and minds abroad as well as at home.

Mysore countryside, February 1967

When introducing us to the villagers, the candidate, a handsome young man in a beige tweed jacket and brown trousers, made no excuses or explanations. He announced Godfrey as a correspondent of *The Statesman* of Calcutta and New Delhi and me as a journalist with *The Christian Science Monitor* (which did not publish my articles). Godfrey's pipe, smoked while the candidate spoke, produced a certain amount of amusement. He and I were considered foreigners by the villagers. The candidate was put into that category as well.

On a second tour with another candidate from a different party, we were offered lunch, seated at a table with cutlery and plates while our host, the candidate and his entourage sat on the floor and ate with their fingers from fresh, broad banana leaves. We joined them. Godfrey was neither comfortable on the floor nor adept at eating with his fingers. "Anglo-Indians consider this going native," he would say as an excuse.

At one small, distant village surrounded by fields, women and children lined up to gently, politely, pinch my arm since they had never seen such a pale-skinned woman before.

The race was contested by Indira Gandhi as Congress head. Godfrey said later party elders had decided to elevate "the girl" whom they thought, wrongly, they could manipulate. They had not counted on the considerable experience she had gained from Nehru's tutelage during her years as his hostess and confidante.

Since polling took place over five days we were able to observe voting at India's southern-most station at Kanyakumari, known also as Cape Comorin, where the Arabian Sea meets the Bay of Bengal and the Indian Ocean. We then moved on to the coastal hamlet of Kovalam in Kerala where we stayed at a five-bedroom government rest house on the beach. The only other guests were a bearded pundit and his US female follower who were definitely not on a spiritual mission for they never left their room.

The morning before we arrived one of the fragile fishing boats had not returned. While several boats went out to look for the missing fisherman, the women, their high-pitched voices rolling Malayalam words off their tongues, congregated round the well next to the guest house. From our room we could hear the hiss of the rope, the slap of the bucket as it hit the water far below and the thump of the bucket as it struck the stone edge of the well when it reached the surface. Their voices and the splash and crash in the well went on all night long while the women kept vigil. At dawn, the drowned fisherman's body washed up on the shore. The next day the villagers cast their votes in a palm-sheltered booth set up for the occasion, illiterates choosing candidates by party symbols. Indira Gandhi won by a landslide. I found I could tolerate India better than an impatient Godfrey could.

The proposal that he should return to Delhi as *The Statesman's* defence correspondent fell through. The day we returned to Beirut, my father rang to say grandma Fancher had died. I had bought her a beautiful silk scarf in India.

Chemlan, Spring-Summer 1966

Godfrey and I were sitting on the wall below the last hairpin bend in the road from upper to lower Chemlan. Below us stretched a rolling slope of green-grey olive terraces bordered by the dark ribbon of runway at Beirut's international airport, and the ever-changing blue of the Mediterranean. Just below our feet were neglected olive terraces and a landslide of broken russet sandstone once quarried by the villagers. "Let's build our house here," he stated, in a curious proposal of either long-term cohabitation or marriage.

He decided to buy and build in Chemlan after I told him he had accumulated a large amount of money in his current account at the British Bank of the Middle East. I had discovered his impressive balance when he asked me to cash a cheque for him while I was running errands. He had never bothered to record deposits or withdrawals in his cheque book and was surprised at the news. The owner of the wedge-shaped plot of some 4,000 square metres was only too happy to sell at an affordable price so Godfrey asked his lawyer to apply for permission to buy and we began to draw up plans for the house that came to be known as *Beit al-Hindi*, the House of the Indian. The first house to be constructed in the village for a century, a house made of three arches, cut stones, roof and floor tiles, and wood cannibalised from a missionary school built in the neighbouring village of Souk al-Gharb in 1868, exactly a century earlier.

We spent the summer in the small flat on top of the stone village house rented by Rasha and Walid, climbing mountains on weekends with Munir and Usama, driving down to Beirut weekdays for work.

Jerusalem-Bethlehem, Christmas Eve, 1966

Godfrey and I moved into our favourite room at the American Colony hotel, directly across the stone-paved courtyard from the entrance. Christmas decorations were sparce, as the hotel hosted few guests. East Jerusalem was still a comfortable backwater, ruled by Jordan, rather than a major tourist destination. We walked down the street toward St. George's Anglican cathedral on Nablus road, passing houses which stood on the Green Line dividing the Palestinian eastern and Israeli western sectors of the holy city. It was a time of testy coexistence, interrupted on occasion by a bout of violence between Israel and Syria. For the Arabs, Israel was a no man's land, a dead zone, sealed off by the barbed wire and rubbish along the Green Line, an entity referred to by journalists as "South Wales" or "Dixie," its name erased by the stroke of a felt tip pen from maps in books imported into Lebanon and other Arab countries.

Dinner was at the flat of Usama and Samia in the Augusta Victoria hospital compound where we met Amin Majaj, the mayor of East Jerusalem, and his wife Betty. Usama and Amin, a physician, were conducting research on malnutrition among Palestinian refugee children.

After the meal we drove out to Shepherds' Fields at Beit Sahour near Bethlehem to attend Protestant celebrations in the misty open air. Here, tradition says shepherds grazing their flocks were startled by an angel proclaiming the birth of Jesus at a stable in Bethlehem. Orthodox and Catholics built churches at rival sites said to be the true Shepherds' Fields where they hold services, but we chose the great outdoors.

The next morning, we explored one or two of the caves in the limestone bluffs descending to the Jordan Valley at the archaeological site of Qumran where the 2,000-year-old Dead Sea Scrolls were discovered. The region was quiet for the time being.

Jerusalem, late May 1967

I flew to Amman where I hired a taxi to take me to Jerusalem. Traffic was light on the highway that dipped into the Jordan Valley. The headlights of vehicles we passed had been painted blue as the region tottered to the edge of a new war with Israel, the third since its emergence in 1948.

There had been minor clashes between Syria and Israel early that year. In May, Moscow reported Israeli troops had massed along the Syrian ceasefire line. Nasser had responded with troop deployments in Sinai and the May 19th expulsion of UN peacekeepers from Sinai and Gaza. Egypt also took over UN positions at Sharm el-Sheikh overlooking the passage called the Straits of Tiran, the sole entrance from the Red Sea to the Gulf of Aqaba. Israel had warned in 1957 when it withdrew from Sinai after the 1956 Anglo-French-Israeli war on Egypt that closing the straits would constitute a casus belli. Nasser declared the straits closed on May 22nd.

I found Godfrey in his room across the stone-flagged courtyard at the American Colony hotel. He had arrived a couple of days earlier to report on the situation to *The Statesman*. Afraid he would be trapped without me if war broke out, I decided to join him. We had dinner and went for a walk through the dark empty streets. We entered the Old City through Damascus Gate and at a bakery at the top of shuttered Khan al-Zeit street bought a couple of flat rounds of hot Arabic bread which we nibbled on and fed to white donkeys making their way on their own with panniers of stones from a construction site. At the Church of the Holy Sepulchre we found men covered in fine white cement dust loading the donkeys and slapping them on their flanks to send them on their way.

When we returned to Beirut, I painted our light bulbs and Hajji's headlights with bluing cubes melted in water into a paste, our concession to blackout. Jordan's king Hussein and Nasser concluded a joint defence agreement and Iraqi troops began to prepare for battle.

Beirut, June 5th, 1967

We were listening to the news on the *BBC* when Rasha rang to see if we had heard Israel had attacked Egyptian airfields early that morning and, according to reports, destroyed the country's air force on the ground. Egyptian SAM missiles and radar installations were also taken out. While Egypt's *Voice of the Arabs* falsely proclaimed a victory in a war of destiny, Israel's ground forces advanced from the Negev into Sinai and Gaza. Shooting and mortar fire between Jordanian and Israeli forces erupted in Jerusalem at 9.30 in the morning and at 11.15 Jordanian Howitzers began a bombardment of West Jerusalem, captured by Israel in 1948.

Shortly after her call, Rasha – who had been on the phone with her brother-in-law Usama in Jerusalem – arrived at the flat, determined to counter the misleading propaganda already being broadcast by both sides and western-dominated media. We formed the "Afro-Asian Unity Movement" and asked a printer to prepare stationery. That evening Israeli warplanes struck Syrian airfields, wiping out that country's defensive capabilities.

We wrote bulletins based on information received from phone interviews with Palestinians in Jerusalem, the West Bank and Gaza, Jordanians and Syrians. The material was flown in envelopes daily to Geneva by Middle East Airlines and distributed to Arab and Third World diplomats, news outlets and activists. We gave as our address the post box of former Lebanese prime minister Saeb Salam who was happy to support the effort. Later we received letters of thanks from Arab diplomats based in Europe and elsewhere.

The war ended in the West Bank on the 7th, with the Old City of Jerusalem falling to the Israelis. On the 8th a halt was called in Sinai which also came under Israeli occupation. The battle over Syria's Golan Heights concluded on June 10th. A triumphant Israel continued mopping up on the 11th.

Israel not only won the war on the ground but also the battle for the hearts and minds of opinion makers, politicians and the western public. *Time-Life* staffer David Rubinger's iconic black and white photograph of Israeli paratroopers at the Old City of Jerusalem's Western Wall soon after its capture hit the front pages of the world's newspapers. Few carried stories about Israel bulldozing the homes of poor Palestinians living in the Moroccan quarter next to the site to make a wide plaza so religious Jews could worship. Homeless Palestinians were put on buses, driven to the Jordan River and expelled across a bombed bridge into the Kingdom of Jordan.

Our friend Israel Shahak said Israelis, even those who don't believe in God, believed the war had liberated the land God gave to the Jews.

In Britain's *Sunday Telegraph*, Peregrine Worsthorne, a harsh critic of the decolonisation process, wrote an article entitled the *Triumph of the Civilised* in which he said, "..last week a tiny Western community, surrounded by immensely superior numbers of the underdeveloped peoples, has shown itself able to impose its will on the Arabs today almost as effortlessly as the first whites were able to do on the Afro-Asian native in the imperial heyday."

Super-sentimental photographs and racist articles like "Triumph of the Civilised" defined for many westerners their view on the conflict. Its victims, the Palestinians were forgotten; Egyptians,

Syrians and Jordanians maligned and demonised. While western countries lined up with Israel, as they had during and after the 1948 conflict, Third World nations gravitated toward the Arabs who were not only defeated but deeply humiliated and determined to meet Israel's challenge and regain not only dignity but deterrence.

That traumatic war was a turning point for the region. Israel had demonstrated it was the dominant military power. This forced discredited Arab governments to invest increasingly in armed forces and weaponry, starving the promised socio-economic "take off" of essential funds and leaving citizens undereducated, unemployed and frustrated. Defeat made the Arabs even more determined to stand against Israel, and refuse recognition. In November 1967, the UN Security Council passed resolution 242 calling for Israeli withdrawal from territories occupied that June, an end to belligerency, respect for the territorial integrity of all states in the region, and a settlement of the Palestinian refugee problem. The resolution was ignored.

Sixty-seven was my first war. Godfrey had fought in World War II, witnessed the slaughter in New Delhi during India's partition twenty years earlier, and had a hand in resolving Lebanon's first civil war. Sixty-seven was followed by regional warfare in 1973, 1982, 1991, 2002, 2003, 2006, 2008-09, and 2014 as well as the turmoil of the 2011 Arab Spring against authoritarian rulers, precipitating conflicts in Bahrain, Syria, Libya, Iraq, and Yemen. Covering this region meant becoming a war correspondent.

Beirut-Chemlan, July-August 1967

Soon after Israel's conquest of East Jerusalem, the West Bank, Gaza and the Syrian Golan, Godfrey went to Jerusalem to report on the situation and see how friends were faring, including Usama and Samia at Augusta Victoria hospital. The hospital built in 1907 and located on a vast campus on Mount Scopus next to the Mount of

Olives, had been bombed by the Israelis and the wards on the top floor destroyed by fire. Photos taken of the devastation showed the blasted roof, smashed tiles, blackened timbers, and the scorched and twisted skeletons of iron bedsteads. Patients had evacuated while fire and brimstone rained down on the city. The Afro-Asian Unity Movement dispatched photos of the devastation at the hospital to Geneva for distribution to outlets and diplomats.

Rasha set up an office in the basement of her house where volunteers wrote English language bulletins and leaflets. One of the leaflets produced, *Collusion 67*, was based on an article Godfrey wrote for *The Statesman* but was also published by Beirut's *Daily Star*, *al-Moharer*, and *al-Jarida*. He argued the 1967 war was a result of active western political and military collusion with Israel.

The Johnson administration had not only failed to restrain Israel – which was ready and waiting for a pretext to launch this conflict – but, on May 26th, Washington had also urged Nasser not to be the first to open fire. Interestingly enough, some hours later, the Soviet ambassador in Cairo had told the Egyptians the same thing.

France, and perhaps, the US, had provided Israel with arms and munitions needed to wage the decisive air war. Once the land offensive began, the US and other western powers pressed Israel for a ceasefire only when it had achieved its territorial objectives. Russian demands in the UN Security Council for Israeli withdrawal were dismissed.

Godfrey also suggested Britain's radar facilities on Mount Troodos in Cyprus and US ships of the Sixth Fleet and Russian naval vessels in the eastern Mediterranean would have been able to track the waves of Israeli warplanes flying low towards Egypt's airbases early on the morning of June 5th and warn their respective governments about the Israeli attack. Since the US and Soviet Union had asked Nasser not to initiate a conflict, Godfrey argued these powers, in particular, should have made an effort to turn around the Israeli aerial attack force which took an hour and a half to reach the main Egyptian airbases near Cairo.

Godfrey wrote, "This connivance gave to Israel the initiative that won her the war in the first place and, second, the inaction of the Powers on the morning of the attack ensured for Israel the element of surprise – which made the attack so devastating."

A few hours after the article, a concise version of the pamphlet, appeared in the Beirut papers, the US, Russian and British embassies responded. Godfrey wrote, "The Americans claimed that there was a confusion in [his] calculations between miles and kilometres; the Russians said they had too few ships to know what the Israelis were doing; the British admitted that it was entirely feasible for their radar on Cyprus to pick up the Israeli planes but that they had had no time to do anything with this information."

The Russians said Israel was the aggressor and called for Israeli withdrawal to positions held before the conflict; the US and Britain did neither. Because of the article, and the more detailed pamphlet, Godfrey was attacked by officials from all three countries who sought to question his integrity. I was considered guilty by association with the man western critics accused of being an "Indian communist" who had not only levelled accusations against the US and Britain but also the Soviet Union.

As editor of the AUB alumni magazine, I exacerbated matters by criticising certain university officials of adopting a weak line on the war rather than standing with the Arabs as Bayard Dodge, president in 1948 had done. I lost my jobs at the university and Godfrey and I were dismissed by the board of Middle East Forum. If Godfrey and I had not had influential Lebanese friends I would have been deported from Lebanon as soon as my work permit was revoked.

In spite of – and because of – the regional turmoil, we had a string of guests. I never knew who would turn up at Godfrey's modest top floor flat in a soiled pink block on Makdissi street off Hamra, the main thoroughfare of West Beirut, or who would come to stay with us in Chemlan where we had rented the top floor of the house belonging to car repairman Abu Habib. From the veranda of this old stone building we had a grand view of the coast and the shimmering metallic sea.

When UN Emergency Force commander Indar Jit Rikhye called at the flat he told us he had had no choice but to pull the peacekeeping force out of Gaza once Nasser had formally requested its withdrawal. UN secretary general U Thant "tried to stall," Indar said. "He knew withdrawal would mean war." Units of the UN force were pulling out as the Israelis advanced into Gaza and Sinai, destroying UN vehicles and killing three soldiers. A World War II Indian army veteran, Rikhye observed the Israeli soldiers take up heroic poses on tanks as they drove into Gaza. For him this belied their seriousness as soldiers. He and his staff were trapped under fire on the beach in Gaza until Israeli defence minister Moshe Dayan intervened.

In Chemlan over mounds of crabs simmered in white wine and herbs, Willy Lazarus, the *Press Trust of India* correspondent based in Cairo, described the mood in Egypt after Nasser had assumed responsibility for the defeat and proclaimed his intention of stepping down, prompting hundreds of thousands of Egyptians and Arabs across the region to pour spontaneously into the streets and demand that he should stay.

Abu Abraham, a cartoonist for *The Observer*, *The Guardian* and *Tribune* who joined us for a few days in Chemlan had a great deal to say about pro-Israeli triumphalism in Britain. Over breakfast on the long veranda, he drew a profile of me which hangs on the wall behind me in my Nicosia study below a Jules Feiffer cartoon of me, a pro-Arab Mount Holyoke student in Bermuda shorts and veil. This line drawing was produced by Feiffer in moments at the instigation of roommate Caroline while he was visiting the college.

Abu blotted his copybook with British publications by criticising Israel's conquest of Gaza, East Jerusalem, the West Bank and the Syrian Golan. He depicted the post-war flight of Palestinians from the West Bank and Gaza in a cartoon of the Virgin Mary and Christ child on a donkey being led by Joseph into Egypt with an Israeli soldier in pursuit.

After years of living in Britain, Abu returned to India in 1969 when the split between east and west was particularly sharp and anti-Indian racism was on the rise due to the mass migration to Britain of thousands of Asian British "subjects" living in newly independent African countries.

Beirut, October 31st, 1967

After a hurried sandwich lunch, I drove Godfrey in Hajji to al-Liwaa newspaper edited by Rasha's relative Abed al Ghani Salam. His office was a large room with salon furniture, velvet drapes and a sparkling crystal chandelier. While waiting with our witnesses, Usama, Amin and Leila for the sheikh to turn up, Godfrey and I discussed what we wanted in the marriage contract, the *kitab*. Barred in Lebanon from marrying as a Christian because of a previous marriage, Godfrey had become a Muslim, a simple process of making the declaration of the faith before a cleric and signing a document.

As the turbaned cleric, with a well-trimmed grizzled beard, began to draw up the *kitab*, Godfrey asked Usama to specify the items we had agreed: my right to divorce and payment of a sum of money in case of dissolution of the marriage or death. The suspicious sheikh did not like this pairing of demands, believing, clearly,

Usama was trying to take advantage of Godfrey. The original sum of 50,000 Lebanese pounds, about $17,000 – the figure Usama had included in his own contract – was whittled down to 5,000 Lebanese pounds ($1,700) by the grey-caftaned cleric. His determination to protect Godfrey's interests forced us to suppress grins and hold back laughter. We turned our eyes to the window where a black sky brought heavy rain and a scattering of hailstones. I worried that Hajji, whose canvas roof had been folded down, would be swamped. Once the *kitab* was completed and signed, Abed al Ghani called for Turkish coffee to be served. It came in tiny gold-rimmed cups on a silver tray. As soon as the sheikh departed, Amin brought out a bottle of champagne. "The sheikh is from Tripoli," Amin remarked. "He married us." Abed al Ghani quickly produced flutes. His office was very unlike any newspaper office we had ever seen.

Beirut had been washed clean by the sudden storm. The sun was out. The streets were wet, and buildings studded with sparkling diamond drops of rain. "Rain and sun, a fox's wedding, is good luck," Godfrey observed. Amin's driver had put up Hajji's soft top and garnished the front of the car with stalks of orange and white gladioli. Godfrey and I sped out of Beirut to congratulatory honks and flashing lights, paused to buy petrol on the coast road, and made for the Tabarja Beach hotel where we spent a few days together in peace and quiet before returning to a party that began with breakfast and ended at two the next morning at Les Caves du Roy.

Chemlan, July and September 1968

We celebrated groundbreaking for the house at the beginning of July with friends at a picnic on our hillside and spent some time at lodgings in the nearby village of Ainab. From the road above our land, we could watch Syrian labourers mixing cement on a flat area, lifting the mixture in baskets made from cast-off tyres, and pouring it into standing wood slat moulds. The Syrians carefully chipped stone blocks for the exterior puzzle.

The cement walls went up, and the roof slab went on, raw and grey until the blocks of stone were put in place and Marseilles-manufactured roof tiles were laid. The fireplace in the sitting room and the flagstone floor in the room Marya eventually occupied were magnificent examples of a local Lebanese mason's craft. Thick dark stained wooden boards from the old school were transformed into beams by being nailed to wooden blocks sunk in the dining room-salon's sloping ceiling – 12 metres from the floor at its highest point. The cupboards and iron railings were also the work of Chemlanis, both Tabibs and Hittis, a fair balance of village clan factions.

The main entrance of the house was on the second of four terraces, the heavy wooden door had a brass knocker shaped like a hand. Inside was a descending flight of stairs beside a massive limestone rock incorporated into the house. The view through two arched doors was of the countryside, trees and slopes with rocky outcrops. On the first floor were the dining-living room, the master bedroom, a bathroom with a strawberry and cream marble tub for two, the kitchen, and the room for offspring. Below were the study, library, washroom, and toilet with a shower.

John, our architect, drove us to the site sometime in early September to show us how the work was progressing. But as Godfrey stood at the back of the main room, he sighed, "I didn't imagine it would be so small." A serious Armenian, John retorted, defensively, "Wait till you bring your furniture. Furniture gives perspective. It's 15 meters from back to front, you know."

A few days short of three months after the groundbreaking, we moved in and invited Rasha and Walid for drinks in the evening. The books were our only possessions out of place. The roof tiles were still being laid and a hashish-addicted painter was repeatedly whitewashing the rooms on the lower floor. We hired a Druze labourer called Wadi'a and his elderly father to repair the olive terraces but had to dismiss them when they threatened to drive the terraces through the house. Our contractor, the Chemlani artisans who worked on the house, acquaintances in the village, and friends from Beirut were invited to the housewarming. Constantine, who came for a visit some time later, warned us about new houses: "The first year you give it to your enemy, the second, to a friend, and the third you move in." We suffered *Beit al-Hindi's* mistakes and faults and enjoyed its space, beauty and warmth.

Chemlan was a bucolic interlude between wars. We walked the village byways and made friends with year-round residents. We harvested our olives and took them to be pressed at the mill in Ainab where I forced the owners to clean the great stone bowl and wheel before transforming our good green olives into first rate oil. Most villagers took their olives when they were bitter black or brown and I did not want their residue to pollute our sweet oil. It was so precious that it was sampled by the owners of the press in tiny liquor glasses as it poured out of the centrifuge in a cloud of fine bubbles at the end of the pressing process. We asked butcher Selim to cook *awarma* (flakes of lamb preserved in melted fat from the animal's tail) which we fried with eggs during winter and added to spiced dahl to make a filling dish served with rice. I flattened figs and dried them on shallow baskets to make puddings for Christmas. While Godfrey continued to report for *The Statesman* on regional political developments, I wrote occasional feature articles for other publications on olives, nursing in the Middle East, and Arab food.

Beirut, January 4th, 1970

Named after Sulafa's younger daughter, Marya was a cheerful baby who slept through the night, fussed little, could sit up from day one and turn over in her basket soon after. Her passport photo showed her to be a bit sad. Perhaps, like her mother, she did not like having her picture taken.

Chemlan, March 1970

After a long lunch at Cliff House with Soraya, Michael Wall came to *Beit al-Hindi* where he proposed that Godfrey report regional events for *The Economist*. This was a welcome offer since *The Statesman* had given Godfrey three months notice at the end of 1969. The paper's new owners, a collection of industrialists dominated by Tata, had elevated to the post of managing editor CR Irani, a member of the right-wing Swatantra party opposed to Nehru's domestic and foreign policies. Irani decided Godfrey had to go because he was too critical of Israel. Under Irani's tutelage, *The Statesman* slipped from being among the most influential newspapers in India to the margins.

Shortly after Godfrey began writing for *The Economist*, foreign editor Brian Beedham came to Beirut. During a visit to Chemlan, he told us someone at the British embassy, he did not say whom, had suggested Godfrey was unsuitable, almost certainly because of *Whose Suez*? Brian shrugged it off. He was not a man to be influenced or intimidated.

Chemlan, August 15th, 1970

We hung out the Indian flag, arranged samosas and quiches on silver trays, and checked if we had put enough bottles of wine in the fridge. Willy, Clovis and Hala, Prue and Ian, Munir and Therese, John and Aza, Sulafa and Soraya arrived in stages for our quadruple celebration. Marya's name day, the feast of the Virgin celebrated with mountaintop fires across Lebanon, which coincides with Indian Independence Day, "VJ" or Victory over Japan day, and Prue's birthday.

As a substitute for baptismal Jordan River water, Godfrey's former driver (whose job I had acquired) brought a bottle of corked white wine from the Cremisan monastery he had bought in Jerusalem in 1948. Although Marya was not inducted into the Christian faith, we opened the bottle of undrinkable wine and touched her forehead with a few drops, her godfathers and godmothers standing by. Only the Greek Orthodox, Protestant, and Sunni were present, the Hindu was in India. Godfrey and I had decided not to dictate our daughter's faith but had appointed advisers who could answer questions about their faiths. Godfrey had suffered greatly from his Christian fundamentalist father's efforts to impose his beliefs on his children.

Baghdad, November 1976

Five months after settling in Cyprus, Godfrey and I flew to Baghdad to attend a major conference on Palestine sponsored by the Iraqi government. Marya remained in Nicosia with Diana and Sophocles and went to school with their daughter Christina.

Godfrey and I were given a large room with a Tigris River view at the Baghdad hotel, a white colonial pile formerly frequented by British crime novelist Agatha Christie and her archaeologist husband Max Mallowan. Godfrey's first reaction was of horror when he turned on the water in the shower: mud poured out and kept coming. Tigris mud, certainly. We called down to reception, asked for the number of Abed's room and told him about the water. Fifteen minutes later the water flowed clear. "The filter had to be changed," he explained. Abed was an AUB classmate, a publisher and the leading Palestinian figure in the Iraqi branch of the pan-Arab Baath party, gripped by a bitter feud with the Syrian wing.

The opening session of the conference took place in the modest hall in the hotel itself. Speeches were predictable. When participants stood to leave, Abed, who had been sitting two rows in front of us, waved us over to meet a medium tall man in a brown suit. "Saddam Hussein, vice-president of Iraq," announced Abed. We shook hands. His handshake was not notable, neither a vice nor a limp rag. It was significant that he sat a few rows from the front without a posse of bodyguards and filed out of the auditorium with the rest of us.

A wide range of people from across the world had assembled for the conference. The great South African singer and human rights activist Miriam Makeba, her hair plaits ending in coloured balls that clicked when she moved her head, sang one evening, filling the hall with rolling applause. Also, in attendance was her former husband, Black Power advocate Stokely Carmichael, the handsome revolutionary who had led the US Black Panther movement. A buxom Russian woman with a chest full of medals asked me where I came from. "America," I replied. "You mean the United States," she retorted, rightly, pointing out that I had claimed the entire "New World."

Godfrey and I rode up in the hotel lift with Italian writer Alberto Moravia whose novel Agostino, I had read in my Italian class at Mount Holyoke.

Late one night, Abed invited us to join a gathering in his room, where we were served the usual Iraqi tipple, highball glasses half filled with Black Label, straight. We were introduced to Zuhair and his British wife. Godfrey gave Zuhair, the nickname the "laughing Baathi" after he told a string of jokes. Baath party members were generally sombre, serious types, rather like Abed.

Nicosia, November 1981

Abed rang from Casablanca to say he planned to come for a visit to celebrate our birthdays, Godfrey's on December 2nd, mine on the 16th, and his in between. "We'll discuss the book," he said, a biography of Saddam Hussein he had been pressing Godfrey to write. Godfrey had given Abed a sheet of paper on which he had written two columns of positive and negative attributes possessed by the Iraqi president. Godfrey said he would do the book if both could be used. Abed argued the negatives were impossible but Godfrey would have access to the president himself.

On December 6th, the *BBC* announced Abed's assassination in his Beirut office. He had been shot 17 times. During his phone call Abed had said he had been given guarantees of his safety by Damascus before he dared return to Lebanon, where Syrian intelligence had a free hand and Syrian soldiers manned checkpoints.

Baghdad, August 2004

Lamia decided to join me on my expedition to visit our mutual friend Zuhair who lived near the *Umm al-Qura* (Mother of all Cities) mosque in the west of the city. "Zuhair and I were in the same group," she said. "We celebrated the revolution and had great hopes..."

Hopes dashed by mad dictator Abd al-Karim Qasim, by Saddam Hussein and the Baath party, by three wars, destruction, and death. Exile in Britain for Lamia, an archaeologist, who had tried to sort out the chaos in the Iraq Museum following the break in and looting that took place under the gaze of US soldiers in tanks in the days after Baghdad fell on April 9th, 2003.

We found the massive mosque, Saddam Hussein's gaudy folly known previously as the Umm al-Ma'arik(Mother of all Battles) mosque without trouble and were directed to Zuhair's house by mobile phone. It was a beautiful house with a lofty atrium, abandoned by his wife and children who had fled Iraq for Britain. A dusty, dark, dim house with closed shutters and curtains in case of an attack or an assassination attempt. Zuhair made tea and apologised for the absence of biscuits. “I’ll be leaving soon. It’s not safe here.” What about the house? “I’ll keep it. Perhaps, one day, we’ll be able to live in it.”

As we drove back to central Baghdad, I thought how different my apolitical youth was from the lives of Lamia and Zuhair who had been deeply involved in the affairs of their struggling country from their secondary school days, often at risk of detention or worse. My friends and I were safe, secure, dangerously innocent.

East Jerusalem, Spring 1988

The first Palestinian rising, the Intifada of the Stones, began on December 9th, 1987, at the Jabalia refugee camp in the northern Gaza Strip when an Israeli lorry struck a car and killed four Palestinians. Godfrey and I waited several months before travelling to Jerusalem and Gaza to cover events.

We had previously stayed at the YMCA on Nablus Road but decided to shift to the National hotel because we could often meet the leaders of the intifada lunching at the roof restaurant. Faisal Husseini was the man every journalist wanted to interview. He normally responded to questions with terse remarks, giving very little in these encounters. We would make an appointment to meet him in the garden of his Mount of Olives house for a solid discussion on where the rising was going and what its local leaders – rather than the exiles of the PLO who were based in Tunis – expected to accomplish.

The first intifada was essentially a protest movement involving marches, strikes, civil disobedience: refusal of Palestinian labourers to work in Israeli settlements and Palestinian citizens to pay Israeli taxes. Palestinian weapons of choice against armed and armoured Israeli troops were stones and Molotov cocktails. Israeli minister of defence Yitzhak Rabin called upon Israeli troops to break the arms and legs of Palestinian protesters, condoning savage beatings. Israel closed Palestinian schools and universities, clamped down curfews, and responded with lethal rubber coated steel balls and live fire. Palestinians organised underground schools, expanded the civil disobedience campaign, and boycotted Israeli goods.

Years later I met Faisal at the Beit Hanina home of his cousin and my university classmate, Dyala, and asked him why the Palestinians had not adopted Mahatma Gandhi's peaceful resistance model. He replied, "We tried but found his methods did not work. We are not Indians, the Israelis are not the British, and the situation is completely different."

Algiers, November 11th-15th, 1988

Godfrey and I installed ourselves in a shabby room with a stormy sea view in a semi-derelict hotel on a collapsing bluff, the low level of accommodation allocated to the hundreds of journalists covering the 19th session of the Palestinian National Council (PNC), the Palestinian parliament-in-exile.

At the conference centre located at the *Club des Pins* 25 kilometres west of the Algerian capital, Palestinian commentators – including celebrated author Edward Said speaking in English, French and Arabic – were confiding their views on the meeting to a posse of television teams. Old friend, Lakhdar Brahimi, then Arab League under secretary general, was well met in the atrium of the conference hall, for he became our main source of information on the protracted negotiations over the Palestinian declaration of independence due to be issued during the landmark gathering.

The meeting was historic for several reasons. While Palestinian PNC members from the Israeli occupied areas were prevented from attending, Palestinians arrived from across the diaspora of the Arab countries, Europe, North and South America, Asia and Australia.

The session was convened by Arafat and his clique based in Tunis but the demand for meeting had been put forward by the authors of the intifada, more than 3,200 kilometres away from the venue. Palestinian rivals were on hand: Arafat and his lieutenants who dominated the Palestine Liberation Organisation (PLO) had to contend with PLO dissidents George Habash of the Popular Front, and Naif Hawatmeh of the Democratic Front. Popular committees running the intifada dispatched proxies; fundamentalist Hamas sent six people. More than two dozen delegates arrived from Damascus despite a deep rift between Arafat and the Syrian government. This was the most inclusive Palestinian gathering ever. Although the independence declaration's text was drafted by beloved and respected Palestinian poet Mahmoud Darwish, every word was scrutinised and debated until intifada and leftist demands were satisfied or rejected.

Godfrey did not make the daily bus journey to the Club des Pins. He preferred to sit on our balcony, smoke a cigar, and enjoy the brisk breeze from the Mediterranean. I hung around the conference centre until I nabbed someone I knew who could tell me what was happening. If I found Lakhdar, he would take my arm and disclose where the discussions had reached while walking round the atrium. The squabbling carried on day after day. A plenum convened late on the 14th with the aim of issuing the declaration but the debate continued. Habash was somewhere else arguing over what would happen after the proclamation. I was standing outside the hall when he and a couple of other delegates entered. The declaration was issued at 01.40 on November 15th and was hailed by cheers, the raising of the Palestinian flag, and playing of the national anthem. We journalists squeezed into the back of the auditorium to snatch an impression of the scene before fleeing to the press centre to file. I returned to our hotel at 03.00, tired, excited, happy in the hope that the Palestinians had, finally, stopped fighting each other long enough to change their tragic and terrible history.

The PNC went overtime because Arafat was determined not only to maintain his control of the "Palestinian case" for self-determination but also secure the flexibility required to press the US, Israel's loyal ally, to recognise the PLO as the representative of the Palestinian people, and urge Israel to negotiate an end to its occupation and the emergence of a Palestinian "mini-state" in the territories occupied in 1967 – East Jerusalem, the West Bank and Gaza. This amounted to acceptance of the "two-state solution" and indirect recognition of Israel.

In a trade-off with the intifada and Habash, Arafat agreed to issue a statement reaffirming the Palestinians' right to resist Israel's occupation while rejecting all forms of "terrorism" in exchange for an agreement to issue a qualified endorsement of UN Security Council resolution 242. This had to be paired with the right of Palestinians to self-determination as well as other resolutions as the basis for future negotiations.

Once the delegates to the PNC were on their way home, Arafat challenged the US and Israel to take up the PLO's peace initiative. He stated, "Let it be clear that, however long it takes, no force on earth can deprive my people of their right to statehood. Let it be clear also that I can return to the PNC and say that moderation does not pay... It is very important to say that there will be no peace without the Palestinians and no Palestinians without the PLO."

Israel responded by banning gatherings of more than ten people, fireworks and flag raising and warned violations would mean imprisonment. A curfew had been imposed on Gaza during the PNC meeting and Palestinian refugee camps, towns and villages in the West Bank were placed under curfew after the declaration of independence was issued.

Arafat was invited to address a special session in Geneva of the UN General Assembly which adopted a resolution, in spite of opposition from the US and Israel, replacing the PLO designation in the UN system with the country name of Palestine. By mid-December, 75 states had recognised Palestine and 93 by February 1993. Nevertheless, it took protracted negotiations over the PLO's Charter, a US-led war to oust Iraq from Kuwait, and the Madrid peace conference to bring the sides together around the negotiating table. Israeli prime minister Yitzhak Shamir pledged to negotiate for a decade while building Israeli settlements in the occupied territories.

Tunis, September 2nd, 1993

I was the first journalist to lay eyes on the Oslo Accord, negotiated covertly in Norway between a team of experts fielded by Israeli deputy prime minister Yossi Beilin, and two figures, Ahmed Qurei and Hassan Asfour, dispatched by Arafat's deputy Mahmoud Abbas. While it was initialled on August 20th, its terms had remained secret.

I had been asked, on September 1st, by *The Irish Times* to fly to Tunis to cover a meeting between Irish members of parliament and Arafat. In the rush before I left home in Nicosia, I rang a Palestinian friend in Amman to ask if he knew anyone in Tunis who could brief me on the Accord. My contact did not answer so I left his number with Godfrey to see if he would have better luck and began my journey across Europe to Tunis. Although it was 11 at night by the time I reached the hotel, I spoke to Godfrey who gave me a number without a name and said to ring early the next morning. I called at half past eight and explained who I was. The man said he would be at the hotel in half an hour. He came with a briefcase, introduced himself as Hassan Asfour and showed me the all too brief basic document.

I accompanied the Irish MPs to Arafat's headquarters. As we sat in the waiting room Brian Lenihan, who had been three times Ireland's foreign minister, suggested I simply go along with them into the meeting and see if anyone noticed. Once the introductions were made, Palestinian foreign affairs chief Farouk Kaddoumi asked who I was and promptly told me to leave even though Arafat did not seem to mind having a journalist in the room. I was later briefed on what was said in this, his first encounter with a European delegation after the initialling of the Oslo Accord.

I told the MPs the story of the Accord was not only the text but also how it had been negotiated. The process, moderated by Norwegian diplomat Terje Rød-Larsen, was conducted in English, spoken well by the Israelis but poorly by Qurei and Asfour. He said they had repeatedly rung Palestinians in Washington, who had been conducting separate discussions with other Israelis, to ask what different words or phrases meant. In consequence, the document did not tie Israel to concrete commitments and left the Palestinians with no means to enforce their reading of the accord or sustain their belief that Oslo would mean an end to occupation and liberation.

Under the Accord, an interim Palestinian self-governing authority was to be established while the sides negotiated a final deal. Israel was meant to pull its army out of parts of the West Bank and Gaza. Key issues like the final status of East Jerusalem, the fate of Palestinian refugees, Israeli settlements, security and borders were to be agreed by the end of 1998.

East Jerusalem, September 13th, 1993

I arrived early for the ceremony marking the signing half a world away on the White House lawn of the Oslo Accord by Palestinian chief negotiator Mahmoud Abbas and Israeli foreign minister Shimon Peres, with US president Bill Clinton, PLO chairman Yasser

Arafat and Israeli prime minister Yitzhak Rabin looking over their shoulders. The high point of the event came when Clinton coaxed Arafat and Rabin to shake hands.

Palestinians hoped the Accord, providing them with self-rule, would ultimately end the Israeli occupation of East Jerusalem, the West Bank and Gaza; Israelis hoped the Accord would lead to an end to Arab hostility toward their country.

A small crowd had already assembled in the parking lot of Orient House, an elegant 19th-century mansion built by the Husseini family in East Jerusalem. The lower floor of the building had been taken over by the Arab Studies Centre headed by Faisal Husseini, the leading Palestinian figure in the occupied sector of the city and was recognised as its de facto PLO office. Faisal, whose family has documents proving 1,000 years of residence in the holy city, and his associates had collected a vast library of documents on Palestinian property ownership and other issues connecting Palestinians to this city and land. Although the PLO failed to seriously take on Israel over Jerusalem, Faisal used to put himself in the front line of the daily battle of Palestinian families against the Israeli authorities and settlers seeking to appropriate Palestinian homes and land.

I climbed the left-hand staircase to the second-floor veranda to secure a view of the proceedings while a chubby Palestinian boy scout in uniform, carrying a folded Palestinian flag, ascended the steps on the right side and awaited orders. As Palestinian notables assembled on the steps and the crowd below thickened and spilled out into the street, a band played the Palestinian national anthem, *Mawtiny* (My Homeland) and the scout opened the red, white, black and green flag, attached it to a rope and pulled, lifting it to the top of the pole erected for this occasion. The flag unfurled and hung limp in the still air. People in the throng gasped, sighed. Flying the Palestinian flag in East Jerusalem was illegal. Someone in the crowd began to hand out small flags on sticks, multiplying by hundreds the illegality of the act of raising the flag.

Once the ceremony had concluded, youths on the far edge of the crowd unrolled a Palestinian flag many meters long and began to march with it along Salah ed-Din street, the main thoroughfare of this sector of the city. Another youth appeared on a horse, a symbol of Arab freedom. We followed, walking past open shops where people had been watching the Orient House and White House lawn ceremonies simultaneously on split screen television along with millions of people the world over. We strode past the Lawrence hotel and turned the corner at the post office where armed Israeli soldiers stood silently by, clearly confused by the turn of events. A few audacious Palestinian lads put red and white carnations in the barrels of the soldiers' weapons. The huge flag was carried to the walls of the Old City and draped over Damascus Gate.

Gaza, July 1st, 1994

I made the journey to Rafah in a rattletrap taxi held together with chewing gum and hair-pins. Once in Rafah I joined the throng waiting for Arafat, who was late for his appointment with Palestine. We just managed to see the folded peak of the black and white checked kaffiyeh on top of his head when at 15.15 he stepped onto Palestinian soil for the first time in 25 years and greeted the thousands of Palestinian political figures and citizens who had waited in the heat for his return. Arafat reviewed a contingent of Palestinian Liberation Army soldiers before getting into an open limousine and speeding along the rutted road, skirting Israeli colony blocks, and avoiding slippery patches of sand. My mad driver managed to keep up with Arafat's entourage by dodging between other racing vehicles and rushing along the road's verges. We arrived in Gaza City in time to view his progression along Omar al-Mukhtar street from the roof of one of its tallest buildings. Gaza businessman Mansour Shawwa observed, gloomily, that the Israelis were granting Palestinians limited freedom in less than one percent of Palestine by agreeing to pull out of parts of Gaza and Jericho in the West Bank.

On July 5th, I joined a few hundred Palestinians to see Arafat arrive in Jericho aboard an Egyptian helicopter that kicked up the sand at the makeshift landing area, marked with an X. He assured Palestinians who had come to greet him that Jericho would be the "first step" in the liberation of the entirety of the West Bank and East Jerusalem and spoke of the unity of Gaza with these areas before returning to Gaza where he had initially based his government.

Jerusalem, January 20th, 1996

Ahead of the first ever Palestinian presidential and parliamentary polls, Israel did its utmost to undermine these existential events. Early that month, Israel had declared a five-day closure of the West Bank for "security" reasons. This prevented members of the election commission from carrying out their work in Palestinian enclaves where voting was due to take place. Campaigning was limited in Jerusalem, annexed by Israel in 1967 and proclaimed its exclusive capital. Overall there were more than a million registered voters, two presidential candidates, Arafat and independent Samiha Khalil, and 676 candidates running for the 88 seats in the legislative assembly.

Since Israel had decided only 4,000 of the 49,000 Palestinians eligible to vote in Jerusalem could do so within its expanded municipal boundaries, my AUB friend Dyala, Godfrey and I had to drive to a school on a hilltop in Ram, outside the municipal limits. Walking slowly with a stick, Godfrey, who had suffered a stroke, and I went into the polling station to watch Dyala vote in a Palestinian election for the first time in her life. For all Palestinians who cast their ballots, it was a momentous occasion, a hopeful step on the road towards an end of the Israeli occupation, independence and statehood.

Well aware that Arafat would win by a landslide, Dyala cast her vote for Khalil, a woman born in a West Bank village. She had been detained by Israel half a dozen times for resistance activities and had founded a major Palestinian welfare organisation. Khalil received over 11 percent of the vote, Arafat 88 percent.

Of the 88 legislators, 50 came from Arafat's Fatah, and 16 were Fatah members excluded from the "official list" who ran as "independents." Among the initially declared winners was Rawya Shawwa, an authentic independent from a prominent Gaza family. But late that night another of Arafat's men was allocated the seat. When Rawya learned of this, she gathered influential supporters and went straight to Arafat's residence in Gaza. In 2006, she was re-elected to the legislature despite a Hamas landslide. Neither Arafat nor Hamas could stand against a Shawwa in Gaza.

Deadlines slipped for implementation of the Oslo deal, Israel continued colony construction, and Israeli troops remained in most of the West Bank and Gaza. By September 28th, 2000, Palestinians felt they had waited long enough and revolted against Israel following a visit by Ariel Sharon to the Haram al-Sharif mosque compound on Jerusalem's acropolis, regarded by Jews to be the site of the Biblical Jewish temples. During this incursion, Sharon was accompanied by dozens of Likud supporters and hundreds of armed and helmeted police. Palestinians in the compound were detained there for hours after Sharon left. Rioting erupted in the Old City where Israeli soldiers clashed with rock-throwing Palestinians. The next day four Palestinian youths were slain. The second intifada, the uprising of the gun and bomb, had begun.

5

INCARCERATION

London, March 21st, 1968

Godfrey and I were visiting friends living at 6 Abbey Road, in St. John's Wood, next to the EMI studios where the Beatles were the heroes of the moment, when news came of the battle of Karameh. Mild supporters of Israel, Suvi and Chandru were not impressed but Godfrey and I saw it as a potential game changer.

Having shut down most Palestinian resistance networks in the West Bank, Israel invaded the town of Karameh and its refugee camp in response to attacks mounted by the Fatah faction on Israeli targets. Jordanian military intelligence had, however, identified the Israeli buildup on the western shore of the Jordan River, forewarned the Palestinians, and prepared to repulse any offensive. When Israeli forces crossed into the East Bank early that morning, Jordanian and Palestinian fighters were ready to take them on. Although the Israelis destroyed the town and the camp, the objective of the operation, they were forced to mount a ragged withdrawal. Having repulsed the Israeli incursion, Fatah and the Jordanian army claimed victory, restoring Arab morale and readiness to fight the occupation. Since the word *karameh* in Arabic means dignity, the victory amounted to the first step in the restoration of Arab honour after the humbling defeat of the Arab armies in 1967.

Arafat exploited the victory to transform the Palestine Liberation Organisation (PLO), which had been firmly under Egyptian control, into an independent body composed of armed factions, making the guerrilla war of attrition the chosen means to fight Israel. Recruits flocked to Fatah and the other groups.

Beirut-Jerusalem, June-July 1968

Shortly after midnight on June 5th, 1968, the first anniversary of the 1967 war, a young Palestinian, Sirhan Sirhan shot and killed Robert Kennedy in the kitchen of the Ambassador hotel in Los Angeles. After the shooting, Sirhan cried, "I can explain. I did it for my country. I love my country." Initially it was suggested the shooter was Cuban but by the evening of the fifth, we learned he was Palestinian. The younger brother of the assassinated president, Robert Kennedy had, as a cub reporter, visited Palestine in 1948 and written about the war that brought Israel into existence, and during the 1968 US presidential campaign he had repeatedly made statements supporting Israel.

Godfrey was asked to write a book about this event which had shocked people round the world, particularly the Arabs. Some tried to justify the murder, others claimed Sirhan was not the assassin and the US authorities had accused him because he was an Arab in the vicinity of the shooting. Godfrey began his research on June 14th by paying a brief visit to Pasadena, California, where Sirhan had dwelled with his mother and siblings. Mary, a high school friend of mine living in San Francisco, flew to Los Angeles to drive Godfrey around and help him with logistics. Sirhan's mother and brothers were subject to a judicial gag order and could not meet Godfrey although two brothers did answer some questions on the phone. An elderly neighbour was forthcoming and gave Godfrey a picture of the Sirhans.

After Godfrey returned to Beirut, we went to Jerusalem to continue his investigation. The first person we saw was Sirhan's father, who had separated from his wife Mary, and returned to the West Bank village of Taibeh where he lived in a large, well built house with very little furniture. The old man spoke for more than two hours. Two things in particular struck me about that encounter.

Bishara Sirhan said he was a master mechanic who had become a foreman in the department of public works in the British colonial administration of Palestine. He was proud of the fact he and his teams used to repair water pipes and electricity pylons blown up by Palestinians fighting the British during the 1936-39 Palestinian revolt against London's support for the Zionist project.

Sirhan also revealed that late in 1947 – before the declaration of the state of Israel – he and his son, then three, had entered the Old City through Damascus Gate when a bomb exploded on the steps killing several Palestinians and wounding many others. The child fainted and had to lie down on the ground for a few minutes but when he awoke and agreed to make his way home he was horrified by blood, flesh and bones on the steps and asked his father to blindfold and carry him. That was the third of several terrible incidents which Sirhan Sirhan had witnessed that month, his father said. While going through AUB library's microfiche of issues of *The New York Times* to provide Godfrey with material for his book, I found the incident that had so nearly taken the lives of the two Sirhans had been reported in detail by *The New York Times'* correspondent Dana Adams Schmidt.

The day after our visit to Taibeh, we went to the Musrara quarter of Jerusalem, the site of the Sirhan home before the family was expelled during the 1948 war. After that conflict the Sirhans spent eight years in extreme poverty living in one room in the Old City before emigrating to the US where they were settled by a Protestant evangelical church in Pasadena.

During a second visit to Jerusalem, Godfrey found a former neighbour who described in detail the Sirhan family's desperate circumstances while they lived in Musrara and afterwards in the Old City where many Palestinians driven by Israel's pre-state army from West Jerusalem had found refuge.

Amman, July 1968 (I think)

We crossed the Allenby bridge back into Jordan and drove to Amman where Godfrey and I met Clovis and PLO spokesman Kamal Nasser on the terrace of the Intercontinental hotel. I asked Kamal why the PLO always exaggerated Israeli casualties from Palestinian operations in the occupied territories. He replied, with a wicked grin, "Divide by ten."

He suggested Godfrey meet Arafat and I go to a PLO camp for young foreign supporters of the Palestinian cause who had been fired up by Karameh. I had my first glimpse of Arafat that afternoon when the short, stocky Fatah leader, clad in uniform and headdress, toddled down the main aisle in an auditorium before addressing a large gathering. This was during the brief honeymoon period enjoyed by Jordan and the Palestinian resistance.

The camp was in the desert on the outskirts of Amman. It was not a training camp for fighters but a place young people from several countries in Europe and Asia exchanged ideas and argued. Dinner was bread, processed cheese and tomatoes served on metal plates washed up by Hanna Mikhail (Abu Omar) a Palestinian intellectual who had left academic life in the US to join Fatah. "It's the first time I see an Arab man washing dishes," I joked. "Revolutionaries must be prepared for any task," he responded. In June 1976 he and his companions disappeared while on a boat to embattled Palestinian camps in north Lebanon.

By the light of a lantern, I argued for some time with Abu Daoud, another leading Fatah figure, about the backing Indians gave to the Palestinians – which he took for granted. The government, I contended, supported the Palestinian cause but many Hindus were anti-Muslim and pro-Israel because of Pakistan. He had visited India and met only friends of the Palestinians.

Godfrey was bleary-eyed the next morning because the meeting with Arafat had been at two or three in the morning, typical for Arafat.

Chemlan, August 29th, 1969

Godfrey and I were dining with friends the night we heard on the *BBC* news that a Trans World Airlines flight en route from Rome to Athens had been hijacked and diverted to Lydda by two Palestinians, Leila Khaled and Salim Issawi, the Che Guevara commando unit of the Popular Front for the Liberation of Palestine (PFLP), headed by George Habash. A refugee from Haifa, Leila – who was armed with a gun and grenade – ordered the pilot to fly over her home town and teased the Israelis by proclaiming to air traffic control where she was and there was nothing they could do about it. Once the plane had landed at Damascus airport, Leila ordered the rapid evacuation of the aircraft as a bomb had been placed on board to blow it up. A former AUB student, Leila had been trained in a flight simulator, so she was able to direct the pilot and read the gauges on the control panel.

Some weeks after she was released by the Syrians, Leila, a slender attractive young woman whose almond-shaped eyes were enhanced by kohl, came to our house in Chemlan to be interviewed by Godfrey. We sat around our copper tray dining table and listened to her story. The incidents I recall were humorous ones.

On the morning before the flight she had wandered around Rome and shopped at an expen-sive store on the Via Veneto where she bought a hat, sunglasses and a large shoulder bag. Once back in her hotel, the frugal refugee donned two pants suits and put other clothing in her handbag, so she could keep the new items once the operation ended.

Her job during the takeover of the plane was to stand at the front holding her gun and grenade but when she rose and reached for the pistol, it slipped down her leg inside her trousers. The waistband had grown loose since she had been too nervous to eat for two days. She laughed as she bent to retrieve her weapon, presenting to the pilot only the top of a large round hat. When she straightened up, the pilot saw a young woman in a white sleeveless suit and floppy hat. She proclaimed herself to be the "new captain" and handed the pilot the pin of the grenade she was holding to make it clear she meant what she said.

The hijacking and the deterioration of the security situation in Jordan due to the presence of armed Palestinians brought an end to the collaboration between Amman and the resistance factions. Gun totting men claiming to be fighters ambled around Amman collecting funds while others openly called for the overthrow of King Hussein.

Godfrey's interview with Leila was rejected by a British Sunday paper and shelved until she and Patrick Arguello, a dual US-Nicaraguan citizen, hijacked an Israeli El Al airliner flying from Amsterdam to New York on September 6th, 1970. The aircraft was diverted to London after Israeli guards shot Arguello dead and overpowered Leila. By that time, Godfrey's article was in the process of being incorporated as an appendix to his book, *Why Robert Kennedy Was Killed: The Story of Two Victims*, published by the Third Press in New York.

The El Al plane was one of four commandeered by PFLP commandos. On the same day a TWA airliner flying from Frankfurt and a Swiss plane that took off from Zurich were hijacked and forced to land at Dawson's field, a disused facility near Zarqa in Jordan. A Pan American flight departing from Amsterdam was seized and flown first to Beirut and then to Cairo. On the 9th a BOAC (British Overseas Airways Corporation) airliner, with British school boys on board, was diverted to Dawson's field during a flight from Bahrain to London. The objective of the final operation was to free Leila who had been jailed by the British authorities. Most of the 310 passengers on the hijacked aircraft were handed over to the Jordanians who declared martial law on the 16th. Over the next ten days the Jordanian army and security forces cracked down on the Palestinian resistance groups in an all-out offensive dubbed Black September.

The Jordanian army, comprised of both Bedouin and Palestinian troops, remained unified while Iraqi and Syrian forces the PLO expected to intervene on the side of the resistance failed to act. Palestinian armed groups were crushed ruthlessly. Palestinian refugee camps hosting fighters were shelled. Arafat and his men fled to Lebanon where they established a state-within-a-state in the camps. Fatah formed a clandestine cell called Black September and plotted revenge against Jordan and attacks on Israelis, including the operation, said to be designed by Abu Daoud, carried out at the Munich Olympics. There, on September 5th, 1972, eight Palestinians entered the Olympic village and took hostage nine Israeli athletes; all the Israelis and three Palestinians were slain in a bungled rescue attempt.

Nicosia-Beirut-Jerusalem, June-July-August 1982

Godfrey, Marya and I were at home in Nicosia when Israel invaded Lebanon on June 6th. The pretext was an assassination attempt against Israeli ambassador to Britain Shlomo Argov by gunmen dispatched by Abu Nidal, a bitter enemy of Arafat. His forces had been observing a US-mediated ceasefire with Israel reached in July 1981. Israeli prime minister Menachem Begin blamed the attempt on the PLO and gave his defence minister Ariel Sharon the go-ahead to launch a ready-made operation called "Peace for Galilee." Sharon had begun preparations and deployments for this offensive as early as February and had simply been waiting for a casus belli. He told Begin the objective of the offensive was to drive Palestinian forces 40 kilometres northwards from the border and create a wide buffer zone within 36-72 hours. This was a lie.

Once the Israelis had crossed the border, Sharon ordered his tanks and troops to proceed to Beirut. He had a far more ambitious agenda than the war plans he had put to Begin. Sharon was determined to destroy the PLO infrastructure in Lebanon, drive Syrian forces from the country, install Maronite Christian ally Bachir Gemayel as president, and compel Lebanon to sign a peace treaty with Israel.

As usual Godfrey and I turned on our radios and listened to the *BBC* hour after hour while the Israeli army bombed Tyre and Sidon, levelled Palestinian refugee camps, and pounded the southern suburbs of Beirut where the PLO had its headquarters. Roger Hardy, a young British journalist, contacted us with the idea of writing a book on the war as the Israeli army bombarded West Beirut from land, sea and air and laid siege to this, the mixed Christian and Muslim sector of the Lebanese capital. The idea was to bring out the book in the fall while interest in the summer's events remained high.

Since Beirut hosted scores of foreign newspaper and television correspondents, this war became one of the most well covered in history, to the detriment of the Israelis who had planned for most eventualities but not for a hostile press from day one. For the book, Godfrey and I decided we would alternate analyses with quotes from newspaper coverage of events in Lebanon with material gathered from agencies and broadcast media. This was easier said than done as there was no internet to surf sources.

We bought *The Guardian*, *The Times*, *The Sunday Times*, and *International Herald Tribune*, papers available in Nicosia, and clipped relevant articles and relied on the "collections" of Israeli Dissident Israel Shahak for translations from the Hebrew press. Somehow, somewhere we managed to pick up articles published in *The New York Times*, *The Washington Post*, *The Baltimore Sun* and other papers not available in Cyprus.

Since Beirut airport was closed, Godfrey, who needed to report on the war for *The Economist*, took a boat from Larnaca to Jounieh in East Beirut, which was dominated by the Gemayels' Maronite Phalange party allied to Israel. I stayed at home with Marya and worried but when Godfrey returned, I went to Jerusalem where I collected material from *The Jerusalem Post* and Palestinian *Al-Fajr* as well as Shahak himself. Once we were both back at home, Godfrey and I made small stacks of newspaper clippings, communications from UNRWA and other UN agencies, and items in Shahak's "collections." Marya painted stones to put on the piles laid out in the sitting room where Godfrey always worked on a folding camping table. I wrote in the study, surrounded by books. Books about the region and Islam, novels, and plays. We wrote by hand on paper. The computer revolution had not yet happened. I typed up the results on an electric machine, whiting-out typos with Tippex.

The 1982 war set the pattern for Israel's subsequent attacks on Lebanon (2006) and Gaza (2008-09 and 2014). The appropriate name for Sharon's strategy should have been "Shock and Awe," the term adopted by the George W. Bush administration for its invasion and occupation of Iraq in 2003. The shock was administered to civilian areas, where PLO fighters dwelt with their families, by Israeli warplanes, naval vessels, artillery, and tanks ahead of troop operations. Since he had not honestly informed Begin or the government of the full extent of the operation he had launched, Sharon was obliged to minimise Israeli dead and wounded and to achieve his military objectives at speed.

He had every advantage: a well-trained army, superior weaponry, total control of the skies and sea, and the full backing of US secretary of state Alexander Haig and, at the outset, of president Ronald Reagan.

Tyre, Sidon, Nabatieh, Damour, and targets in West Beirut and their adjacent refugee camps were devastated by massive Israeli firepower. Tyre and Sidon were hammered for several days, West Beirut for weeks. The liberal Israeli daily *Haaretz* carried an article by Professor Yehoshua Porath on June 25th in which he wrote, "The heavy bombardments, the enormous destruction and the high number of casualties among the [Palestinian] refugees and the Lebanese population, were supposed to make it easier for the Israeli army to occupy the [chosen] area with a low number of casualties. An immoral act was done!" Israelis critical of the operation were some of our best sources.

In some areas, Israel dropped leaflets warning civilians to flee but Israel also used what journalists on the ground at the time called "terror weapons": airburst bombs, fragmentation bombs and shells, vacuum bombs, cluster munitions and white phosphorous bombs and shells – the latter generally employed in open battlegrounds against tanks rather than in urban settings.

The onslaught was meant to disperse the 60,000 Palestinians living in the camps in the southern half of Lebanon and damage or destroy the camps, so inhabitants could not rebuild and remain a national grouping distinct from the Lebanese. Israeli colonel Dov Yirmiya wrote that when cabinet secretary Dan Meridor visited Sidon on June 18th, he was asked to define the government's policy toward the Palestinians. He replied, "They should be driven eastward," gesturing toward Syria. "Let them go there and don't let them return."

When they moved into urban areas, Israeli tanks and troops based themselves and installed headquarters and arms dumps in civilian residential areas just as the Palestinians had done. On July 11th, Godfrey saw an Israeli artillery piece located 90 metres from the Hotel Alexandre in East Beirut open fire on West Beirut or the mountains overlooking that sector of the city. During his stay in the hotel, he was also present when live Palestinian rounds whizzed through the terrace cafe thanks to the Israeli placement of its cannon.

Due to the need for speed, the Israeli army took advantage of ceasefires to seize territory and even concocted breaches of ceasefires by the Palestinians to break the terms of temporary truces.

Finally, Israel obstructed humanitarian and medical relief efforts intended to help tens of thousands of Palestinians and Lebanese expelled from their homes. The tally for the human cost of the invasion was 12,000 killed, 40,000 wounded, 300,000 homeless, 100,000 without shelter, and several hundred thousand destitute.

While this war was a "walk-over" for the Israeli army and hardliners in the Likud because Arafat and his fighters were forced out of Lebanon, "Peace for Galilee" was a public relations disaster for Begin and Sharon and for Israel's friends in the international community. The debacle became a catastrophe when after the departure of PLO defenders, hundreds of Palestinians were massacred by Israel's allies in the Lebanese Maronite Phalange and the surrogate South Lebanon Army militias while Israeli troops encircled the Palestinian Sabra and Chatila neighbourhoods south of Beirut.

For the first time in the history of Israel, its politicians, soldiers and citizens criticised "Peace for Galilee" as a "war of choice" not of necessity and an unnecessarily brutal campaign. Shortly after Israeli troops surged across the border, questions began to be asked by the Labour party opposition and five cabinet members. Dissidence was met by organised pro-Likud, pro-army events and propaganda that flooded the media. This did not intimidate or counter anti-war elements, including serving members of elite parachute, commando, and armoured units who staged public protests. Academics helped organise popular demonstrations. Begin was described as "delusionary" and divorced from reality. Rallies against the war staged in Tel Aviv, Israel's most liberal city, attracted 20,000, 100,000 and 250,000 during July and August. Israel's peace camp demanded negotiations with the Palestinians and Arabs and no more wars. "Peace for Galilee" ended on August 12th, after Reagan told Begin to halt the slaughter.

The book, *The Battle of Beirut: Why Israel Invaded Lebanon*, the first on this war, was published in November by Zed in London.

Nicosia, 1982

Nicole, Abdullah and Yasmin came to escape the war. Yasmin, just two, was traumatised by constant explosions, the roar of low flying warplanes, the whine of shells. During an Israeli bombing, a shower of red hot shrapnel greeted them in their home as they were hurrying down the stairs to the shelter.

We took them for a picnic near a small dam in the countryside half an hour's drive from home, but the summer sun had dried the grasses and made them sharp and brittle, prompting Yasmin to call the outing a *picque nique*, a prickly outing. She took shelter beneath an olive tree when a plane flew overhead, leaving a ragged white tail. Yasmin was a child of war.

On September 11th, 2001, she was in New York City staying with a friend who lived in a university flat not far from the World Trade Centre's Twin Towers. When they heard the explosions, these war-veteran Lebanese women shrugged: planes breaking the sound barrier in the fashion of the Israeli air force over Beirut. Yasmin summoned the lift to go down to the nearby bakery for croissants, but the concierge ordered residents of the building to depart immediately, leaving their possessions behind. The girls walked across Manhattan to another friend's apartment where they stayed until flights resumed.

Beirut, July 12th-August 14th, 2006

As soon as news was broadcast of Hizbullah's capture of two Israeli soldiers on patrol along the Israeli side of the border with Lebanon, I rang Paddy Smyth, then foreign editor of *The Irish Times*. "I must fly to Beirut tonight, the airport'll be hit tomorrow," I told him. "Let's wait until tomorrow," he replied. "Tomorrow will be too late," I thought. I was half an hour's flying time from Beirut but could not go the next day because Israel had bombed the airport that morning. The paper asked Mary Fitzgerald, a correspondent then in Jordan, to travel overland through Syria to Beirut. She was replaced by Lara Marlowe who also took the land route. I fumed until the Indian navy began shuttles between Beirut and Larnaca, evacuating civilians and delivering aid. As the West Asia correspondent of *The Deccan Herald*, Bangalore's home town newspaper, I asked for an interview with the admiral on board the flagship of the four-vessel squadron. He agreed to give me passage but suggested I contact the French as they had a ship set to sail that night.

The French official at the port asked, "Can you go now?" "No, I have to drive to Nicosia, pack and close up my house. " "Can you be ready by five?" she demanded. "Yes." She took my phone number and said, "We'll call you."

I rushed to Nicosia, took Rikki, my cat, to the minder half an hour's drive from town, put my plants on the stair landing for my neighbour to water, and packed. The command came: "Be at the port by six." I rang Andreas who drove me to Larnaca where three male journalists were waiting on shore for a dinghy to convey us to the Siroco, an amphibious assault ship anchored outside Larnaca bay. We had a rough ride in an inflatable dinghy driven by a sailor in Sterling Moss mode, but we arrived safely and were swallowed into the belly of the ship. They put us into a cabin with four bunks – my name, Michael, had confused them – and invited us to dine in the junior officers' mess: three well-cooked courses and two kinds of wine, red and chilled pink. After dinner we were given a tour of the ship and a glimpse of the bridge with its banks of computers and light filled panels. One of my roommates snored as Siroco, its sister ship Mistral, and two frigates sailed through Israel's naval blockade.

My first encounter at the Mayflower hotel was with the Cypriot Doctors without Borders team trying to arrange for a shipment from Larnaca to Beirut of urgently needed medical supplies. I suggested ringing the Indian embassy to request carriage on one of the Indian warships. When it arrived, the consignment was cleared by the Palestinian Red Crescent Society to avoid bribes and delays in customs or warehousing. A colleague and I travelled to the northern edge of Sidon to visit two hospitals where the supplies had been delivered.

At the edge of the Palestinian camp of Bourj el-Barajneh that abuts on the Dahyeh, the south Beirut quarters that form the Hizbullah stronghold, the border was defined by a half-built flyover stretching above a wide concrete expanse littered with rubbish. Bourj, home to 18,000 Palestinians originally from Acre, Jaffa and Haifa, had offered refuge to hundreds of Lebanese fleeing apartments in high rise blocks in the Dahyeh, Israel's main target in this war. The Hamadeh family from Kfoun, near the embattled border town of Bint Jbeil, had also found sanctuary in Bourj, which lies near Sabra and Chatila. Israel sought to avoid mention of these two camps this time around.

Bourj residents dwelled in raw breeze-block rooms jumbled into two- to three-storey structures. Since land was at a premium, there are few proper streets, people made their way from place to place on foot through a warren of narrow alleyways, roughly paved and slippery with water and slime. The buildings were knit together overhead by a cat's cradle of electricity and telephone lines. Small shops were stocked with shrivelled vegetables, green apples and leopard spotted bananas. Women applied to butchers for a few cubes of lamb or a handful of mince from sides of lamb and beef hanging in shop doorways.

Following my visit to Bourj, I went to see the UN's Larry Hollingworth who was based at the Movenpick hotel on the beachfront. He described the overall humanitarian situation after Israel had driven most civilians from their homes, villages, towns and lands in the south. I told him about the possibility of bringing in supplies from Larnaca on evacuation ships and using the Palestinian Red Crescent as a clearing agent. I also pointed out the hotel's halls were wider than the narrow, tortured alleyways of Bourj el-Barajneh ten minutes drive away. He shrugged, "I agree that this is the wrong place for us to stay. We're put here for security reasons." He refrained from saying the Israelis had been told firmly not to bomb the Movenpick, a large enough landmark to be easily identified.

Two ships carrying fuel for Lebanon's power plants remained anchored off Cyprus. Their captains had demanded funds to pay $15 million in insurance premiums and guarantees of safe passage Israel refused to grant. The US navy offered to escort the ships to Beirut port through the Israeli bombardment and blockade. One captain accepted, the other refused but agreed to offload his cargo onto small vessels prepared to deliver the fuel to Beirut and Tripoli. The World Health Organisation urged speed as 60 percent of the country's hospitals would cease functioning if the fuel did not arrive in a week.

Access between regions was difficult because Israel had destroyed the connective tissue of roads and bridges. The entire region between the border and the Litani River was cut off when Israel blew up the last bridge. Israel warned vehicles travelling in this area would be attacked. The northern Bekaa Valley and the Roman city of Baalbek were also isolated. Both these regions were heavily Shia and supportive of Hizbullah.

By August 8th, an estimated 915,000, more than a quarter of Lebanon's population, had been displaced; 565,000 were living with families, 131,000 in schools and public buildings, and 220,000 had left the country; 150,000 went to Syria where Syrian households hosted them. The dusty little fenced park in West Beirut's Sanayeh was filled with refugees camping in the open, some making tea on primus stoves, others sitting in the shade provided by blankets strung between trees.

Armed with assault rifles and anti-tank weapons, Hizbullah guerrillas fought the Israeli invaders to a standstill in the south and lobbed missiles into northern Israel, forcing 250,000 Israelis to evacuate their homes and seek refuge in the centre and south. Hizbullah proclaimed a famous victory but had to admit there might have been no war if the movement had not staged its cross-border attack on the Israeli patrol and abducted two soldiers.

At around three in the afternoon, of August 13th, after Israel's cabinet had accepted the Security Council's ceasefire resolution, Israeli warships fired 18 rockets in quick succession into the southern suburbs of Beirut in the heaviest single strike since the war had begun a month earlier. The explosions generated by combined strikes resonated as one and their impact shook the whole of West Beirut. While lunching at a restaurant on Hamra street with my colleague Karin, who had arrived on the French warship Mistral, clientele and staff were jolted into silence. We later learned at least a dozen civilians were killed. Believing the ceasefire would take effect in the morning, they had returned to their flats in the Dahyeh. At six the next morning, I was awakened by the whistle of metal canisters flying through the air, ending in explosions. I pulled on clothes and rushed into the street to find shredded Arabic leaflets. Israel was determined to have the last word whatever it was.

Later that morning I went on a tour of Dahyeh with one of the hotel drivers. Around the ruins of residential buildings, shops, and office blocks, Hizbullah had already strung yellow tape proclaiming "The Divine Victim Restricted Area No Trespassing." The movement's construction arm was already shifting debris.

Karin and I secured a passage back to Larnaca aboard the Siroco. At dinner in the senior officers' mess, I asked the captain if we would sail through Israel's blockade "bombed up," ready for action. He paused, surprised at the way the question was phrased, before answering, "Yes." I had got the "bombed up" from the Indian admiral during my interview.

Gaza, November 15th, 2008

School children streamed out of buses, strode through the museum's black gate embellished with graceful lines of Arabic poetry written in gold, and flowed into the entrance hall. They paused to take in the massive marble base of the largest Roman column found in the Strip and the stumps of fallen pillars placed on a bed of stones at the centre of the hall.

In small groups they passed through the hand crafted wooden door of the museum – the *madhaf*, into a high rectangular room filled with antiquities from Gaza. Teachers offered a few words on Gaza's long history as a land bridge between Egypt and the Levant while the children examined stone anchors, Bronze Age implements, Attic pottery, and bleached marble heads of classical Greek statuary, found at the bottom of the sea or excavated from building sites.

These artefacts formed a link between Gaza's proud past as a centre of civilisation and its sad, sordid and often brutal present.

The children filed out of the museum into the bright morning light to leap, shrieking onto inflated toys in the playground before taking their places at tables at the cafe for a snack and carton of juice. Here at the *madhaf* children escaped from poverty and crowded refugee camp homes to have a glimpse of the lives led by children in the US and Europe where museums are plentiful, and cafes abound.

Jawdat Khoudary, the contractor who built the museum, said, "My dream is to have a national museum. It should have been done by the government, but it is not top of the agenda."

So, he built his personal *madhaf*, which quickly became al-Madhaf. "A little museum is better than nothing."

The museum, located on the coast near the Shati refugee camp, was the first in Gaza. "In three months we've had 15,000 visitors."

Constructing the museum was an act of resistance against Israel's siege and blockade of the Strip and its 1.5 million people.

"We started without materials," he said. When Palestinians toppled Israel's wall between Gaza and Egypt in 2007, Khoudary managed to bring in some bags of cement, banned by Israel. He sent teams to raid mounds of rubble from demolished buildings. Since Gaza has no quarries and no trees, he gathered rough rocks from fields and old railway ties from warehouses. For ceilings, he used sheets of copper once employed by carpenters to decorate furniture. "We could not bring in flagstones, so we cut the stones we used for the walls." The original idea was to build only a museum, but next came a restaurant and garden, and, ultimately a hotel and conference centre. Conferences are highly popular in Gaza where trapped Palestinians' only option was to make plans for development, the betterment of different sectors of society, and cleaning up the environment, plans they could never implement because of Israel's siege and blockade.

Nicosia-Jerusalem-Cairo-Gaza, December 27th, 2008 – January 28th, 2009

In June 2008, Gaza's Hamas rulers and Israel agreed to a ceasefire which was largely observed until Israel mounted an operation into Gaza on November 4th, precipitating fire fights and fresh rocket strikes on Israeli territory. Israel responded. This escalated into a sustained period of violence between the two sides. Hamas set conditions: an end to Israel's blockade of Gaza, the opening of the Egyptian border crossing at Rafah, and a ceasefire in the West Bank. Israel refused to consider these demands. By December 25th, Israel had completed preparations for an all-out assault on Gaza on the basis of plans laid down six months earlier. The scenario followed the pattern established in 1982 when Israel launched its full-scale invasion of Lebanon to end the ceasefire with the PLO-Fatah and deny the Palestinians status and credibility.

The Israeli campaign, dubbed "Cast Lead," began, as usual, with air, land and sea bombardment of Gaza's tightly packed residential districts, which I covered from home in Nicosia by telephoning Gazans to find out how they were faring. Israel's ground invasion began on January 3rd. I reached Jerusalem a few days later and promptly obtained an Israeli press card which normally permits journalists to enter the Strip through the Erez terminal on the northern Gaza border. Israel, however, had decided to ban journalists from visiting Gaza and Egypt soon followed suit. Only those present at the onset of hostilities were in position to report the Israeli assault at first-hand.

I stayed in Jerusalem with my friend Dyala and covered events in Gaza by phone, speaking to human rights activists, ambulance drivers, and friends. I visited Ramallah and surfed television channels for the latest. Without any help from my subject, I wrote a long piece about UNRWA's operations chief in Gaza, John Ging, a brave Irishman who spoke his mind in television interviews. When asked for an interview, he replied, "Don't write about me, write about the Palestinian people."

On the day Hamas and Israel declared unilateral ceasefires, I joined a group of Scandinavian journalists determined to enter Gaza through Erez. If rejected, we had decided we would drive down the Negev to the Eilat-Taba border crossing and through Sinai to el-Arish just south of the Egyptian border crossing to Gaza at Rafah. It was a long, tiring drive – accompanied on the Taba-el-Arish leg by an Egyptian security man in suit and tie but carrying no weapon. We arrived at el-Arish at about two in the morning of the 18th. En route Swedish radio correspondent Cecilia Udden, who had good contacts in Cairo, found out what documents we would need to gain entry to Gaza: waivers from embassies and letters from an Egyptian journalists' organisation. The latter and the Nordic embassies faxed documents to the hotel; I had to dash to Cairo to get my waiver in person from the US embassy, spend a night at the Marriott, and hurry back. While I was on this errand, the Egyptians continued to prevent hundreds of determined journalists from crossing into the battered and beleaguered coastal strip. Discouraged, Cecilia and her colleagues drove to Cairo with the intention of catching a plane – I don't recall their destination.

Armed with my documents, I packed my bag and went to Egypt's Rafah terminal which was besieged not only by journalists but also by scores of humanitarian workers who had come to treat wounded and deliver medical supplies and ambulances. In the courtyard just inside the gates of the terminal, a line of ambulances remained parked, awaiting clearance. Finally, the word came: let them in; the paperwork took several hours before we were welcomed by Palestinian immigration officers in the neat Gaza terminal. When Cecilia and her colleagues heard the Egyptians had decided to allow journalists into Gaza they abandoned their flight and rushed back to Rafah too late to catch the first wave to make the crossing.

While other correspondents filed onto a bus, I took the usual ramshackle taxi to Gaza City, driving in pitch dark most of the way with an occasional patch of illumination from a roadside stand or garage or a tree wound round with fairy lights. Gaza City had also been plunged into darkness and my driver, from Rafah, did not know his way. When we came upon the Shawwa Cultural Centre the streets were enveloped in dust, making visibility poor. However, as we circled the centre I caught the scent of perfumed tobacco burning in water pipes (*shisha*) and directed the driver to Marna House where the garden restaurant had a few customers sending up smoke signals. The next morning, Gaza awoke to Israeli gunboats shelling the coast, wounding four children.

The level of destruction of residential and industrial areas and infrastructure was horrific. The parliament building in central Gaza City was in ruins, mosques were gutted and burned. His small son Ali sitting in his lap, Eyad Sarraj, head of Gaza's community mental health centre, said "99 percent of Gazans" were suffering from post-traumatic stress. "What about Ali?" I asked. "I keep him with me always."

Al-Madhaf had been hit and holed, ceramic pots broken by shrapnel when the Israelis had bombed the nearby sports centre.

When I met UNRWA's chief Karen Koning AbuZayd in her office, I asked if Israel had used white phosphorus, she replied by saying, "If it looks like white phosphorus, acts like white phosphorus and smells like white phosphorus, it must be white phosphorus." There had been a great deal of controversy and criticism over Israel's liberal use, once again, of this weapon, meant to be employed only on battlefields outside urban areas.

At UNRWA's field headquarters, John Ging scolded me for failing to put into my biographical article quotes he would have liked included. I made the point he had refused to cooperate. He spoke so rapidly about the agency's efforts to carry on and Palestinian sufferings, I realised that he was also dealing with PTS and told him so. He took me to see the still smouldering ruins of the agency's warehouse struck by multiple phosphorus shells during Israel's bombardment of the neighbourhood. He said after the first rounds had struck the roof of the vocational training centre where hundreds of people had sought refuge, UNRWA contacted the Israeli military, told the duty officers their shells were hitting the compound and warned them about the danger of exploding the nearby fuel dump. When fresh rounds struck the workshop next to the fuel storage area, staff members kicked phosphorus gel out from under fully loaded fuel lorries and drove them out of the compound. "If they had been hit, the whole place would have gone up," John said.

Israel's operation had killed 1,445 Palestinians; 13 Israelis had died.

Nicosia, July 2014

Israel launched its next major Gaza war with air strikes on July 8th following the slaying in the West Bank of three Israeli teenagers by suspected Hamas members and the retaliatory burning to death of a Palestinian teenager by three Israelis. The war adhered to the established pattern of Israeli-Arab engagements with Israel using massive fire power ahead of a ground invasion by troops and tanks enjoying constant air cover. According to UNRWA 1,500 civilians were killed, 501 of them children out of a total of 2,262 Palestinians slain; 11,000 were injured. Five Israeli civilians died, one a child. A Thai worker and 66 Israeli soldiers were killed.

During the 51-day Israeli operation, half a million Palestinians fled their homes. About 128,000 homes were damaged and 12,000 totally destroyed.

Two other *Irish Times* correspondents reported the war from Gaza, and I was in Cairo to report on the efforts to achieve a ceasefire. Egyptian diplomats and military men took charge of the negotiations which began in early August and ended on the 26th with a fragile ceasefire which the sides interpreted differently. The Palestinians received a pledge from Egypt to press Israel for an end to the siege and blockade of Gaza so that the authorities, UNRWA and Palestinian citizens could rebuild damaged and destroyed homes, schools, power and sewage installations, and other infrastructure. The Palestinians also demanded the release of former detainees, rearrested by Israel after the abduction of the three Israeli youths, opening of Gaza's port and airport, and the convening of a donors' conference to raise $6 billion needed to rebuild Gaza.

Israel's maximalist demands were unrealistic: the disarmament of Palestinian resistance groups and the demilitarisation of the Gaza Strip.

The talks took place under tight wraps at intelligence headquarters in the Cairo suburb of Heliopolis. The Israelis, who flew home every evening, had rooms at the Fairmont hotel in Heliopolis, the Palestinian delegation at the JW Marriott hotel in New Cairo. Both were a good hour's drive from the city centre.

I joined a handful of journalists staking out the Palestinian delegation, composed of representatives of PLO factions as well as non-PLO Hamas and Islamic Jihad. Before going to their hotel, I had managed to ring Rami, a Palestinian-Egyptian activist with contacts in the delegation. He secured for me a brief interview with Bassam al-Salihi from the leftist People's Party who said, "The main question is how to end the [Israeli] blockade and allow people to move freely without restrictions, including between the West Bank and Gaza. The Israelis want never to end the blockade." He expressed concern over Egypt's inability to exert influence over Israel.

When we journalists attempted to ambush Democratic Front member Qais Abdel Karim (Abu Leila), he refused to talk until I reminded him that we had met during a conference in Cyprus. "Twenty years ago," he said and opened up. In his view the Egyptians were "too focused on the ceasefire" so they had failed to deal with the Palestinian demands for the post-ceasefire period. The ceasefire broke down precisely because of this.

Fresh efforts to stalk the Palestinian delegation ended in failure although I did manage to speak to Abu Leila on the phone. At mid-month, the Egyptians put forward their own proposals for the opening of crossings between Israel and Gaza, an end to Israeli restrictions on imports of building materials, and resumption of trade between Gaza and the West Bank. Israel would expand Gaza's fishing grounds from three to 12 nautical miles from the coast and would not object to the transfer by the Palestinian Authority, based in the West Bank, of salaries owed to Gazan civil servants appointed by Hamas. The issues of opening the airport and port were deferred. Israel's demand for disarmament and demilitarisation were not addressed because the Palestinians insisted they were "final status issues" to be negotiated in a peace deal. Egypt's proposals were not accepted by Israel.

Former Palestinian minister and negotiator Ghassan Khatib told me on the phone from Ramallah, "It's going to take time. Ending this war is not going to be as easy as launching it because of the internal politics of the two sides. [Israeli prime minister Binyamin] Netanyahu must appear tough enough so that he will be victorious enough not to pay a heavy price [to end Palestinian rockets]. Hamas must reach an agreement that lifts the closure" of Gaza so the movement cannot be accused of settling for an easing of the blockade that could have been "reached in the first week of the war."

Negotiations punctuated with exchanges of fire continued until the sides agreed to a month-long truce, Israeli opening of the goods passage into Gaza to allow in building materials, expansion of fishing grounds, and the opening of the Egyptian crossing at Rafah to allow Palestinians to leave and enter the Strip. On the first-year anniversary of the war, Palestinians had only been allowed enough construction materials to repair damaged homes. No totally destroyed home had been rebuilt. Gaza fishermen were frequently harassed by Israeli naval patrol boats within the 12-nautical mile area and the Rafah crossing operated only occasionally.

6

SANCTUARY

Nicosia: July 10th, 1976

When we swung into the drive of the Hill hotel in central Nicosia we noticed pro-Phalangist slogans in Arabic and French on the low wall across the street. Exiting the front door was an enforcer who had fled Beirut for fear of retaliatory assassination. The civil war had preceded us. We parked our luggage and dining table top in the entrance, attracting the attention of a Lebanese guest who sneered, "Those copper trays go for fifty pounds in Beirut." Ours was at least 150 years old, an antique fashioned in Morocco by Jewish craftsmen. At its centre a six-pointed star. Not fifty Lebanese pounds.

We quickly retired to our rooms and I let T.S. out of the case onto the flat roof of a lower section of the hotel. He scuppered away, his beige body blending into his brightly sun-lit surroundings until only his dark tail and ears could be seen. I was a bit nervous turning him loose but T.S. normally came when called, especially if dinner was his reward.

The next morning, we visited an estate agent who took us around available lets: boxes with flat tops, mostly. Then a house with character. A fifties' style two-floor building where the landlord lived downstairs and tenants upstairs. A flat with two fireplaces, one in the study, the other in the living room; a dining room, three bedrooms. The price was a bit over budget but the landlady, Eleni, who proffered small cups of Turkish coffee and orange *glyko* on small glass plates with tiny forks, was prepared to let us rent for three or six months, as long as the war in Lebanon lasted. We moved in with our trunks and table top the next day and went to a second-hand dealer to buy a bed and order basic furniture – divans for the salon and bunk beds for Marya – from his carpentry shop.

Then we went shopping. We bought six settings of crockery and cutlery, kitchen utensils, camping gas for cooking, a picnic cold box to keep food cool, food, and a plastic washing up bowl and soap. Half a dozen green and white checked tea towels. Clothing hangers. Three folding chairs and a stool. The bed was delivered that afternoon. Godfrey described it as a cross between a hospital and a brothel bed. It had a sturdy iron frame painted cream and gleaming aluminium trim at head and foot.

We camped in the empty rooms as best we could – refugee style. Marya chose to sleep in the small bedroom on my thin Hajj mattress until her bunk beds arrived. We emptied our trunks into closets and onto bookshelves in the study and set one trunk on top of another to make a base for our dining table tray. On his own in Nicosia while Diana and the children were in Britain, Sophocles came for a dinner of stew cooked on camping gas. The bare wooden floors creaked beneath our feet, the curtain-less rooms echoed with our voices. We went to the bank and withdrew funds from three of Godfrey's monthly retainers. We had a house, a dozen trunks worth of possessions, and money. We were fortunate refugees.

I crossed the Green Line dividing the island between the republic and the Turkish occupied north to collect the remnants of furniture from our Kyrenia house from storage rooms belonging to Sabri, the Turkish Cypriot who had sold British writer Lawrence Durrell his splendid house in Bellapais. The fridge was there, a squat, rust tinged, musty example hardly worth stealing, two tables and four chairs, not our chairs which were new but old cafe chairs with slightly bent knees: far more interesting and valuable than our new rush seat numbers. The rest of our scant furniture had long since disappeared along with the cement mixer belonging to the Turkish Cypriot contractor, the kitchen sink and bathroom tiles due to be installed in the house which was under renovation at the time of the Turkish invasion.

We had bought the house in November 1973 and were in the process of reconfiguring the 125-year-old traditional mud brick structures consisting of a two-storey building, a bedroom on each floor, and a kitchen and bathroom located across the flagstone paved courtyard. The buildings were to be connected at the back of the courtyard by another two-storey section with a double-storey Cypriot arch. The roof of the single storey was to be transformed into a wooden fenced roof garden with a view of Kyrenia castle. We had planned to hold a house warming at the end of August. By then the Turkish army had divided the island.

Refugeedom did not thrust us into a foreign country but gave us back Beirut as well as new lives in Cyprus. By the time we arrived, the island had received thousands of refugees from the Lebanese civil war. Many of our friends had preceded us. Prue, Ian and Charlie and the rest of the *Middle East Economic Survey* team had come several months earlier. Journalists from newspapers and agencies had set up shop here and formed a foreign correspondents' association. Ghazi opened a Lebanese restaurant that became a club for exiled Beirutis half an hour's flight from home. Refugee children flocked to English and French language schools.

Cyprus was already a country of refugees. While Turkish Cypriots living in the south had been forced by Ankara to move to the Turkish-occupied north after the 1974 Turkish invasion, Greek Cypriots living in the north had been made refugees in the south.

Diana and Sophocles, Rachel and Andreas, and Stilvi and Joris – who became close friends and our "extended family" – were victims of division and ethnic cleansing. Sophocles' bus company lost vehicles, Stilvi and Joris land; Andreas was cut-off from his family's village.

The village home and orange groves in Argaki near Morphou belonging to our landlady, Eleni, her mother *Yiayia*, husband Nicos, and children Stella, Zenon, and Anna were on the wrong side of the ceasefire line as was our mud brick house on Constantine Prophyrogenitus Street in Kyrenia. The name of the street was longer than the four-house street. We Jansens could claim to be double refugees.

We were also adopted by Eleni and Nicos, who lived downstairs in the 2,000-year-old village of Ayios Dhometios, which had become a Nicosia dormitory suburb where people from the Morphou area had settled. We celebrated Christmas and New Year's Eve together, picnicked on Easter, and camped in summer.

Our architect Theo, twice a refugee within Cyprus, observed, "You have to tell your children they will be a refugee at least once in their lives." Theo and his wife, another Eleni, lost their home in the Neapolis neighbourhood of Nicosia during inter-communal clashes in the 1950s and Theo's Kyrenia business during the 1974 war. His mother had been expelled from Turkey in 1922 and his wife had fled Palestine when troubles between Palestinians and Jewish colonists erupted. Theo and Eleni's daughter Evie married a Palestinian whose Greek mother, a child during the expulsion of the Greeks from Asia Minor, had been adopted by a Palestinian couple who had fled to Beirut following the establishment of Israel.

In the wake of the Turkish invasion and occupation, Cypriot lives were governed by austerity.

Money was tight. Seventy percent of the island's economy, its tourism facilities, manufacturing sector, and citrus orchards had been in the north. Water was in short supply as the Turks were sitting on the aquifers. The south provided the north with electricity in exchange for water until new sources were developed in the south. Food was plentiful but homegrown rather than imported. Unlike war-torn Beirut, Nicosia had few luxuries.

Greek Cypriot refugees crowded in with relatives until they could earn enough to rent their own flats. Rents were high due to the influx of Lebanese. Refugee couples worked two or three jobs while grannies minded children who studied hard and excelled at school as they saw education as their only safe prospect – like many Palestinians.

The Jordanian desert, October 8th, 2012

Clouds of dust rose with the passage of every vehicle along the narrow, rutted road to al-Zaatari camp, engulfing the line of newcomers waiting to be admitted. An armoured scout car stood sentinel outside the gate of the vast fenced enclosure. A cheerful soldier glimpsed at our credentials and waved us through. Our passes, issued by the interior ministry, were checked by an officer of the Jordanian charity in charge of the camp.

Between 300-500 Syrians arrive daily said Dr. Karim, coordinator for the Moroccan field hospital where refugees were treated for gunshot and shrapnel wounds and trauma as well as sunburn. Since its establishment the medics had received 20,000 hurt and ailing refugees and delivered 25 babies. The most frequented treatment tents, ranged round a rectangular courtyard, were for paediatrics and skin complaints. "Syrians are fair people, they cannot take exposure to the sun," Dr. Karim stated.

Residential tents, once white but now dyed red by desert dust, were pitched along streets. Vendors selling fruit and vegetables squatted in make-shift shelters consisting of plastic sheeting stamped with the letters UNHCR, UN High Commissioner for Refugees, stretched over aluminium frames. Boys of nine or ten hawked cigarettes from tables set up on street corners. Each neighbourhood was supplied with chemical toilets and blue breeze-block compounds with showers. Taps fixed to outer walls dripped water into puddles. Laundry hung on lines between tents.

Three young women, in headscarves and spotless caftans, said they were from the town of Taibeh in Deraa province as wind dashed sand in their faces and forced them to turn away. "Sand and dust are our curse," asserted Mariam, as we took seats on cement blocks in the shade of an awning in front of their tent. "No chairs," observed Sawsan, a young mother of two. Yusra had four children, Mariam one boy, who insisted he is eight but is, in fact, nine. Time is lost sitting in a refugee camp with little to do. The charity provided two cooked meals a day in takeaway cartons as well as ingredients for supper for all 30,000 residents. The number was expected to double by year's end.

"We will cut off Bashar's head, if we get a chance," stated Sawsan, referring to Syrian president Bashar al-Assad. This was the Zaatari refrain. If he stepped down, who would you want to be president? Turkey had proposed former vice-president Farouk al-Sharaa. They favoured Sharaa.

He is from Deraa and they believed had no blood on his hands. One of the men who joined us said he was fifty-fifty for Sharaa. Muhammad, an army conscript who fought in the terrible battle of the Baba Amr quarter of the central city of Homs, said, "I spent seven months in prison because I am from Deraa." He did not elaborate. When I stood to depart, Mariam stuffed a packet of biscuits into one jacket pocket and a small carton of orange juice into the other. "You are our guest," she said. As I walked past a tent where women were baking thin flat rounds of bread which they sprinkled with sugar, they insisted I should have a piece. Arab hospitality survives refugeedom.

I met my colleagues at the shelter transformed by Ibrahim Naimi into a coffee shop. Mattresses were ranged along plastic sheet walls, cement blocks served as side tables, empty sardine tins as ashtrays. A shelf at the back held a transistor radio, small bags of sugar, and a packet of coffee powder. He boasted he had 50 customers a day for coffee and water pipes. "In Syria, I ran a coffee shop in a prison," he stated. "People here pay in Syrian, Jordanian, dollars, euros, whatever they have." His family was originally from the Golan, occupied by Israel in 1967.

Fig Tree Bay, August 1976

We pitched our borrowed tent with difficulty in the soft sand, trying to drive the metal stakes deep to stabilise sagging canvas. Marya followed Christina, Michael, Katy and Ion to the water's edge and tentatively put a foot into the Mediterranean, its restless surface glittering sliver in the late afternoon sun. Neither Marya nor I had been camping before and Godfrey 's last stint under canvas had been during World War II when he was an officer who did not have to put up his own tent. Diana and Sophocles, Rachel and Andreas had their tents up before we managed but we did, finally, succeed. T.S., wearing a collar and restrained by a lead, tried to make sense of our new habitat by digging deep into the sand. Balu remained in quarantine. The only other campers on the beach were three young Cypriot National Guardsmen on a few days' leave.

Once our tents were up, rubber mattresses inflated, clothes and towels stowed, and folding chairs and table set up in front of our tent, we staggered up to the cafe to sip cold beers and order fresh fish for dinner.

Our new friends had invited us to join them at the beach while we awaited delivery of our divans and bunk beds. Nicosia was sweltering hot and our flat bare. Marya was aloof, shy of their four children who had grown up together, but the sea released the three of us from the cares of the war we had abandoned when we boarded the freighter that had delivered us to peaceful but divided Cyprus.

Amman, October 9th, 2012

Shadi led Menahil, an Iraqi refugee, and me into the handsome stone-faced apartment block in a leafy neighbourhood of Amman and up four flights of unfinished stairs to his flat. As we slipped off our shoes at the door, his two round-eyed daughters stared at us. Clinging to their mother's skirts, they followed us into the sitting room furnished with a wide screen television set and three thin mattresses covered in flowered cotton, cushions. The windows were curtained with sheets. We bent nearly double to lower ourselves onto two of the mattresses while Shadi said he, Mona and the girls had come from the Damascus suburb of Muadamiya, a place I had visited twice since the Syrian conflict began in 2011.

"We came six weeks ago. We had no problems near our house, but we could hear clashes at night. I have a sister in Sweden who invited us to visit. The embassy rejected our request for visas because of the bad situation in Syria. We will stay here and apply for humanitarian asylum. We want to live in Sweden but if there is no progress with the embassy, we will return home." He had a job selling clothing in a shop, earning $280 a month, an average wage for low-level employees in both public and private sectors.

Mona brought us small cups of Turkish coffee on a tray and sat beside Shadi. "It's very expensive here. The rent is very high. We are homesick and want to return to our family and friends."

Nadia, a thin-faced woman in a headscarf, and her four children from the "hot" Damascus suburb of Qadam, dwelt with her sister in a flat three-floors below. We stepped over a discarded rag doll and sat down on a sagging divan covered in threadbare brocade. On the wall opposite was a jagged line of black mould, on the windows thin, semi-transparent curtains of faded, dusty material.

"There were no Free Army [rebels] in our quarter," stated Nadia, a Jordanian married to a Syrian of Palestinian origin. Nevertheless, her house and the houses of her sisters were destroyed during clashes. She did not say who was fighting whom. She fled in a taxi with her children and reached Amman safely but miscarried. Her husband, a policeman who had served on the force for 20 years, was arrested. "We don't know his fate. We lost his salary and pension."

Menahil and I climbed back up to the top floor where Muhammad awaited us. His wife and sister had gone to bed. Here the divan and chairs were modern, the television modest and the fridge was in the sitting room. He had arranged chocolates carefully on a plate and offered them round before telling us his family's story. Their house at the centre of Homs sustained damage when the adjacent building was shelled or bombed. They moved to Damascus with the help of the Free Army but later fled to Amman, he said in a matter of fact tone.

"I used to work here before I got married and made good money as an electrician. Con-struction is down so I was jobless for six weeks. Now I have a job, but employers pay less than before. We are exploited." He walked us down the stairs to the ironwork front door and unlocked it. "We have thieves in this area."

Latakia, July 1976

As the Russian car ferry pulled out of the Syrian port, our Volvo, known affectionately as "the tank" was clamped firmly to the deck where I found myself standing at the rail next to an elderly man watching the land disappear as water roiled below the bow of the ship.

"Why are you going to Cyprus?" he asked. I live there now. I came to Damascus to collect my car which we left with Syrian friends before we left Lebanon. "Due to the war?" he asked. Yes, we lived in a village above Beirut, Chemlan. But mortars began to fall, our daughter had no school, and my husband's newspaper could not transfer his salary to Beirut. We used to collect his salary in Nicosia but when the planes stopped... Well, we had to leave.

"Your husband is a journalist, then?" Yes, for *The Economist.* He's called 'Our Levant correspondent.' "Perhaps you knew my son. He knew many journalists in Beirut. Ghassan Kanafani?" Of course, we both did.

We were up and getting ready for the day when the *BBC* had announced his death in an early bulletin on July 8th, 1972. His car blew up, killing Ghassan and his 17-year-old niece, Lamis Najm. At mid-morning, we drove to Beirut and the office of *Al-Hadaf*, the newspaper of the leftist Popular Front for the Liberation of Palestine (PFLP), to condole with his colleagues. Everyone who knew him was in shock. Ghassan was a poet, a writer of short stories and novels, and a political activist. He was a PFLP spokesman, a man of words, not a fighter. Ghassan was 36.

Israel's external intelligence service, Mossad, eventually claimed the assassination. The motive was said to be the massacre carried out by three PFLP-recruited Japanese Red Army members at Israel's airport near Tel Aviv. Twenty-six people were killed and 80 injured. Two of the attackers died while a third was captured. A photo of Ghassan with one of the Japanese was published in the press a few days after the airport operation.

I had met Ghassan when I was collecting interviews on the experiences of Palestinians expelled from their homeland after the creation of Israel. One individual stood out among the many I met. He and his family had refused to leave. He was a middle-aged man who lived in hiding near his village in northern Palestine and said he conducted strikes on Israeli pipelines, electricity pylons, and other structures. Since he had been a fighter during the 1948-49 war, he was a wanted man who dared not show his face. "I buried arms near my hide-outs," he said. "The Israelis never asked about the children born to my wife after I disappeared," he laughed.

Fayez Kanafani and I talked about Beirut, about Ghassan's wife Anni and children until the sun sank beneath the molten sea. My cabin mate for the night was a Lebanese woman from the Greek Orthodox Koura area between Beirut and the northern port of Tripoli. Like hundreds of thousands of Palestinians, including the Kanafanis, she had left her home and village with nothing. But she fled while under attack from her own Christian countrymen, the Maronite Phalange militia. "I ran away in my nightgown," she said. The Palestinian example had made us carefully plan our exit from the Lebanese civil war.

Chemlan-Beirut-Larnaca-Nicosia, June 1979

Hajji, my MG sports car, was given special permission to enter Cyprus which had banned the entry of vehicles more than three years old. In a letter to the office dealing with the importation of cars, Nicos, a friend in the Planning Bureau, wrote Hajji, born in February 1949, was a "classic car," and would be "a national treasure."

My permission to import her and my list of Lebanese phone numbers in hand, I flew to Beirut, still in the grip of civil conflict, and, without knowing whether he was still alive, rang Selim, the mechanic who had kept Hajji going until we moved to our house in the mountains. Selim answered. I explained that Hajji had been abandoned in a garden at the bottom of a steep slope in Chemlan. He was game for the extraction.

We were taken to the village by Abu Hamzeh, the driver who had conveyed us to Tyre where we had boarded the cargo ship for Cyprus and entered refugeedom. This time Abu Hamzeh came without his pistol and knife tucked into his socks. Selim and his team drove a large four-wheel drive vehicle to haul Hajji up the hill. They brought a battery, petrol, oil, brake fluid and tyres. Battered, stripped of her speedometer and other instruments, a small dent at the top of her radiator from shrapnel, Hajji was a sad sight. Selim and his team got to work and after some time we heard her resonant roar, a small miracle in this brutalised land. Once back on the main road, Hajji was ready to go under her own steam.

She sped off carrying two mechanics, a door flying open at right-hand curves, and no brakes, swooping downhill, negotiating the twisting alleyways of the village of Bchamoun, and whizzing across a narrow natural bridge slung across a deep valley, the men whooping like kids on a roller coaster. She zoomed – without pause – down the forested slopes to the coastal highway and made for Selim's garage where she would be repaired enough to make it to the airport and fly by cargo plane to Larnaca.

After her road tax was paid and leave papers were stamped, Hajji, dozens of boxes of books and a few pieces of furniture were loaded onto a pallet and lifted into the hold of a cargo aircraft bound for Larnaca. I had caught a passenger flight that landed earlier, collected the old girl at the airport, and drove to a lay-by outside Larnaca where she was put onto a lorry, taken home and dropped off at the Thomas Savvas' garage across the street from our house. It took the heroic Thomas nine months, working overtime after his daily patients had been treated, to bring Hajji, my refugee MG, back to her old self. Marya and her friends demanded Hajji convey them to school until her crank-shaft broke and we had to order a new one from Britain.

Yarmouk Palestinian "camp," August 1st, 2012

Karin and I met Jamil at Palestine Square, a ten-minute drive from our hotel in the heart of Damascus. At the centre of the square was a curious sculpture featuring a ball. On one side stood a burnt-out police station, watched over by armed guards and surrounded by yellow tape universally used to corral crime scenes.

We began our tour at the corner of Yarmouk street, one of the two main thoroughfares of this built-up city housing 160,000 Palestinians and at least 800,000 Syrians, Sudanese, Somalis, and other nationalities settled just south of the capital. At the nearby entrance to Palestine Street stood an arch, the smiling face of the late Palestinian president Yasser Arafat at its centre.

Pieces of thick glass from the window of the pharmacy at the top of Yarmouk Street littered the sidewalk and were scattered on the display of medications and shampoos. "A bullet pierced the metal shutter during the clashes," stated the white-coated pharmacist. He planned to apply to a government office for compensation. His shop was one of the few open.

Spray-painted graffiti decorated the closed shutters. "Strike or burn," ordered one. "Down with pigs," stated another, directed at the government. Here and there the unimaginative slogans had been x-ed out.

Jamil remarked, "The shops closed for six days and then reopened. Owners have to work, or they cannot pay rent or feed their families. They will open at noon." This was the daily fasting and night time feasting month of Ramadan.

"The Free Syrian Army is not accepted here," he added. Palestinians refuse to be drawn into the conflict between the government and rebels although some sympathise with the opposition.

Jamil said his family was divided, with his mother supporting the revolutionaries and his father adopting neutrality.

A street sweeper was scraping tidy piles of rubbish in the dust along the kurb in the hope that garbage lorries would soon return to collect mounds of stinking, fly-and-rat infested refuse which had accumulated over the previous 18 days.

Outside the Palestinian Liberation Army hospital, we met Ibrahim, a grizzled ambulance driver whose family had originally come from Nazareth. "During the clashes I had to pick up 21, maybe 22 people from the street. Three were dead and the rest wounded. It's dangerous work, my ambulance was shot by a sniper, up there," he pointed to a building across the street. "Now it's quiet. But we never know what will happen after an hour or two."

We passed two mosques where there had been anti-government demonstrations several months earlier and made our way to the UN-run Palestinian school – named for the village of Qastel in Palestine – with a wide, tiled courtyard and blue ribbed metal roofing. Some 350 refugees from neighbouring areas were camped out here. At the height of the clashes there were 750. While the UN provided some aid, the bulk came from Palestinian organisations although most families were Syrian.

Uniformed soldiers checked identity documents of drivers and merchandise in lorries at the corner of the street that formed the border between Yarmouk and the Hajar al-Aswad district, where fighting had erupted 24 hours earlier. Glass shards were scattered on the ground and the walls of buildings were pock marked by bullets, but no major damage had been inflicted.

On both sides of the broad road were car repair garages and lots selling second-hand cars. "This is the place people used to come to buy cheap cars," Jamil remarked. As we turned back into Yarmouk we skirted a blackened building. The former headquarters of the pro-government Popular Front-General Command headed by Ahmed Jibril whose fighters were supposed to keep the peace and protect Yarmouk from outside forces, ensuring Palestinian neutrality.

Jamil led us through a narrow alleyway, into a building and up a flight of stairs where he asked us to wait while he warned his mother he was bringing guests. A few moments later he ushered us into the entrance of his family flat where we slipped off our shoes before moving into the well-furnished salon. His mother, Leila, came out of the kitchen to greet us, slightly fussed but welcoming. She had been preparing the evening Ramadan breakfast. She disappeared and returned with two glasses of *toot*, cool mulberry juice. "It's very hot today, you must be thirsty." She brought none for herself or Jamil since they were fasting.

We spoke of Palestine and the plight of Palestinians in Syria, of Arafat whom I had met several times, Habash of the Popular Front and Hawatmeh of the Democratic Front. She was particularly taken by the fact that I had met Arafat. After we had consumed traditional small cups of Turkish coffee, thanked our hostess, slipped on our footware, and started down the stairs, Jamil said, "I told you my mother is the revolutionary in the family."

Damascus, May 2013

Jamil rang to say he was stuck in a traffic jam between the eastern side of the Old City and the new city, but his sister would meet me near the Italian hospital and take me to the flat. Lora, a very handsome young woman in casual dress, met me by the mosque on the corner and we walked to an old building. The sitting room was large, with cream coloured walls and a high ceiling elegant with decorative moulding.

Lora is an architect who was employed by a local firm, Carla, the youngest sister, a student at Latakia University in the north who was afraid to attend because she did not want to be separated from her family. A third sister, Sarah, worked in a bank in Dubai. The sole son, Jamil arrived, a bit fussed from his long, hot ride in a bus, and they related the story of how they reached this house in central Damascus.

On December 16th, 2012, a small group of renegades from Jibril's unpopular Popular Front-General Command had opened the way for the entry of rebels from the Free Syrian Army and al-Qaeda affiliate Jabhat al-Nusra. "It is rumoured Abu Hashem, a family friend, had been paid by Qatar," remarked someone. The government responded by shelling and bombing Yarmouk. One bomb targeted a mosque. "Fifty were killed. People freaked out," said Carla.

On the 17th, tens of thousands left Yarmouk, walking slowly in long lines. Leila and Carla, who had been at home – cooking calmly – during the takeover, gathered a few things and walked for three hours. "There were thousands and thousands, so many heads in front of and behind us. It was heartbreaking, another Naqba. Yarmouk camp was the biggest Palestinian settlement outside Palestine," Leila said.

Jamil and Lora found them in the chaos and led them to Bab Touma, St. Thomas' Gate to the Old City and to a boutique hotel, empty since the onset of the conflict in March 2011. They remained there for several weeks before moving into this flat.

Jamil continued, "The Free Army stole so much. It divided up Yarmouk into quarters and systematically robbed the houses. Most fighters come from Hajar al-Aswad. The Eagles of the Golan are really bad guys."

"Many people hated Jibril and his men before the fall of Yarmouk, but Ahmed Jibril protected Yarmouk for eight months," asserted Lora, angry over the betrayal by some of their countrymen. "When the Free Army and Nusra entered, the government did not support Jibril, so the camp fell."

"There are 70,000 people now in Yarmouk, 8,000 families," observed Leila. "There used to be a million," 112,550 Palestinians registered with UNRWA. Leila and Carla returned a couple of times to get summer clothing and other possessions. There were long lines of people entering Yarmouk and, again, many checkpoints. "We didn't send Jamil because he could be taken at the checkpoints."

Leila and Lora had cooked a splendid meal of Palestinian dishes.

"This flat belongs to relatives who are in Cairo. We pay half the rent of $500," stated Jamil. "But they plan to return in six months or so... We'll have to find something else."

Bavaria, September 2015

On September 11th, 2014, Leila, Jamil, Lora and Carla put themselves into the hands of smugglers in a bid to travel from Syria to Germany. They departed from Bab Touma in a minibus driven by a smuggler and made for the border with Turkey, passing through checkpoints manned by government soldiers and armed anti-government fighters, who extracted small bribes in cash and cigarettes to allow them to pass. The women put on black cloaks and two heavy veils to go through territory held by Islamic State (*Daesh*) and al-Qaeda's *Jabhat al-Nusra*. Jamil worried about his jeans, banned by *Daesh* in areas under its control. Kidnapping by these groups was a great risk. Lora and Carla were pretty, and Jamil was of fighting age.

At the first place they tried to cross into Turkey, the border was too heavily patrolled by Turkish troops, at the second a Turkish soldier had intercepted the family, put the muzzle of his gun against Jamil's chest and ordered them to turn around. On the third attempt they scrambled through a hole in the barbed wire and slipped along trenches near Bab al-Salameh.

Once in Turkey, they travelled by bus to Ankara and Izmir where they stayed in some neighbourhood hosting smugglers who arranged risky boat passages to Greece, refugees' first European destination where they could remain legally for six months. The family was ordered to shift to the smaller coastal towns of Bodrum and Didim to board a rubber raft bound for the nearest Greek island called Farmakonisi. The boat sank at some distance from the Turkish shore and the passengers were rescued by the Turkish coastguard, taken to a police station and fingerprinted. The family searched for lodging late at night, their clothes stiff with dried salt, discouraged, exhausted, and convinced the smugglers were in cahoots with the Turkish police and shore patrol.

A few days later the four boarded a second rubber boat with another 38 people but this boat sank near shore and all the passengers managed to reach land safely – although Leila cannot swim. This time they slept as best they could on the ground near the launch location of the boats.

When on the third try in a rubber boat with a decent motor they neared Farmakonisi, other passengers slashed the boat with knives, so it would sink, and they could not be sent back to Turkey. This time they were rescued by the Greek shore patrol. They were put up at a stinking army barracks at a military post on the island, fingerprinted, given visas for six months, and sent by ferry to Athens. There they remained for 36 days, resting, meeting friends from Damascus, and investigating which route would get them safely to Germany.

They chose to go by 18-hour ferry to Venice and proceed by public bus, entering southern Germany on November 9th, without passing through immigration. There was at that time free travel between European Union countries which were parties to the Schengen agreement. After spending a night in Munich, they proceeded toward Berlin in a minivan with Bulgarian license plates but were intercepted by a police patrol. Many smugglers used vehicles with Bulgarian plates. The family was taken to a police station where they were again fingerprinted and the process of obtaining German asylum began.

Their first accommodation was a cubicle enclosed in blankets in an exhibition hall where, after examinations by doctors, they remained for 15 days. They were then taken to Nuremberg to share a three-bedroom flat with a Ukrainian family of four and a Serb family of four, although each bedroom had only three beds. Finally, around November 23rd, my friends were transported by bus to a pleasant, well-appointed two-bedroom flat in a Bavarian village where I visited them in September 2015.

Leila, Lora and Carla stayed in Bavaria where the rent was paid by the government and each person received a fixed amount a month for expenses. Lora, an architect, worked as an unpaid intern at a nearby firm while Carla searched for a course she could follow. Jamil moved to Berlin to begin a master's course at a German university. All became proud recipients of light blue German refugee passports on which they could travel freely throughout the European Union and apply for visas for journeys elsewhere. Their handsome dark blue Syrian refugee documents were accepted nowhere. In several years' time, the family hoped to secure German citizenship and cease being stateless Palestinians.

7

LIBERATION

Beirut, September 29th, 1970

Godfrey, Marya, strapped into her baby chair in the back seat of the car, and I drove from Chemlan to Beirut, a black flag flying from the aerial, causing the slender metal rod to thrum with the wind. Godfrey feared we might meet demonstrations in the streets and should make a show of mourning. Beirut's streets had filled with bereft millions attending Nasser's funeral.

Nasser had died of a heart attack overnight after engaging in intensive negotiations with Jordan's king Hussein and PLO chairman Yasser Arafat to reach a ceasefire in the brutal war between the Jordanian army and Palestinian guerrillas launched after the leftist Popular Front's civilian airliner hijackings. The deadly 11-day conflict was dubbed Black September not only because the Jordanians subdued the PLO and its allies but also because of Nasser's demise.

Despite the breakup of the United Arab Republic in 1961 and Egypt's defeat in 1967, Arab nationalists did not break faith with Nasser. Many blamed Syria rather than Egypt for the divorce. The March 1962 liberation of Algeria, after 132 years of French colonial rule, had kept pan-Arab nationalism alive. Egypt had provided military aid to the Algerian National Liberation Front (FLN) and

Nasser and FLN leader Ahmed Ben Bella had emerged firm friends and allies.

Algeria was a beacon for other Arab and African states still fighting for independence while Nasser not only became a leading figure in the global decolonisation drive but also a founder, along with India's Nehru, Yugoslavia's Tito and Cyprus' Makarios of the Non-Aligned Movement (NAM) formally established in Belgrade in 1961.

Cairo, Summer 1973

Eager to collect and spend a few hundred Egyptian pounds Godfrey had earned for articles written for *Al-Ahram*, he, Marya and I flew to Cairo. It was our first visit to Egypt since Nasser had been succeeded by Anwar Sadat, a very different sort of president with a very different agenda. In July-August 1972 – under a deal said to have been cooked up between Washington and Moscow – Sadat had expelled thousands of Soviet officers and troops deployed since 1969 to bolster the Egyptian armed forces which had failed so miserably to defend the country against Israel in 1967. Russian advisers remained, however, and Russia stepped up the flow of arms supplies to Egypt.

While Godfrey was meeting experts at *Al-Ahram's* Centre for Political and Strategic Studies, Judge Jasper Brinton drove Marya and me through the nearly empty district where Russian officers had formerly dwelled with their families. The judge, then 95, served for 27 years on the Mixed Courts, a colonial era relic which tried cases involving foreigners, and founded the Egyptian Society of International Law. He and his wife Geneva lived in a book-filled flat in Zamalek.

Father, grandfather and great-grandfather of Beiruti friends, Judge Brinton crossed Qasr al-Nil bridge and turned onto the riverside boulevard, steering his ancient convertible with verve, ignoring stop signs and red lights. Perhaps Egyptians who scurried out of the way understood the judge was a prominent actor in their history. Or, those who lived along his normal routes simply scattered out of self-preservation.

He had decided to take us to visit another Philadelphian, archaeologist George Scanlon so Marya, aged three, could see what an excavation was like. "Never too early," was the judge's reasoning. Fustat in Old Cairo was the first capital of Egypt after its conquest by the Muslims. Marya was not impressed with George's Fustat ruins but clamoured to see his houseboat on the Nile.

Zarqa-Amman, October 6th, 1973

I had just completed my visit to Miss Coates' farm where she had demonstrated how to find water with a forked stick for an article I intended to write and was passing through the streets of this Jordanian town when the driver switched on the car radio. "*Harb*" was the word the announcer kept repeating. War! Egypt and Syria had attacked Israel from the air and land in a bid to recapture the Sinai Peninsula and the Golan Heights seized by Israel in 1967 along with Gaza, the West Bank and East Jerusalem.

Since Godfrey was set to travel to Jordan on assignment for *The Economist*, Brian said, "Take Michael along. Have a weekend holiday." We left Marya at home in Chemlan with Sitt Asmah, our octogenarian baby-minder, departing on Friday, due home on Sunday, two days away from Marya. Our car was parked at Beirut's international airport, something we never did if we were travelling for any length of time.

Godfrey and I rushed back to the hotel, Amman's Intercontinental, where we followed developments by listening to *BBC* bulletins hour after hour on our transistor radio and checking a news agency telex in the lobby. Amman's airport closed as the first warplanes dropped their bombs on Israeli positions. We were stuck, separated from Marya, hopefully not for the duration. We telephoned Chemlan and spoke to Asmah and Marya, assuring them that we were alright and would return as soon as possible.

The war began with simultaneous Egyptian and Syrian air strikes on Israeli army positions in Sinai and the Golan. The offensive, launched on Yom Kippur, the Jewish Day of Atonement, and during the Muslim fasting month of Ramadan, was the first ever initiated by Arab powers against Israel. Arab involvement in Israel's 1948 war of establishment followed the expulsion by Israeli forces of 250,000 - 300,000 Palestinians from their homes between April 1st and the declaration of the state on May 15th. In 1956, Britain, France and Israel attacked Egypt after Nasser's nationalisation of the Suez Canal, and in 1967 Israel launched the war by striking Egyptian airfields.

Arabs across the region had been calling for an offensive against Israel that would not only win back lost territory but also regain Arab dignity and self-respect after the humiliating defeat of 1967. This made the war doubly inevitable. Shortly after taking power, Sadat, an arrogant man who favoured classy military uniforms resplendent with unearned medals, had suffered personal humiliation when he offered Israel peace in exchange for Sinai but had been rebuffed by Israeli prime minister Golda Meir.

The unexpected attack shocked Israel and the world powers, particularly when the Egyptian army, under the command of general Saad el-Shazly, crossed the Suez Canal and breached the "Bar Lev line." This consisted of fortifications along the eastern bank of the canal designed to prevent the Egyptians from doing precisely what Shazly's troops had done. Shazly restored Arab honour and compelled Israel to examine the dismissive attitude its military chiefs and politicians had formed of Arab armies.

During the first hours of the operation, Syrian troops captured Israel's fortified surveillance facility on Jabal al-Sheikh (Mount Hermon) and Syrian tanks advanced deep into the Golan, seized by Israel in 1967.

By dawn on the 7th, 100,000 Egyptian soldiers and 100 tanks had crossed the canal into Sinai and advanced about 15 kilometres. As fighting raged Jordan, Iraq and Saudi Arabia mobilised forces for the offensive.

There was not much we could do but fume and fuss. Ibrahim, a friend from AUB days then with the Jordanian information ministry, promised to get me on the first flight out once the airport reopened. Restless and fed up with the hotel, Godfrey and I walked to a nearby restaurant for dinner. Wine was served in a teapot and drunk in cups as it was Ramadan when public consumption of alcohol, prohibited to Muslims, was frowned upon.

On the 8th, the Israeli army – which had more modern US tanks and longer-range artillery – began to respond effectively to the Syrian offensive.

On the 9th, we drove to the Syrian border with the aim of getting to Beirut by crossing Syria, but Israeli jets had bombed Damascus and Homs, killing hundreds of civilians, including several Indian ladies attending a coffee party in a residential neighbourhood. We were turned back by Jordanian immigration: Syria had closed its borders, especially to Indians.

Asmah panicked when an Israeli warplane shot down a Syrian fighter that had crashed on a hill several kilometres from our house. She took Marya to her little dwelling, sheltered by other village houses, but Godfrey's sister D arrived in a taxi and carried Marya to Beirut. We told both to get her back to *Beit al-Hindi.*

The next day, Israeli troops crossed the 1967 ceasefire line with the aim of reaching Damascus while Iraqi and Jordanian forces prepared to deploy. Egyptian units had hunkered down in their positions in Sinai as Israeli aircraft, roaming freely, bombed and strafed them. Casualties were high.

Ibrahim was as good as his word. He found me a seat on a flight to Frankfurt, arriving in the evening, I slept the night in a cheap hotel in a room with seven beds and the next day, caught a plane to Beirut, collected the car from the airport parking lot and drove up to Chemlan. Across the valley, the wreckage of the downed Syrian jet still smouldered.

Godfrey returned home after another three or four days. By that time the Israelis had turned the tide of battle on both fronts, thanks to US resupply of ammunition and spare parts and the failure of the UN Security Council to impose a ceasefire-in-place that would have pressed both sides to halt where they were.

Although Israel was able to maintain its grip on occupied territory, the Arabs had "won" the war. They had launched a credible, well-coordinated, properly planned offensive on two fronts, deeply shaking the overconfident Israeli military. The Arabs had proved their soldiers did not drop their weapons and flee if confronted by the Israeli armed forces but were prepared to stand their ground and fight. This was a lesson it took Israeli generals and politicians years to absorb, a lesson repeated in 2006 when Israel attacked Lebanon after Hizbullah had abducted two Israeli soldiers patrolling the ceasefire line between the two countries.

Chemlan, July 15th, 1974

Godfrey waved me down as I drove past Ian and Prue's summer house. "Makarios has been toppled by a coup," he said through the open window. "They don't know if he's alive or dead." Who did it? "The Athens junta using the Greek contingent in Nicosia."

Makarios survived, escaped across the mountains and was airlifted off the island by Britain, which – along with Greece and Turkey – had committed to defend Cyprus ahead of independence in 1960. Godfrey fussed and fumed for two days before taking a flight from Beirut to Nicosia. His excuse: "I must visit Glafkos. Make certain he is still alive, safe." Clerides, speaker of parliament, was under house arrest.

The world waited for Britain, which had forces on the island, to intervene. US secretary of state Henry Kissinger reportedly told his counterpart Jim Callaghan, "Don't be a boy scout, Jim," leaving the door open to Turkey to act on its own. Ankara attacked early on the morning of the 20th. When I finally reached Godfrey by phone at the Ledra Palace hotel on the Green Line that divides Nicosia between Greek and Turkish Cypriot sectors, he reported, "I've filled my bathtub with water, in case the supply is cut. The hotel is full of visiting Cypriots and tourists. The staff fled and left baskets of rolls on the kitchen table. Nothing else. National Guard snipers on the roof attract fire from Turkish paratroops who have been landing all day. A couple of rounds were fired through the lobby, hitting the band's instruments."

It took the UN 48 hours to arrange a local ceasefire and dispatch tough French-Canadian troops in armoured vehicles leading a convoy of lorries to rescue the hotel guests. Godfrey rang me as soon as he had reached the British base at Dhekelia. "They've put us in empty barracks and fed us bully beef stew. It was the best meal I've ever eaten. They'll fly us to Britain in the next few days." He landed at the British airbase at Lyneham and travelled to London where he wrote his war and escape dispatch for *The Economist*.

Godfrey was no stranger to war. He had been an official war correspondent based in Burma during World War II and was a student of war. Our shelves boast many metres of books on war. He rarely spoke about his "war," except to say he had a "good war." He did not know if he had killed anyone when shooting blindly toward Japanese soldiers in the jungle or firing a machine gun during his sole stint as a tail gunner in a flimsy British fighter plane. "The most frightening experience I've ever had," he remarked.

From the balcony of the hall of Singapore's Municipal Council building he witnessed the Japanese surrender in September 1945, after the US bombing of Hiroshima and Nagasaki. He saw Japanese officers handover Samurai swords to their opposite numbers in the allied forces and general Seishiro Itagaki and lord Louis Mountbatten sign the document of surrender. Godfrey was dispatched with his Royal Indian Air Force unit to Hiroshima. He and the other Indian officers wore their side cap crown badges upside down to register their support for India's independence.

As an Indian diplomat in the first post-independence batch, Godfrey, press attaché in Cairo, walked along the top of the wall of the Old City of Jerusalem in 1948 when Jordan's Arab Legion was battling Israel's underground army for possession of the city.

Kyrenia, February 13th, 1975

Eileen handed me a clumsily stapled booklet. "I thought you might write about this, so I made you a copy of my diary." Throughout the Turkish invasion, she had been in her small house with a wide picture window looking out onto the new Turkish Cypriot quarter. On the street outside a "snow drop," a white helmeted Turkish soldier, paced up and down in front of the house, waiting for her teenage daughter to show herself. "I'm afraid, mum, I'll come with you to Bellapais. I don't want to be here alone."

Refrigerators filled with food that rotted after the invasion still haunted street corners and many homes had boarded up doors and windows, meant to deter looters who specialised in stealing doors and shutters. We parked on the main street and walked to our little house, the blue street door was gone along with the contents of the building site. Eileen sighed. The war had taken her job with Theo, our Greek Cypriot architect, and his Turkish Cypriot contractor as well as her husband Khalil's job with the telecommunications company.

We followed the coast road before turning uphill along the winding road past the lemon groves of Kazafani. Finally, we entered the narrow street at the entrance of Bellapais and arrived at the square, where the Tree of Idleness had once sheltered Greek and Turkish Cypriot men sipping thick Turkish coffee and playing cards until their women summoned them for lunch or dinner. Where tourists armed with battered yellow-covered copies of Lawrence Durrell's *Bitter Lemons* had absorbed the atmosphere and admired the 13th century Abbey, gold and ivory against the backdrop of the azure Mediterranean, white gulls wheeling above the ruined cloisters. The church had sheltered wounded Greek Cypriot guardsmen until Finnish UN soldiers had escorted them to safety before the Turkish troops arrived and took charge.

Eileen introduced me to a British couple who had remained throughout the Turkish invasion and the early days of the occupation. They gave me a day-by-day account of what had happened in the village for the novel I intended to write about the events of that summer. The Turks had rounded up 1,000 Greek Cypriots from the coast and nearby villages and dumped them here in picturesque Bellapais. Those who wanted to leave were dispatched to the Greek Cypriot lines in buses. Men and boys opting to stay were taken away in buses to sheep pens near Nicosia and interrogated, women and children marched to the Bellapais hotel down the hill where they stayed until their houses could be searched for weapons and robbed of small, valuable objects. Details were filled in by other residents, foreign and Greek Cypriot, until I had a picture of the situation during and just after the war. Details and colour which I took home to Chemlan and fashioned into a first draft while the 75-millimetre Howitzer planted on the top of the hill looming above us loosed shells at the Maronite mountain north-east of us. Writing to the music of Mikis Theodorakis broadcast by Cyprus radio kept me sane during the long, hot summer of 1975, the Battle of the Hotels in December, and the terrible months that followed.

Dherynia, April 20th, 1975

It was a glowing spring morning when Godfrey, Marya and I set out for the ceasefire line village of Dherynia where Greek Cypriot women and their supporters were due to march in protest against the division of Cyprus following the Turkish invasion and occupation of the north. Nearing the site where Women Walk Home participants were to assemble, we were waved into a field to park our hire car. Buses from all over the free areas of the island converged on the location, unloading dozens, scores, hundreds, eventually 35,000 women. There were older women in black, middle-aged middle-class women in suits and sturdy shoes, young women in bright red, green, and blue jackets and jumpers. Some carried white flags: Cypriot and Greek flags were banned. Others bore placards bearing the slogan, "We come in peace."

We were directed to the head of the line where foreign delegations had assembled. Palestinians in their beautifully embroidered national dresses stood out amongst the Britons, French, Italians and Lebanese in jeans and jerseys. The organisers distributed national flags to participants. I was handed the Indian flag, as Marya, then five, was too small to carry the banner. Lila Clerides, the Indian-born wife of the House speaker and the only other Indian on the scene joined us. At the head of the long line four to six women across were notables who had come to show support for the cause of ending the Turkish occupation of the north and reuniting the island.

The stars included lady Amalia Fleming, World War II Greek resistance leader, anti-Greek junta activist and wife of British doctor Alexander Fleming who discovered penicillin, and Greek actress Melina Mercouri, another enemy of the Greek generals whose coup on Cyprus had precipitated the Turkish invasion. The presence of Mercouri at the front of the slow march reminded me of the popular 1960 Greek film, *Never on Sunday*, in which she led a march of Pireaus prostitutes striking against work on the Christian Sabbath. If only someone had played the theme song written by Greek composer Manos Hadjidakis.... Melina Mercouri at the head of a column of thousands of largely conservative Greek Cypriot women, many in the black of mourning for their homes, lands and lives on the other side of the line made permanent by international collusion with Turkish military might.

We were halted by UN troops in blue berets. We did not breach the line, not this time, but Diana bit the arm of a UN soldier who had tackled her to prevent her from crossing into the buffer zone.

Nicosia, 1974-onwards

Turkey portrayed its long-planned invasion of northern Cyprus as a "peace operation" intended to rescue the island's Turkish Cypriots from the threat posed by right-wing Greek and Greek Cypriot elements who had mounted the coup against president Makarios. While liberating the Turkish Cypriots, the Turks also began systematically looting and destroying the cultural heritage of the occupied north. Archaeological sites, museums, libraries, churches, chapels, monasteries, and private collections of religious art and antiquities were pillaged.

The first phase of cultural cleansing began on July 20th, the day Turkish troops landed on the northern coast. Cultural cleansing proceeded in parallel with the ethnic cleansing of 162,000 Greek Cypriots. About 500 Greek Cypriots were allowed to live in the north, most of them elderly.

Pillage was both random and conducted by professional thieves and smugglers. Dutch icon smuggler Michel Van Rijn was in the north during the war, staying with Turkish Cypriot friends. As he made his way to Nicosia during a ceasefire along roads clogged with Greek Cypriot refugees, he saw Turkish soldiers throwing icons looted from churches onto pyres. While visiting the north in September, Godfrey found homes and churches open to looters and vandals. Nothing had been done to secure either when I went to the occupied area in February 1975. Looters not only carried away cultural treasures but also, in the process of plundering, destroyed artefacts, religious buildings, and archaeological sites.

During the second phase of cultural cleansing, lasting from 1977-79, specific items were targeted by well-organised local networks of icon and antiquities smugglers connected with Aydin Dikmen, a Turkish black-market dealer based in Munich.

The third phase began in 1980 but has, to an extent been curbed. Theft continued from known and newly discovered archaeological sites and excavations deemed illegal by the internationally recognised Cyprus republic are being conducted by Turkish and Turkish Cypriot archaeologists. There has, however, been a laudable effort, launched under UN auspices, to prevent churches in the north and mosques in the south from falling into rack and ruin and to repair iconic buildings, like Othello's tower in the Turkish-occupied old city of Famagusta. But the people to whom the churches and mosques belong remain separated by the Green Line that bisects the island.

Akhna, March 19th, 1989

Women Walk Home "commandos," who had spent the night at Cape Greco, climbed into the backs of closed lorries early in the morning for the drive to Akhna forest with the aim of crossing the ceasefire line delineated after the 1974 mainland Turkish army invasion and occupation. We hoped to evade the notice of UN peacekeepers – who had increased patrols and put up helicopters – cross the line and reach the deserted Greek Cypriot village of Akhna while the UN and the Turkish army were focused on a well-publicised mass protest due to take place elsewhere. This was mounted by hundreds of women in tourist buses which cruised the line until they reached the plain near Lymbia where the hilltop church of St. George, the target site, had been converted into a Turkish army post flying the red and white Turkish flag. A sight Greek Cypriots encountered every time they drove from the capital of Nicosia to Larnaca where the international airport was located.

Soon after we in the commando unit, clad in jeans, t-shirts and jackets, had clambered up the slope to the village, we found two little Turkish Cypriot girls with posies of wild yellow daisies. But they were soon replaced by a posse of helmeted Turkish soldiers ordered to obstruct the women who were to follow us. While we waited for reinforcements, we surveyed the church, which had been stripped of icons and furniture, windows smashed and the building left open to the elements. The floor was scattered with broken stones and bird and rodent droppings. We wandered around the gutted homes of former Akhna residents, now refugees in Dherynia, Larnaca, Limassol, Nicosia, London and Sydney. The main body of the Akhna prong came walking, plucking flowers from the fields, carrying posters and banners proclaiming "Peace" in Greek, Turkish and English.

I left mid-afternoon after I had found a ride to Nicosia as I had to file a story to *The Irish Times.* At Akhna and Lymbia there were scuffles between the women and Turkish troops and Turkish Cypriot police in neat blue uniforms. At Lymbia nine women were injured, one who had a broken leg. More than 50 women, including Diana, were arrested at both locations and released after mediation by the UN.

When my cleaning lady, Kirya Olympia came to the house that week she asked why she had not seen me in the crush atop the hill in Dherynia. "I was at Akhna," I replied, happy that at last this small, elderly Greek Cypriot woman had finally taken action against refugeedom.

The twin-crossings campaign was the fourth and final event staged by Women Walk Home since the initial march of 35,000 at Dherynia. The aim was to protest the Turkish imposed ethnic division of the island between Greek and Turkish Cypriots and call for reunification and freedom of movement and settlement for both communities throughout the country. Since 1974, Turkish Cypriot leader Rauf Denktash had permitted little interaction between the communities, arguing the 82 percent Greek Cypriot majority posed a danger to the 18 percent Turkish Cypriot minority which required the protection of 35-40,000 Turkish troops.

Nicosia, June 4th, 1993

Marya and Brian were married by Nicosia's deputy mayor within the walled city at a tradi-tional Cypriot town house refurbished nicely to host civil ceremonies. Brian in suit and tie and Marya in a cream-coloured Edwardian, high-necked, long-sleeved dress bought in Oxford while we were attending her graduation from St. Hugh's College. A circlet of pink and white flowers rested gently on her hair.

The wedding breakfast of champagne, croissants and strawberries dippled in chocolate was a small, family affair but 90 guests dined on Indian and Lebanese food at tables set on the flat roof of the house. Members of the extended Cypriot family, friends from Cyprus and Beirut, and neighbours came. Politics were represented by a friend from the PLO and two Iranians from the expatriate opposition Mujahedin e-Khalq. We were obliged to invite the Iranians when they turned up the day before the wedding while we were preparing the house. They arrived at the party with a massive bouquet of spring flowers. Godfrey and I had rejected June 5th, a more convenient Saturday, as ill-omened because of Israel's 1967 war which had initiated the Arabs' slow slide into tragedy and chaos.

Nicosia, December 18th, 1996

Cyprus was buoyed by the landmark judgement of the European Court of Human Rights at Strasbourg holding Turkey responsible for denying Greek Cypriot refugee Titina Loizidou access to and "enjoyment" of her property in the Turkish-occupied town of Kyrenia since 1974. The court took the view that Ankara exercised control over northern Cyprus, 36 percent of the territory of the island and regarded the Greek Cypriot government in the south as the sole legitimate authority on Cyprus. Ms. Loizidou's lawyer had submitted claims of $1 million compensation and $200,000 costs during six years of litigation. Ms. Loizidou had participated in all the Women Walk Home protests against the Turkish occupation and was among the women detained at Lymbia.

Nicosia, December 1997-London, Spring 1998

Van Rijn and his partner Patricia met me in the Hilton hotel lobby. He had, grudgingly, been hailed as the hero of the sting operation in Munich that had led to the repatriation of 32 pieces from the frescoes looted from the 12th century church of Antiphonitis and the 6th century mosaic medallion of St. Judas (Thaddeus) stolen from the church of the Virgin at Kanakaria. During the interview he related the bare facts of the tale of the sting mounted by him, Cyprus' honorary consul in the Netherlands Tassoula Hadjitofi, and the Cypriot and Munich police. This operation had recovered hundreds of Cypriot antiquities pillaged after the Turkish occupation. Although the bulk of these treasures remained in a secure police lock-up in Bavaria, van Rijn had taken the 32 pieces of fresco to Holland where they were exhibited in a museum before being handed over to the Cyprus Orthodox church, their rightful owners.

Following the publication of my article in *The Irish Times*, Michel asked to call on me at home. Godfrey did not like the idea. Fortunately, Michel arrived with Patricia, whose presence probably discouraged Godfrey from making inappropriate comments. Michel presented me with a copy of his memoir, *Hot Art, Cold Cash*, published in London in 1993, and asked if I would cooperate with him in writing an account of the sting. I responded by saying I did not co-author books but suggested that he could tell me the full story and I would turn it into a book. He agreed and proposed that Godfrey and I fly to London for a week or ten days where I could tape his narrative and, perhaps, meet other conspirators. After Michel and Patricia had left, Godfrey grumbled, "We Jansens don't mix with crooks." Although he had suffered a second stroke during the summer of 1996 and walked with difficulty, he agreed to travel to London.

Michel found us a nice Mayfair flat with a view but an uncertain elevator where he and I spent day after day talking and recording, going over and over each incident, each stage in the year-long process of recovering Cypriot icons, wall paintings, mosaics and other looted artefacts. Godfrey grew tired and somewhat fractious over being cooped up with us, afflicted with our droning voices, but tolerated Michel because this was a story I wanted to write.

It was a genuine pot-boiler packed with double dealing and intrigue, a detective story, a fable of our time. In February 1997, Michel had approached Hadjitofi with a proposal to recover three mosaics and 44 pieces of fresco in exchange for protection from a vengeful Turkish dealer in stolen art called Aydin Dikmen and a license to operate a casino in Cyprus. She raised $500,000 from the Cyprus Orthodox church to buy back important items.

Dikmen had it in for van Rijn because during legal proceedings in the US, Michel had exposed the Turk as the vendor of the 6th century mosaics of the saints James and Matthew, Jesus as a boy, and an angel with a broken wing looted from the church of Panagia Kanakaria located at the edge of the Karpass Peninsula in Turkish-occupied northern Cyprus. The Cyprus Church won the landmark case and reclaimed the mosaics from Peg Goldberg, an art dealer in Indiana.

For the sting, Michel had enlisted Gaspar, a Briton of Hungarian origin, to act as intermediary. Told that Gaspar's client wanted a number of artefacts, Dikmen, who was hard pressed for cash, agreed to sell the Judas mosaic and to discuss other items once this deal had gone through. Driving from Holland into Germany in his armoured Mercedes, Michel delivered the cash – $200,000 – to Gaspar who handed over the mosaic at a parking lot in Weisbaden.

The next exchange, involving a mosaic portrait of the Apostle Andrew, took place two weeks later in Munich. On this occasion,

Dikmen, a consummate forger, pulled a fast one and delivered a fake. Michel saw immediately, as he put it, a "living and breathing" Andrew had not emerged from the parcel – for which he had made a down payment of $25,000. The final stage of this operation involved the purchase of fragments of two frescoes, the Tree of Jesse and the Last Judgement. Michel hired an executive jet to take the loot to Rotterdam where the items were handed over to the Cypriots to whom he proposed a grand deal promising $3 million to Dikmen for his entire Cypriot collection. The aim of this operation, was to assess his inventory, locate it and turn him over to the police. The operation, co-ordinated with the Munich and Cypriot police and recorded by a television team, was literally a smashing success – ultimately involving breaking of walls in Dikmen's flat to extract hundreds of looted treasures stolen from round the world.

While Godfrey and I were still in London, I took Michel to meet my agent. She was delighted with the book idea and promised to take up the project with publishers during a coming event. She suggested an advance of £50,000 might be achievable. Her enthusiasm was short-lived. No one was interested. Perhaps because Michel's first book had required a great deal of cutting – from 700-odd pages to 484 – and had not made the bestseller list. Instead of a book, I produced a magazine article and sat on the material for several years until I put together a monograph on what happens to the world's cultural heritage during war.

Nicosia, January 19th, 1991

Paddy Smyth rang at half two in the morning and asked for an Arab reaction piece on the launch of the US-led war on Iraq. Despite the US troop buildup in Saudi Arabia and creation of a so-called "coalition of the willing," Godfrey and I somehow did not believe that George H.W. Bush would go to war. Consequently, neither of us had offered to go to Baghdad to cover the conflict.

We hurried to the sitting room and switched on the television to watch sinister green images caught by night vision cameras installed in the noses of bombers tracking missiles as they travelled to and exploded on targets in Baghdad, an open city with a population of seven million. If Bush had confined his war objective to the liberation of Kuwait, forces assembled in Saudi Arabia should have focused on Iraqi Republican Guard units deployed in the emirate and units dug in along the border, supply routes and communication lines. Liberating Kuwait was the stated objective, regime change the undeclared goal.

Our friends Nuha, Ma, and their family were in Baghdad, sitting ducks in elegant homes on the Tigris. I watched the strikes and listened to the cold-blooded commentary for a few minutes and filed a piece on our telex about the angry reaction to expect from Arabs who still clung to the secular faith of Arab nationalism although some of their governments had aligned with Washington. Godfrey, who had left *The Economist* in 1988, filed stories to *The Deccan Herald* in India later in the day.

We remained glued to *CNN* thanks to a newly installed two-metre satellite dish on the roof, divan – rather than couch – potatoes, sleeping little, drinking too much coffee during the day and brandy at night, eating too much chocolate. Maggie O'Kane, then a freelancer, was reporting for *The Irish Times* from Baghdad. I was providing analysis and ringing Arab commentators for their reactions.

It was clear from the first moments of the war that the Bush administration and its western and Arab allies were determined to crush Iraq, the core country of the eastern Arab world and a regional military power. At the time the first bombs struck Baghdad, the Iraqi economy was already staggering from sanctions imposed on

August 6th, 1990, four days after Saddam Hussein ordered his army to invade Kuwait.

Revelling in 88 percent support on the home front, Bush had widened his stated war aim by claiming he intended to erase Iraq's nuclear weapons potential, eliminate its chemical and biological weapons programmes, and wipe out its conventional arsenal. Bush had also decided to cripple Iraq's civilian infrastructure by bombing electricity, water purification and sewage treatment plants, telephone installations, chemical plants and machine tool manufacturers. The bombing of these facilities had nothing to do with the "liberation" of Kuwait but were designed – along with the punitive sanctions regime – to transform Iraq into a weak if not a failed state.

Finding themselves under near constant bombardment, Iraqis came to realise more was at stake than Kuwait. This stirred Iraqi nationalism as well as popular opposition to the war across the Arab world and criticism of Arab governments that had joined the US coalition – Saudi Arabia, Egypt and Syria.

Regional commentators and citizens argued an Iraqi withdrawal from Kuwait might have been secured without war. As Bush deployed troops in the Saudi desert, there were a number of attempts to resolve the crisis. Saddam Hussein had initially proposed the evacuation of Kuwait in exchange for Israel's pull-out from Palestinian and Arab territory. He had proposed the withdrawal of Syrian forces deployed in Lebanon since 1976 and had offered an Iraqi withdrawal if sanctions were lifted, Iraq was given access to the Gulf and Kuwait agreed to handover to Iraq the section of the Rumaila oilfield that lies within Kuwait.

Bush either ignored or rejected all Iraq's proposals as well as mediation efforts by Jordan and other countries. Consequently, the encounter in Geneva on January 9th between US secretary of state James Baker and Iraq's Tareq Aziz produced no meeting of minds. Confronted by Bush's massive military buildup, demand for an unconditional Iraqi withdrawal from Kuwait, and rejection of negotiations over terms, Aziz – under instructions from Saddam Hussein – refused to discuss Kuwait with Baker.

Godfrey became a casualty of this distant but all-consuming war. He suffered a moderate stroke from the late nights and long days of viewing the war on Iraq in our sitting room, pressure of filing, distress and anger.

The war ended with Iraq's defeat, destruction of its military machine, and devastation of its infrastructure. Sanctions were not lifted, and Iraq was ordered to pay massive reparations to Kuwait for damage inflicted on its oilfields and infrastructure. Bush began to put together his strategy for re-election in 1992 but was defeated by Democrat Bill Clinton.

Amman-Baghdad, April 1992

I secured our visas in record time from the Iraqi embassy which had booked a taxi to take us to Baghdad early the next morning. "You pay only $100," the consul told me. We had been invited by a Jordanian doctors' association to attend a conference on the impact on the health of the Iraqi population of economic sanctions and the 1991 US-led war to drive Iraqi forces from Kuwait following Iraq's August 1990 invasion of the emirate.

There were still no flights to Baghdad due to international sanctions and the 1,000-kilometre drive was an ordeal that could last anywhere between ten and sixteen hours. We departed at dawn in an ancient Iraqi taxi and arrived after nearly five hours at the restaurant in the Jordanian town of Ruwaished, the traditional pause on the journey to Baghdad. Most tables were taken by drivers and their passengers drinking tea or Turkish coffee and eating kebabs: the same fare was served for breakfast, lunch and dinner.

The journey at 160 kilometres an hour along the broad highway through Anbar province, Iraq's largest, was enlivened only by the sight of bands of camels roaming the desert behind the chain-link fences that flanked the road. The driver slowed for Ramadi, a tribal town known for lawlessness an hour's drive from Baghdad.

Although Godfrey had travelled to Baghdad by bus at least twice during the 1980-88 Iran-Iraq war, he was as amazed as I was by the networks of ugly concrete underpasses and overpasses that had embraced the fabled city of The Thousand and One Nights (*Alf Layla wa Layla*). We checked into the Palestine hotel on the Tigris and rang Naji al-Hadithi, head of foreign press in the information ministry.

While he was still with *The Economist*, Godfrey had met Naji on several occasions in London when he was cultural attaché at the Iraqi embassy. Rightly proud of the country's regional primacy in the arts, the government had mounted excellent exhibitions of paintings, engravings and sculpture and held musical events in major world capitals. We had a chat with Naji over cold drinks on the balcony of our room in the hotel. "Come to the office tomorrow and we'll work out a programme." During that meeting, classical music blared from a hi-fi on one side of the room while *BBC* newscasters read out headlines in crisp tones. Naji was determined to confound any bugs.

At the conference, doctors reported on the dramatic deterioration of the health sector following the imposition of a stringent sanctions regime on Iraq and the accelerating decline since the 1991 war. The key post-war document was a report issued during the summer of 1991 by the UN. This revealed Iraqis, who had enjoyed a high level of health care before sanctions and the war, were afflicted with a lack of clean water, electricity, medicines, and medical and dental equipment. The incidence of disease caused by polluted water had quadrupled. Malnutrition among children and pregnant women was rising due to the lack of essential foods. The team assembling the report, headed by Prince Sadruddin Aga Khan, former UN high commissioner for refugees, warned the food supply crisis required urgent international intervention. The document was ignored by sanctions-committed western powers.

In addition to attending the conference, we went to the Shia holy city of Karbala which had been devastated when Shia militants had risen against the government. Incited by Bush and actively supported by Shia Iran, the revolt had been crushed brutally by the regime. Thousands died, tens of thousands fled to Iran, and hundreds of thousands were displaced.

A year after the rising, Karbala was once again a thriving city, the shrines of the martyred grandson of the Prophet Muhammad, Hussein and his half-brother Abbas, had been restored on a wide plaza where shops and homes had stood before the rebellion. As we approached the mosque of Hussein, an officious guardian told us non-Muslims could not enter. Godfrey growled, "I'm an Indian and my wife is a hajji." The mosque, which had been cruelly mauled in the fighting, was newly minted, its golden domes warm in the spring sun, inside, its crystal chandeliers clean and sparkling unlike the dusty, fly specked chandeliers that had hung in the cavernous interior in 1976 when last I had visited. History had been erased and replaced.

As we left Karbala, I asked the driver to stop on the roadside, so we could buy dates. He nodded but ignored vendors and, after some time, plunged into a forest of date palms criss-crossed by irrigation channels. He stopped the car in the shade, got out, told us to wait and disappeared into a dun-coloured house, reappearing with two cups of sweet Turkish coffee and a bag of frozen fresh yellow dates from the previous harvest. Here on the outskirts of Karbala electricity had returned. To the strains of Arabic instrumental music blaring from the car radio, the three of us feasted on the dates and threw the pits out of the windows as we drove back to Baghdad.

On the 28th, Saddam Hussein's birthday, Godfrey, whose mobility had been curbed by his stroke during the 1991 war, stayed at the hotel while I joined other conference guests for a tour of street parties in the capital. We rode first in a bus and then walked from square to square, meeting Iraqis feasting on kebabs, hummus and salad, waiting for the signal to serve hundreds of cakes distributed by the Baath party. As darkness fell on Baghdad, the cakes were cut the moment the city's lights blazed, staying on night and day in defiance of the western and Arab powers that had reduced the country's electricity production to 15 percent of pre-war output with the aim of bombing Iraq to the "pre-industrial level," to quote Prince Sadruddin.

Baghdad, January 1993

Godfrey and I made the arduous road journey a second time to the Iraqi capital to attend another conference focusing on health issues. When I returned to the hotel after a visit to the press centre, Godfrey propelled me to the restaurant where planked fish (*masgouf*) was on the menu. We had just returned to our seventh-floor corner room with wrap around windows when Godfrey said, "Come, look at this. There is something flying down the river. Slowly." Indeed, there was a bullet-shaped object hovering over the moon-lit Tigris, a peaceful apparition – until explosions began. I hurtled down seven floors worth of stairs, caught a taxi and hurried back to the press centre where buses were waiting to carry journalists to target sites. We were taken to the smouldering ruins of a facility for making machine tools, hardly a weapons site, and other areas struck by the missiles before we returned to the press centre. A German journalist, wounded in the attack, was visited in hospital by Saddam Hussein late that night.

The next morning, Godfrey rang Naji to see if our appointment with the minister of industry was to go ahead on schedule. Naji rang back, "The appointment holds." Amer al-Saadi was in army uniform when we met him at his office.

Nicosia, May 1996

In April 1995, the UN Security Council had adopted a resolution permitting Iraq to sell a substantial amount of oil to purchase desperately needed food and medical supplies.

In May, a reluctant but hard pressed Iraqi government signed a memorandum of understanding accepting the terms of the resolution. Resolutions adopted in 1991 for limited oil sales and close monitoring of purchases had been rejected by Iraq on the ground they breached the country's sovereignty.

In connection with the 1996 development Lesley Stahl said to US ambassador to UN Madeline Albright on the *CBS 60 Minutes* programme, "We have heard that half a million children have died [in Iraq from the harsh sanctions]. That is more children than died in Hiroshima. And, you know,is the price worth it?"

Albright replied, "I think this is a very hard choice, but the price - we think the price is worth it." The "oil-for-food" programme did not go into effect until December 1996 and remained in force until well after the US invasion and occupation of Iraq in 2003.

8

INCARCERATION

Amman-Baghdad, March 1979

While Godfrey was covering events in Tehran, *The Economist* asked me to travel to Baghdad to report on the Arab League's foreign ministerial meeting convened in response to the conclusion of the peace treaty between Egypt and Israel. Brokered by US president Jimmy Carter and signed by Egyptian president Anwar Sadat and Israeli Prime Minister Menachem Begin, the treaty was seen by the Arab public and governments as a betrayal of the Arab front against Israel. The slogan of the times was: "No war without Egypt, no peace without Syria." The Arabs were convinced that without the threat of war, there could be no peace, the Palestinians would continue to live under occupation, and countries which refused to submit to Israel's terms for coexistence would be attacked.

En route to Baghdad, I stopped in Amman to meet with the chief of Jordan's Royal Court Sharif Abdel Hamid Sharaf who, on his return from visits to Baghdad and Riyadh found that his secretary had given me an appointment. Writing for *The Economist* opened many doors. He told me Jordan, Iraq and Saudi Arabia had agreed to form a moderate bloc at the summit to punish the Egyptian government for its separate peace deal with Israel without alienating Egyptians, who largely opposed the deal and distrusted Israel. He said Arab countries would sever diplomatic relations with

Cairo, Egypt's membership in the League would be suspended, the League's headquarters would move out of Cairo to Tunis, and $4 billion would be cancelled as Egypt's share of the fund for frontline states at risk of Israeli attack.

After arriving in Baghdad and checking into the Salam hotel, I found a cheerful Zuhair in the dining room with a group of Iraqis visiting from Latin America. As the ruling Baath party's foreign minister, he was in charge of cultivating expatriates with the aim of convincing them to return or invest in the development of Iraq.

The conference was dominated by fiery speeches from PLO chairman Arafat who called on the Arabs to punish both the US and Egypt. Popular Front leader Habash urged the Arabs to direct "military blows" at the US, Israel and the Egyptian regime. Syrian deputy prime minister and foreign minister Abdul Halim Khaddam argued the treaty was an attempt at "reorganising the Israel occupation" and urged the Egyptians and Arabs to "bring down the Egyptian regime." Kuwait also adopted a tough line. Nevertheless, the deal hammered out by Jordan, Iraq and Saudi Arabia held. Its ramifications were wide. All Arab organisations associated with the League also moved out of Cairo, League members worked to isolate Egypt within the Non-Aligned Movement, the Organisation of African Unity and the Organisation of the Islamic Conference. Egyptian firms that dealt with Israeli companies were placed on the League's boycott list.

As the conference dragged on, Zuhair invited me to visit the Baath party headquarters where he took me along the corridor to catch a glimpse at his desk of the *Ustaz*, the Professor, the revered Michel Aflaq, who in 1947 along with Salahedin al-Bitar, had founded the party, the second oldest pan-Arab party after the Syrian Social National party. Zuhair sent me back to my hotel in a white Volvo, the make and colour favoured by regime and party. At that time, top government officials rode round in Mercedes accompanied by a police outrider on a motorcycle rather than a posse of security vehicles packed with gunmen.

When colleagues in Tehran saw *The Economist*'s Levant Correspondent had two articles in the weekly magazine, one from Tehran and the other from Baghdad, they asked how he managed to be in two places at once: "My wife is in Baghdad."

Nicosia, February 18th, 1978

Anger and resentment against Egypt had been building since Sadat made his surprise visit to Jerusalem on November 19th, 1977, and addressed the Israeli Knesset on the following day. Western powers hailed the event as "historic" and "heroic".

Ten days earlier when he told the Egyptian parliament he was prepared to go to Jerusalem to make peace with Israel, his ultimate political goal after the 1973 war, no one had taken him seriously. Not forewarned, the Arabs were stunned and bitter. Anti-Sadat demonstrations erupted across the region. Talks that eventually produced the Camp David agreement and the peace treaty, were seen as a unilateral move binding no other Arab country.

Among the Egyptians who accompanied Sadat to Jerusalem was Yusif Sebai, chief editor of a number of Egyptian publications, including influential official daily *Al-Ahram*. In spite of the furore generated by Sadat's initiation of talks with Israel, Sebai was determined to attend an Afro-Asian solidarity conference in Nicosia. He was shot to death at mid-morning by a gunman outside the bookshop at the Hilton hotel while making his way to the conference room. The shooter and his partner went into the hotel ballroom and took around 30 delegation members hostage, threatening to kill them if the Cypriot authorities refused to fly them out of the country.

The gunmen and eleven hostages, including an Egyptian and two PLO officials, were put on a Cypriot commercial airliner and flown to Libya where it was refused landing rights. After being rejected by half a dozen other countries, the aircraft refuelled at Djibouti and returned to Cyprus. While Cypriot officials were negotiating the culprits' surrender, an Egyptian military aircraft filled with troops landed on the tarmac, a jeep carrying four commandos rolled off a ramp, and sped toward the commandeered plane. A platoon of commandos followed on foot. Sadat's aim was to kill or capture the armed assassins whatever the cost to the hostages and crew. The Egyptians were met with a barrage of fire from the Cypriot National Guard. Fifteen were killed and a number wounded. Cairo was not only infuriated but also humiliated when it was found some Egyptian soldiers had gone on the mission in pyjama trousers and flip-flops. The terrified assassins surrendered to the Cypriots and released the hostages unharmed.

As events unfolded the evening before the surrender, Godfrey, Marya and I went over to the house of Diana and Sophocles to help her produce a series of press releases based on information she received by phone and fax from the press and information office, an arm of the ministry of Interior. Marya went to bed while we drafted one release after the other – including a scoop interview with the British pilot, and faxed them to the press office. The next morning we had coffee with one of the 19 hostages freed at the hotel before the others had boarded a bus for the airport. Our source, an Iraqi, told us one of the team was Palestinian and the other an Iraqi with a Basra accent. Baghdad-based Abu Nidal's Palestinian renegade group claimed full credit for the assassination although it was almost certainly done in collusion with Iraqi intelligence.

I followed the trial of the men before a bench of senior Cypriot judges who called scores of witnesses but not an eight-year old boy who had been in the bookshop reading comics when Sebai was killed, and had witnessed the shooting. The men's death sentence was commuted to life imprisonment but they were released and deported after serving several years in prison.

Beirut, March 27th-28th, 2002

At the heavily guarded door of the Phoenicia hotel, Marwan from the Lebanese press office greeted me with a question: "Do you have an appointment with any of the delegates?" I nodded. Mr. Haddad from Syria, I responded, hoping he had come to the summit. I paused at the bank of phones just inside the entrance, asked for his room and waited. No reply. But I evaded the security men who were trying to keep track of importunate journalists. I did reach him later in the morning and had a useful half hour talk over coffee in the lobby. "How did you manage? The Syrians are talking to nobody," asked a colleague who had seen us sitting together. "The old daughter network," I responded. "My daughter and his daughter were best friends at school in Cyprus where he had headed the Syrian mission for many years." My other successful interviews were with friends made over decades, and not scoops staged by journalists who represented major world newspapers or broadcast media; but were fresh to the region.

Nabil Shaath of the Palestinian delegation pointed out that the US and Israel keep objecting to a Palestinian state on the ground that the "Palestinian right to return" would mean "Israel would be flooded with Palestinian refugees and cease being a Jewish state. But they know millions of refugees would not return." UN General Assembly Resolution 194, paragraph 11 of December 1948 speaks of their "return" only at "the earliest practicable date" and calls for compensation for their losses.

Marwan put me in the custody of two security men when I went up to the suite of Iraqi foreign minister Naji Sabri al- Hadithi who had agreed to meet for two minutes. Ignoring the chatter of advisers in his suite, he told me that Iraq had been working with UN monitors to secure a clean bill of health on the issue of weapons of mass destruction; which George W. Bush's administration sought to use as a pretext to attack his country. He argued, "There are no weapons of mass destruction in Iraq, no facilities for the production of such weapons. And there is no intention by the Iraqi government to acquire or use these weapons." During the summit, Saudi crown prince Abdullah effected reconciliation between Iraq and Kuwait and Arab leaders stood with Iraq on the weapons issue, fearing a fresh war in the region.

The summit also adopted the Saudi peace initiative, calling for full Israeli withdrawal from all Arab territory occupied in 1967 – the Palestinian territories plus the Syrian Golan Heights – in exchange for full normalisation of relations with the Arabs.

Israeli prime minister Ariel Sharon responded by reinvading the West Bank on the morning of the 29th, claiming the offensive was in response to a suicide bombing 36 hours earlier at the Israeli coastal resort of Netanya where 23 mainly elderly pensioners were killed. Sharon began his operation with a frontal attack on Arafat's compound, the *muqataa*, in the West Bank city of Ramallah, breaching the outer walls, rendering all but a few rooms uninhabitable and confining Arafat to them. I flew home to Cyprus, repacked my bag and made for Jerusalem via the Allenby bridge connecting Jordan to the West Bank.

Jerusalem, March 31st – May 8th, 2002

I checked into the Christmas hotel in East Jerusalem and rang around to find out how to get to the battlefront in Ramallah. Based at the

Ambassador hotel, where many visiting journalists stayed, Basma served as coordinator for not-quite-clandestine visits to Ramallah and the sealed off towns and cities of the West Bank. I promptly jumped into a minibus carrying European members of parliament, a blue paper EU flag stuck to a side window. We drove to the border between Israeli annexed East Jerusalem and the West Bank Kalandia checkpoint, turned to the right and, after the driver surveyed the scene, rushed up a hill from where he waited and watched for Israeli patrols to pass. Once he felt it was safe to move, he accelerated downhill, shot across the road and dipped into a quarry on the other side, coming up in Kalandia. All went well until we reached the entrance to Ramallah where an Israeli machine gunner fired over the roof of the minibus, narrowly missing the vehicle. We confined our visit to forbidden territory by stopping at the emergency ward of Shaikh Zayed hospital to interview wounded Palestinians.

Siege and curfew breaking came to be known as crossing "the Tora Boras," what we thought to be mountains but were in reality caves in the White Mountains in Afghanistan where Taliban and al-Qaeda forces hid from US-allied troops during the 2001 war launched by George W. Bush following the September attacks on New York and Washington. Sometimes Basma arranged these risky journeys, other times journalists would team up, convince a taxi driver to take us to, say, the Tora Bora of Beit Sahour-Beit Jala-Bethlehem, where we would alight, climb over a mound of earth blocking the road and make our way through an olive grove to a spot where taxis waited for customers, either residents of these towns seeking to go home after work elsewhere, humanitarian workers, or journalists.

Isolde, then Irish representative to the Palestinian Authority, told me an Irish activist, Caoimhe, had posed as a medical worker and entered Arafat's compound. Armed with her phone number and a card providing units for her mobile phone, I spoke frequently to Caoimhe who was invited to candlelit dinners of beans and bread with the Palestinian president. She said he slept on a thin mattress in his office while the Israelis tightened the siege around his headquarters. Caoimhe left after 16 days as she had arrived, in a doctor's white coat, her red hair flying as she strode out of the *muqataa*, besieging Israeli soldiers' weapons trained on her six foot plus figure. During a post-escape meeting at the YWCA in East Jerusalem, she said she did not see any point on staying on.

Later, Isolde had to contend with a citizen in the besieged Church of the Nativity in Bethlehem, where Palestinian civilians, priests and fighters had sought refuge. Mary, an Irish nurse, had followed Caoimhe's example, entering the church in medical garb. Mary felt it was her duty to treat the wounded. She was prepared to describe over the mobile phone conditions in the 6th century basilica and comment on Israeli efforts to intimidate those trapped inside into surrendering. The Irish angle provided by these brave women was, of course, welcomed by *The Irish Times*.

Nablus, April 9th, 2002

The first relief convoy entered Nablus, led by the silver armoured jeep of the French consulate and a vehicle belonging to Medicins du Monde. Cars, vans and lorries filled with medicine and food came close behind. The convoy had left Jerusalem at dawn but was held up for 40 minutes by an Israeli army patrol and for another hour and a half at an Israeli checkpoint where television and photojournalists were forced to get down and were abandoned by the roadside. Low profile pencil press were allowed to carry on. No one even asked us for identity documents. As we pulled away from the checkpoint, two Israeli army jeeps drew ahead of us, photographers clicking away with their cameras, providing evidence that the army was assisting in humanitarian efforts. We sailed through the final checkpoint and, leaving the Israeli jeeps behind, proceeded slowly into Nablus, a besieged city with a population of 116,000.

The main road had been holed by bombs and littered with rubble. Cars had been flattened or riddled with bullets and pushed onto pavements, shop fronts caved in, houses bulldozed, street lamps felled, and manhole covers lifted. At the Balata refugee camp buildings were blasted and burnt, proof residents had put up stiff resistance to the invading Israelis. At the town centre, the once handsome stone-built Ottoman barracks, the governor's offices, were in ruins. From a distance came the dull thud of bombs striking targets, the crackle of machine gun fire.

On a hill overlooking the old city stood a school hosting the Nablus HQ of the International Committee of the Red Cross (ICRC) and its local partner, the Palestinian Red Crescent. Aid workers gathered round us when we arrived. ICRC delegate Beat Mosimann welcomed us with a smile and spoke freely. "Ambulances are obstructed every time they go out," he said. "They are regularly shot at." He pointed to the bonnet of a UN ambulance that had been pierced by two bullets. "Two others were shot inside the old town, each in two tyres." He had been fired upon three times by Israeli troops, once while carrying a wounded man. "I took shelter behind a garbage bin... It took seven hours to coordinate one evacuation [with the Israeli army] and 12 hours to carry it out. The distance was about three kilometres. The 12 wounded included children. We would clear one checkpoint and be stopped at the next. There are too many soldiers around, too much indiscipline."

The ICRC managed to extract 25 bodies from a small building inside the old city only because Israeli troops involved were accompanied by journalists. As Beat spoke, Israeli helicopters circled the old city, dropping bombs and firing into the warren of streets lined by two or three-storied apartment houses and souks famous for olive oil soap and *knafeh*, a Nablus sweet made of soft cheese and fine noodles and sprinkled with crushed pistachios.

Ramallah, April 14th, 2002

During one of my Tora Bora trips, I went to the Palestinian Medical Relief Committee headquarters in Ramallah with Adam, co-founder with his fiancée Huwaida, of the International Solidarity Movement that strives to bring foreigners to the Palestinian territories to intervene in contentious situations and observe and report on the Israeli occupation. Adam said, "I'm going on foot house to house to see if people need food or medical supplies and report back here so ambulances can deliver the goods or take ill people to hospital. Want to come along?" We both donned white vests proclaiming our affiliation and set off through the battered streets of Arafat's administrative capital where 100,000 Palestinians were held captive in their homes under a draconian Israeli curfew. The streets were eerily empty, their surfaces scoured by tank tracks, littered with bullet casings and broken limbs from trees and scattered rubbish uncollected by municipal lorries. Squashed and burnt-out hulks of cars had been shoved aside by tanks. Adam warned me not to look too closely at the roof of a glass-sided tower block as an Israeli sniper posted there generally held pedestrians in his gun sight. Damage to homes and the surroundings intensified as we approached the *muqataa*. A tank saw us off and sent us on our mission.

Some houses had no water, many no electricity. Elderly people who had been unable to hurry to the shops during brief windows in the curfew needed food. A woman asked for cooking gas, an old man heart pills. These were not poor camp dwellers used to privation, but middle-class Palestinians, professionals living in handsome houses, shocked over what was happening to their town, destroying the Palestinian experiment with limited self-rule and democracy.

A tall, handsome Palestinian woman raised in the Detroit area, Huwaida was back at the flat when we returned. A Jewish man from Brooklyn, Adam had spent a night in Arafat's besieged compound that the American – like Caoimhe – had entered with a medical mission. Several other journalists and activists were camping out in their flat, a short distance from the Shaikh Zayed hospital. While the activists prepared signs for a protest against the Israeli siege of Arafat's headquarters, I turned to the story I had to file. But an email arrived from Birgitta, the Swedish wife of a Palestinian friend saying he had died of a heart attack after falling in his home in Oxford. Stunned and shocked, I stared out of the window for a long time at the empty street, turning to my keyboard only after a pair of Israeli tanks rumbled by, a threat to anyone who broke the curfew.

The kitchen cupboards were nearly bare. There was no way to go out to buy food. Huwaida and Adam had not thought of meals or counted on half a dozen guests. I found lentils, an onion or two, and cumin and made enough dhal and rice to keep us going.

A one-sided conversation between Huwaida and her mother in far distant Michigan provided light relief and lifted the gloom I felt over Michel's early death. I cannot report Huwaida's side of the exchange word for word or in its entirety as it went on for half an hour but I can try to give the gist. Huwaida, "Mom, my wedding dress is in Bethlehem and I'm in Ramallah with the Israeli army in between... I can't get there and the dressmaker cannot get to me. I know the wedding is on the 25th but what can I do?" After a breathless pause she told her mother to get her sister to go to a shop, choose a dress and try it on. "She's the same size as me."

The next morning, we sallied forth from the house and walked through deserted streets to the *muqataa*, collecting en route a few activists carrying placards calling for an end to the Israeli invasion and siege. The protesters closed ranks outside the blasted and burnt compound and waited for US secretary of state Colin Powell. Anticipating his arrival, Israeli soldiers had tidied up the courtyard between the buildings by towing away cars flattened by tanks, restored running water, installed a generator to provide electricity cut off during the previous two weeks, and permitted the Red Cross to deliver supplies. A privileged gaggle of journalists belonging to the secretary's travelling circus turned up before his armoured convoy guarded by gun-toting men in flak jackets.

On foot in light coats and jeans and surrounded by armed Israelis, we watched the arrivals with amusement. Huwaida, her long curly hair blowing in a stiff breeze, berated the Israeli soldiers in English and Hebrew and led the activists in chants calling for Arafat's release and an end to the Israeli occupation. Once Powell had been whisked away, we walked back across Ramallah where journalists in our party and others who had risked Israeli snipers and arrest to reach the compound assembled outside the emergency entrance to the Shaikh Zayed hospital to catch a minibus back to Jerusalem. A clanking, groaning Israeli tank turned the corner, rolled up and slowly swung its cannon until it was pointed directly at us. After a standoff lasting five or six minutes the tank pulled away, leaving us trembling with shock. Since my clothes and computer were still at the flat, I asked my colleagues to hold the bus so I could collect them and return. "Yes, yes," was the reply but when I returned to the hospital with my bags, I found they had disappeared and left me stranded in Ramallah. "Don't worry,“ said the head doctor at the hospital. "A taxi is coming to drive a woman who has just delivered to her home in al-Ram. He'll take you to Jerusalem." The taxi did so by mounting a Tora Bora and weaving through the back streets ofKalandia.

Jerusalem-Jenin, April 17th, 2002

Basma organised two mini-buses to Jenin, the northern West Bank town where Palestinians said there had been a massacre in the refugee camp between April 5th and 11th. Huwaida and other brave souls had managed to walk into the town, besieged, bludgeoned, and blockaded from April 1st but the Israeli army refused to pull out, claiming it was mopping up. Israeli troops, who still ringed the camp, barred lawyers seeking evidence of mass killings, humanitarian workers, and journalists. My travelling companions were human rights activists, and, oddly enough, municipal officials from Italy dressed in suits and ties as though they were going to a conference.

We took a forest route, hoping Israeli troops would not catch us but they did, halting our progress by firing a machine gun burst over the buses. The officer in-charge ordered us out and examined our passports, told us to get back in and follow his armoured scout car. Another took up position behind our little convoy. We were taken to the Israeli army camp at Salem on the hills above the West Bank where the officer returned our passports but took away the drivers for interrogation, leaving us walking in circles in the dust, wondering how long we would be held. When, after a quarter of an hour, an ice cream van drove up, bells tinkling, I begged a ride to the main road where I caught a bus to Tel Aviv. By the time I reached Jerusalem, it was too late to file a piece on my escape.

Jenin, April 18th, 2002

Basma found another minibus prepared to make a second attempt to reach Jenin. "It will be expensive," she warned, but we shared the cost, each paying fifty dollars. This time, the passengers were activists, an elderly Catholic priest from Boston, and a two-man Jordanian television team who were staying at my hotel. We followed the same route as the day before but were not intercepted by the Israeli army, which remained determined to keep foreigners out of Jenin. The Israelis had gouged red earth from the mountainside and bulldozed a hillock across the approach road, preventing vehicles from driving into the town and camp. We left our bus and walked the two or three or four kilometres to Jenin. Many refugee camp residents who had fled during the Israeli onslaught were with us, returning to see what had happened to their homes as well as relatives and friends.

Our objective, the prostrate body of the camp had been partially gutted, its innards had swollen into obscene mounds of earth, debris and rubbish; its bones, buildings, had been crushed to rubble or low walls. On top of one mound I found an old woman wrapped in brown shawls, plunging a long stick into the earth. "This is where my house stood," she said, "I'm searching for my grandson."

Corpses, which had lain for days in shattered homes, had been removed but the sickly stench of death hung in the air, permeated the pores of the skin, clung to hair. Israeli troops had smashed huge holes in internal walls of homes to make passages so they could avoid Palestinian snipers while moving from place to place. Breezeblock walls had been transformed into lacework by bullet holes and shrapnel. Some houses had collapsed, burnt, or flattened. In several cases entire walls had been sheared off rooms that remained intact.

One second-storey flat had light green walls with pictures still in place, tables chairs, rugs and on the floor. The owner, a smartly dressed woman waved as people walked by, shoes crackling on shattered plastic plates and bowls and shards of glass.

In the roofless basement of a house, the blackened spatter of brain on a wall perfumed with putrefaction. Palestinians wandered here and there, refusing to accept what had happened. "We don't even know where the streets used to be," said a weeping man.

After what seemed to be hours, our group convened at an arranged rendezvous and set off to find our bus, walking along a hillside covered in olive trees with scores of Palestinians, including women in embroidered dresses, and mothers dragging small children who could not be left behind. Without warning, Israeli snipers on the opposite slope began firing at us, aiming just above our heads so the bullets showered us with twigs, leaves, and minute pale green flowers from the olive trees. One of the activists and I grabbed the hands of the priest and pulled him up the hill where we hid behind a small concrete building housing irrigation pumps until the shooting subsided and we could make a dash for a barricade where the others were waiting.The Jordanians filmed our flight. No one was shot, fortunately, although twenty or thirty people had been forced to race across the hillside to safety.

Shocked by the ferocity of the Israeli assault that had forced half of the 13,000 camp residents to flee, Palestinian spokesman Saeb Erekat said 500 had been massacred. Humanitarian agencies and journalists took up the charge. By the end of the month, 52 bodies had been retrieved from the wreckage, 21 of them civilians. Israel's friends dismissed the accusation. Since Israel had claimed the killing by Hamas of 23 Israelis at Netanya was a "massacre", the slaughter in Jenin of 21 Palestinian civilians should also have qualified.

Bethlehem, April 19th, 2002

I took a taxi to the Bethlehem-Beit Jala-Beit Sahour Tora Bora and crossed the mound, making for the shaded spot in an olive grove where taxis took visitors to the drop off point outside the gate of the King Hussein hospital in Beit Jala. There I began the uphill trek to Bethlehem through curfew-emptied streets, keeping an eye out for Israeli armoured personnel carriers and scout cars. I stopped for a chat with Bethlehem mayor Hanna Nasser who had last visited his office on Manger Square before April 1st, when the Israeli army occupied the town. He laughed when he greeted me, "I saw you on Jordanian television last night."

The square and the streets leading down to it were off limits to all but Israeli soldiers, except when he and the other four members of the Palestinian committee, trying to negotiate an end to the siege of the Church of the Nativity, went to the battered Peace Centre to negotiate with Israeli officers.

Mayor Nasser denied civilians and clerics in the church were being held "hostage" by fugitives, a claim put forward by the Israelis. "They are civilians and policemen and some armed men… They sought refuge out of fear... I myself took refuge in the church in 1967."

Among those in the church were two ten-year-old boys, 50 teenagers, 40 members of the clergy, 100 policemen, and, perhaps, as many as 30 peace activists. Israel demanded the surrender of the "most wanted" men among the fighters. These men had to stand trial in its courts or accept permanent deportation as the price of lifting the siege. Israel presented a list of men it thought were in the church but the Palestinian negotiators found only 13 of those named were there.

Israeli tanks took up positions around the square and snipers on surrounding buildings. They killed seven fighters sheltering within the church, picking them off at night with laser beams. The church's bell ringer was shot dead in daylight as he tried to cross the courtyard to the basilica to ring the bell for prayer. Pope John Paul II said the violence in the region had reached "unimaginable and intolerable levels." During a gun battle Israeli troops fired a smoke grenade into the church causing a fire that was put out by Palestinian firemen. An Armenian monk wearing civilian clothes was shot and wounded. During subsequent bursts of fire, more Palestinians were injured. A Japanese couple who had no idea of danger approached the church but was rescued by Palestinians. Activists entered the church and ailing monks departed. As Caoimhe had done while in the *muqataa*, Mary, the Irish nurse, provided me with mobile phone descriptions of life in the church in exchange for phone units.

Day after day, as the negotiations dragged on, journalists crouched in the narrow streets leading to Manger Square and the church, and staked out the siege, hoping for something to happen. The sun was high overhead, warm, so we chased the shade as the sun moved across the sky. There were photojournalists, television teams, satellite channel anchors, and humble reporters, a few in body armour. We walked around the town for diversion. If accompanied by a colleague in a flak jacket, those of us without would put him in front, in case we met a patrol of trigger-happy Israeli soldiers.

Peace activists would occasionally cause a stir by rushing to the square with placards demanding an end to Sharon's offensive, called inappropriately, "Operation Defensive Shield." Foreign envoys came to the Peace Centre to negotiate with a hard-nosed Israeli colonel and Palestinian teams whose members changed according to Arafat's whims.

The siege ended early on the morning of May 10th, after 39 days, with the evacuation of 39 militants who had sought sanctuary in the church. The first to leave were the "wanted" 13 – ten from Fatah, and three from Hamas. One by one, 12 men bent low to exit through the Door of Humility, escorted by priests. They passed through a metal detector and boarded a bus. The thirteenth, Jihad Jaara, whose leg had been fractured by an Israeli bullet, was carried out on a stretcher and placed in an ambulance. The men were driven to Ben Gurion airport and put on a British military aircraft bound for Cyprus that, the day before, had offered to give them temporary refuge until European countries would agree to accept them as long term immigrants.

Next to emerge were 26 lower level intifadists who were transferred to Gaza. They were followed by 84 Palestinian policemen, civilians, clerics, ten peace activists and a press photographer, whose identities were checked before they were freed. The majority of Palestinians opposed the deportation of the men to both Europe and Gaza in violation of the Fourth Geneva Convention, which bans the expulsion from his homeland of someone living under military occupation.

Arafat left his imprisonment in the ruins of the *muqataa* and toured the battered but not bowed enclaves administered by the Palestinian Authority. In Bethlehem, he was heckled for the deal reached over the Church of the Nativity. Back in Nicosia, friends asked, "Where did you get your tan?"

9

SANCTUARY

Mecca, December 1973-January 1974 – dhu-al-Hijjah 7th-12th, 1393

I welcomed the New Year walking through the upper galleries of the Grand Mosque, watching tens of thousands of white-robed pilgrims circling the cubic *Ka'bah*, enveloped in a beautifully embroidered cloth, called the *kiswah*. Elderly or ailing men and women were borne by porters in flimsy wooden chairs, riding high on the flowing tide of pilgrims circling, circling seven times.

I had joined the masses rounding the *Ka'bah* before evening prayers and performed the rituals prescribed for arrival in Mecca, the *tawaf* and *say* honouring the holy city. The *tawaf* consists of circling the *Ka'bah*, the *say*, a re-enactment of the search for water for her son Ismail by Hagar, wife of the prophet Ibrahim, by "running," rather, walking in a crowd, between two enclosed mounds called *al-Safa* and *al-Marwa*.

Pilgrims had come from all corners of the world. Brown, black and white men wearing versions of the traditional *ihram*, a two-cloth wrap, and women in white caftans, their hair covered by scarves, faces open to the world. There were clean shaven businessmen, shop-keepers, farmers, bearded Afghan warriors with high cheekbones and sharp noses, Iranian women with the addresses of their *mutawwifs* (guides) stitched to their scarves, Turks roped together to prevent them from getting lost, and buxom African women in low cut caftans. A wave of faith had crested round the world and swept us all into Mecca.

In the morning I prepared for the brief journey to Mina, the pilgrim settlement eight kilometres from Mecca. I packed a few things into a bag and rolled up the thin blue mattress I had bought in the Saudi port city of Jeddah before setting off to Mecca. At the pharmacy of the Pakistani organiser of my Hajj, I boarded a minibus. A sign posted in the window of the pharmacy advertised Swiss liquor chocolates although alcohol was – and is – strictly forbidden in puritan Saudi Arabia.

The road was thronged with cars, minibuses, and open lorries filled with pilgrims chanting the Hajj refrain, the *Talbiyah*:

Labbayk, Allahumma, Labbayk!
Labbayk, la sharika laka, Labbayk!
Inna-al-hamda, wa an-ni'mata laka wal mulk!
La sharika laka, Labbayk!

Here I am, O God, at Thy Command,
Here I am!
Thou art without associates
Thine are praise and grace and dominion
Thou art without associates, Here I am!

At Mina we took up residence in a simple pistachio painted building of two stories. I found a narrow slot for my mattress on the floor of a room housing six Pakistani women and seven children. My billet was a clear, pleasant chamber with striped rugs on the floor, a ceiling fan and rectangular windows open to the elements. Mina was a fascinating place, a town hosting hundreds of thousands of residents for five days to a week every year in a few bare buildings and sprawling tent-neighbourhoods, some housing pilgrims on a national basis. Mina was provided with broad avenues, sanitation facilities, first aid tents, *sabeels* (offering free chilled water), and a fire station. There were goods from the world over and pilgrims selling handicrafts from their homelands to finance their travel. A small Swiss aircraft sprayed the area against insects while helicopters hovered overhead to control traffic and spot pilgrims who required assistance. The tents were of all shapes and sizes and boasted a range of amenities. There were striped tents, and flowered tents, tents partitioned into living, sleeping and bathing areas. Tents with fine Persian carpets and elegant furniture for wealthy Iranian and Saudi pilgrims. Although dressed alike in *ihram* (garments worn by Muslim people during the pilgrimage), all were not equal.

The next day, the ninth of *dhu al-Hijjah* (the 12th month of the Islamic calendar), we embarked on the second leg of our journey, this time on the roof of a minibus bound for ʻArafat and the climax of the pilgrimage. Suddenly we were on the move, chanting "*Labbayk*," chatting, singing, and waving to pilgrims on foot. At ʻArafat, I made for the dark granite hill on the edge of the plain where the Prophet Muhammad had stood to deliver his sermon during his Farewell Pilgrimage. I began the ascent to the top where a white pillar stood, wriggling past African, Asian and Arab pilgrims, some taking shelter from the sun under umbrellas. Keeping pace with me was a man chatting to his wife, paying little attention to our august location until suddenly he glanced up, saw the summit of the mount, covered with men in *ihram*, and burst into tears. A tall African offered me the shade of his vast green silk umbrella. I did not make it to the top. There were just too many people. Back on the plain, I "stood" facing the mount at noon with the multitude in commemoration of the Prophet's life and message. Back in our tent, my Pakistani roommates and I lunched on delicious lamb and chicken biryanis, flavoured with saffron and decorated with cashews and raisins.

After the meal, I toured the encampment. One young man in *ihram* was encased in a plaster cast from his ribs down to one ankle. Patient boy scouts minded the "lost children's tent" and tried to calm their wards with sweets and toys until parents claimed them.

At dusk we climbed onto the roof of our bus and rode to Muzdalifah where we spent the night under the stars and gathered 49 pebbles with which we were meant to stone "the devil", short white pillars, *Jamarat*, surrounded by low white walls, located at wide intervals on the plain at Mina. At dawn, I began the walk from Muzdalifah to Mina for the Feast of Sacrifice, beginning with the symbolic stoning of the *Jamarat*, where the crowds were not at their peak. I had the meat of the lamb I purchased fried at cook shop under an awning, shared a portion, and gave the rest to an old man who held out a pocket of bread and asked for food.

The symbolic stoning of the pillars, a means to release anger and guilt and cleanse the spirit, took place on the next two days when pilgrims shopped, paid visits to friends, went to Mecca to site see, or rested.

I discovered that Hajj is not Saudi Arabia where men and women are strictly segregated, women cannot drive, religious police intervene, dissent is punished by lashes and imprisonment, and murder and drug dealing by decapitation. Pilgrims obtain special visas for the Hajj, which allow them to travel to Mecca and Medina but not to Saudi Arabia itself. The atmosphere of the Hajj is free and easy, liberating spiritually and culturally. At 'Arafat, I saw Egyptian girls driving a huge copper coloured US-manufactured car. Muslims of all colours, shapes and sects mingle and pray together. English is the lingua franca, Arabic the liturgical language.

In years long lost, poets and men of letters used to gather for literary discussions. Young men and women – who do not cover their faces during Hajj – viewed prospective wives and husbands. These days businessmen conclude lucrative deals.

While Hindu pilgrimages in India may gather millions of devotees, the Hajj brings together the largest number of the faithful from all corners of the world for specific rites at a set time.

Hajj

Following the third stoning, I returned to Mecca in the back of a pick-up, went to the hotel where I had spent the first night, and showered and changed into coloured clothing to show I had completed the rituals of the Hajj. As the golden evening folded the nearly empty Grand Mosque into its arms, I joined a few score pilgrims performing the *tawaf* and *say* of the Pilgrimage and took part in the *Maghreb* (sunset) prayer, as pigeons fluttered and soared overhead. On the road back to Jeddah, I began to see the world with the eyes of one who had stood at 'Arafat.

Nicosia-Islamabad, January through August, 1979

Godfrey launched the New Year with an essay on "Militant Islam," published in *The Economist* while he was in Tehran covering the overthrow of the shah. In the essay he made points about Islam's "aliveness" that remain valid today: that as a faith Islam is in its "vigorous early middle age" and has never been "allowed to relax or to become hidebound or fossilised" since it has been under political, spiritual, and cultural challenge from the earliest days of the Christian west.

Godfrey had been in and out of Tehran during the upheaval leading to the overthrow of the shah. Iran's armed forces had begun to shift allegiances by the time the ayatollah arrived on February 1st, turning the tide against the Old Order. Godfrey remained there for another nine difficult days, on occasion dictating copy to me over the phone; which I then called in to Barbara Smith at *The Economist*.

Marya and I met Godfrey in Athens on February 10th only hours after veteran correspondent, Joe Alex Morris of the *Los Angeles Times*, had been killed at an airbase in a crossfire between rebels supporting Khomeini and forces loyal to the shah, who had fled the country. Shocked by Joe's death, Godfrey was glad to have a few days respite driving around Greece.

Back in Nicosia at a weekend dinner party at the home of *Guardian* correspondent Martin Woollacott, Cypriot historian George Georgalides blithely suggested to Godfrey that he should write a book on "militant Islam." On the following Monday, he rang Sonny Mehta at Pan Books who, when asked if he would be interested, replied that he would have liked the book "yesterday." Between the third week of March and the first week of May, Godfrey took digs at St. Antony's College, Oxford, where he had written his first two books, and produced his third which was published that summer in record time. Our first copies of "*Militant Islam*," with the photo of an armed, black turbaned Shia cleric on the cover, arrived in August.

Before the book turned up, Godfrey had received an invitation to visit Pakistan and interview the president, General Zia al-Haq. The general had asked his then foreign minister, Agha Shahi if he knew the Jansen who had written the essay in *The Economist*. Shahi said that they had been best friends at Baldwin Boys School in Bangalore. "Get him here, I want to meet him," the general ordered. So we three flew to Karachi, landing in a monsoon storm that had flooded the airport highway and the streets of the city. We did not travel until the next day to Rawalpindi from where we went by road to Islamabad.

Our most memorable day in Pakistan was August 13th when we attempted to drive to Murree, a popular hill station and the birthplace of our close friend Prue. Our government car broke down in the foothills. We abandoned both car and driver to hitchhike up the mountain first with a Christian cleric who complained about the discrimination Christians suffered in majority Muslim Pakistan. The final leg was through a sudden, surprising summer snow storm in a battered lorry that detoured off the highway to drop us at a traditional colonial-style hotel with wrap-around veranda and a blaze in the lounge fireplace. After high tea with scones and jam, we hitched a ride back to Islamabad with a very *pukka* army officer.

The next morning, Marya and I flew to Lahore for sightseeing while Godfrey conducted his interview with Zia, the first with the general by an Indian journalist. The date was significant as it was Pakistan's 22nd national day. Godfrey was startled when Zia pounded the arms of his chair with his fists, and stated, punctuating each word with a blow, "You Indians know who you are. We don't know who we are." This was an honest admission by the Pakistani dictator who had been trying to inculcate Pakistani identity by promoting his conservative version of Islam. On the 15th we celebrated India's independence with friends in Delhi.

Nicosia, November 20th, 1979

Early in the morning, firing erupted in the Grand Mosque in Mecca, the most sacred site for Muslims across the world. A group of bearded tribesmen drew weapons out of their cloaks and called upon the congregation to recognise one of their number as *Mahdi*, messiah. The leader of the group seized the microphone, "I am the *Mahdi's* brother-in-law. My name is Juhayman. Recognise my brother-in-law, recognise the *Mahdi* who will cleanse this kingdom of its corruptions." Acting on a well-prepared plan, the rebels, ultra-orthodox Salafis seeking to return to the sacred early days of Islam, allowed most of those assembled for the morning prayer to depart. The mosque guards and clerics briefed the authorities on what had happened in the mosque. Awakened two and a half hours after the seizure of the mosque, King Khaled ordered officials to shut down telephone and telex links to the outside world. Bewildered, fearing a widespread uprising, he and his advisors attempted to deal with the crisis on their own.

Radicalised by dissidents in Medina, Juhayman broadcast his demands from the minarets of the mosque. He denounced western influence in the kingdom, the government's toleration of Shias, and the consumption of alcohol by princes, their gambling, business dealings, and travel abroad to foreign capitals where they enjoyed the company of prostitutes. He castigated football and the employment of women outside their homes. Juhayman had been making these complaints for years but had been ignored. Most of his followers had, like himself, served in the Saudi National Guard, or were members of his Otayba tribe. Muhammad Abdullah al-Qahtani, who had been proclaimed *Mahdi*, was killed during clashes in the mosque.

There was no rising in response to the attack and capture of the mosque. Most of the people held hostage were terrified of the rebels and did not sympathise with their cause. The Saudi armed forces – commanded to end the siege without destroying the mosque – took more than two weeks to carry out this task. The official toll was 255 troops, rebels and pilgrims killed and 550 wounded. Diplomats argued that the figure could have been more than 1,000. The 67 insurgents were tried and beheaded. This battle in the holiest place in the Muslim world was just one in the protracted wars over whose version of Islam should prevail.

Nicosia, January 1981

Godfrey began the New Year with a second, signed essay entitled, "*Moslems and the modern world*" in *The Economist* which identified him as its Levant correspondent. The question he was asked to answer by foreign editor Brian Beedham was: Can there be accommodation between "Islam and the western world?" Godfrey replied that the west "seemingly called for accommodation, but it has done so without conviction." He elaborated by making a telling comparison: "...in effect, the west has been following the line of thought of that male chauvinist Professor Henry Higgins when he asked, 'Why can't women be more like men?' Why, the west has been asking, cannot Islam 'get with it' – 'it' being the Zeitgeist, the spirit of the age, in this last quarter of the twentieth century. Islam, it is suggested by western critics, needs to be rethought in modern terms."

Godfrey responded to the last notion by pointing out this is precisely what educated Muslims tried to do during the latter years of the 19th and the first three-quarters of the 20th centuries. While a number of serious Muslim scholars succeeded in rethinking Muslim religious and social practices, most Muslim leaders turned to secularism rather than Islam as the means to create modern, independent nation states. Their efforts were not met by encouragement and understanding but by western imperialism, colonialism and repression.

During the last decade of the 20th century and the first years of this century, western intervention has undermined and nearly destroyed the post-independence secular model adopted by Arab and Muslim states, leaving them prey to Muslim radicals seeking to turn back the calendar to competing regressive versions of the seventh century utopia when the tolerant and forward looking Prophet Muhammad reigned.

Nicosia, July 31st-August 1st, 1987

At dusk on Friday, the eve of the pilgrimage, clashes erupted between Iranian pilgrims and Saudi security police in the streets outside the Grand Mosque in Mecca. Saudi police fired tear gas and used truncheons against Iranians shouting slogans: "Death to America," "Death to the Soviet Union," and "Death to Israel," burning effigies of US president Ronald Reagan, torching cars and attacking other pilgrims and residents. Hundreds of pilgrims completing the rituals of the Hajj were caught up in the turmoil and stampeded, trampling and crushing people gathered on the esplanade of the mosque. The death toll was 402 with 649 injured. Of the fatalities, 275 were Iranians, and 85 Saudis, including security personnel.

The clashes took place in the context of the war between Shia Iran and secular Iraq, the latter financed by Sunni Saudis, Kuwaitis and other Gulf states, and involving US naval intervention in the Gulf. However, some Muslim commentators argued that the violence was driven by deep, centuries-old antagonisms between orthodox Sunnis and Shias, sharpened by Iran's efforts to export to neighbouring countries the ideology of its 1979 revolution despite the fact that 85 percent of Arab Muslims are Sunnis.

Godfrey wrote the political lead on the Mecca incident for the *Middle East International* (*MEI*) and I contributed a think -piece on the desecration of the Hajj by pilgrims violating bans on engaging in political and personal disputes and violence. Hajjis take these prohibitions seriously, claiming that during the Hajj, pilgrims must not quarrel, speak in an angry voice, uproot a plant or kill an insect.

In spite of this ban, Iran's supreme leader Ayatollah Ruhollah Khomeini had, since 1981, called upon Iranian pilgrims to politicise the Hajj, causing ructions with the Saudis in successive years and in the days leading up to the 1987 pilgrimage. To achieve its aim, Tehran boosted Iranian representation from 50,000 to 155,000.

Many pilgrims were fit men of an age recruited by the Republican Guards corps, prompting Saudi suspicions the ayatollahs had every intention of disrupting the Hajj, the most powerful religious experience ever felt by many Sunni and Shia Muslims who angrily resent political disturbances in the sanctuaries of Mecca and Medina.

Shortly after I had filed my piece to *MEI*, I received a phone call from Andy Pollak, religion editor of *The Irish Times*, asking me to write on the significance for Muslims of the clashes. Once this had been published, I asked if the paper would be interested in further regional coverage; which I have been providing ever since. My only regret is that Ma did not see me regularly employed by a paper as solid and respected as *The Irish Times*. The tie to the paper would have reinforced her connection to her Derry-born woodcarver grandfather. I discovered his identity only after Ma's demise while my sister Carla and I went through her papers. Ma was a great one for "roots" but she was also a bit of a snob who preferred to think the family link with Ireland went back to a surgeon called Caldwell, who was on George Washington's staff during the US Revolutionary War.

Nicosia, November 1997

On the sidelines of a conference on Iran and the west, I met Abdolkarim Soroush, the most controversial and innovative Muslim thinker in Iran. A quiet, thoughtful London-trained philosopher, Soroush had been banned from lecturing at Tehran University although thousands would turn out to listen to him speak. So dangerous were his words that hardliners sent thugs to beat him up. The authorities prohibited publication of his writings and, for a time, confiscated his passport. When I asked about his mentors, he said he followed Sir Muhammad Iqbal, the Indian Muslim scholar who wrote "*The Reconstruction of Religious Thought in Islam*."

Dr. Soroush said, "I try to reconstruct and re-interpret Islamic tradition in the light of [scientific and socio-economic] achievements of our age." He considered the faith a "series of interpretations of Islam," undergoing change according to historical experience. In his view, Re-interpretation is essential for every age.

"... according to my interpretation... there cannot be any official interpretation of Islam... or any official class of interpreters of Islam." By saying this he dismissed both Shia and Sunni official interpretations and interpreters. He favoured "secularised" state structures for deeply religious Muslim societies.

He said he was in contact with thinkers like himself, including Muhammad Shahrour, a Dublin-educated Syrian reformer Godfrey and I had interviewed several times. His monumental work, "*Al-Kitab w'al Quran,*" "The Book and the *Quran: a Contemporary Reading*", was a best seller in Jordan and Lebanon as well as Saudi Arabia where it and his subsequent books were banned. Circulation was underground. According to Shahrour, Islam makes no laws but fixes limits, giving adherents, "the greatest possible degree of freedom."

Not surprisingly, Shahrour had been declared an apostate by conservative clerics affiliated with al-Azhar, the primary source of Sunni jurisprudence, in Cairo. Egyptian tele-cleric Yusuf al-Qaradawi, a strong supporter of the Muslim Brotherhood, dismissed Shahrour's writings on Islam, claiming he was promoting "a different religion."

Beirut, October 2008

I interviewed Lebanon's Grand Ayatollah Mohammad Hussein Fadlallah at his office deep in the Dahyeh, the southern suburbs of Beirut, a Hizbullah stronghold. Revered by Shias across the region, Fadlallah, 73, had not only been elevated to the apex of the Shia clerical hierarchy but through piety, scholarship and good works, he had also reached the *marja'yat*, the select company of "emulated" clerics, a figure to imitate or follow.

Although of Lebanese origin, he was born in Iraq and educated in Shia seminaries there. In 1952, he moved to Beirut where he wrote books and established a foundation that built a public library, schools, orphanages, and Islamic centres. Regarded wrongly as the spiritual mentor of Hizbullah, he was targeted by assassins on several occasions. In 1985 he survived a car bomb near his home that killed 80 people.

Able to trace his lineage to the Prophet Muhammad's daughter Fatima and her husband Ali, Fadlallah wore the high black turban of the *sayeds* and a white cloak or *abbaya* over a tan caftan. Pale and frail with a gentle demeanour, the ayatollah was a man of steely purpose and conviction. He was a rare moderate and progressive cleric in a region beset by excess and regression.

He blamed the centuries old, often bloody split between Shia and Sunni on figures who sought to exploit differences for political gain. This resulted in "tribal feuds [leading] some Sunnis and some Shias to regard each other as infidels." They should, instead, "develop a common understanding and bring closer their interpretations of Islamic law and philosophy... We strive to bring together Sunnis and Shias to arrive at the great goal of Islamic unity," he stated.

Speaking in general terms, he continued, "In any religious dispute differences are accentuated by feudalism and extremism, and transformed into political problems." He compared disagreements between Muslim sects to divisions between Catholics and Protestants in Ireland.

"We believe in dialogue between religions. I wrote a book 20 years ago on Islamic-Christian dialogue… dialogue brings minds together and allows people to understand one another. Many religious problems are due to misunderstanding and misinterpretation. Dialogue solves problems if minds are open...violence never solves problems, rather it complicates problems."

He accused the western powers of "trying to control the Islamic world by deepening differences and feuds." Commenting on Iran's political system, he said he does not "believe in the absolute authority of the *imam* [the supreme guide] unless the interests of the nation are endangered."

He also adopted a progressive line on children and women. He said children should be treated with decency and respect and educated. On the position of women, he was a true revolutionary. "A woman is a human being exactly like a man… there is no difference in their mental or other capacities… Women have the right to be respected, educated to the maximum, take part in political life, elect and be elected at all levels and assume responsibility in the administration of the state. Women should have the right to hold and dispose freely of property and to defend themselves if struck by men."

When he died in 2010, the Muslim world lost one of its few moderate, modern mentors.

10

LIBERATION

Beirut, October 1990

Once Syria had joined the US-led coalition massing troops in the region to drive Iraqi forces out of Kuwait, Damascus was given permission by Washington to end Lebanon's civil war by crushing the rebellion of General Michel Aoun; who assumed control after president Amin Gemayel stood down, and seized Lebanon's presidential palace in Baabda. Following an attempt on his life on the 12th and two bombing runs by ageing Syrian Sukhoi Su-7s the next morning, the general fled to the French embassy. Aoun overtly called upon troops loyal to him to ceasefire, but, in a double cross, covertly rang his officers and ordered them to fight the Syrians. Casualties were heavy on both sides with, perhaps, 800 soldiers and civilians killed. At a location called the "Back of the Beast," Aoun's men showed the white flag while surrounded by Syrian troops but when they approached opened fire and killed as many as 150.

In retaliation the Syrians executed the Aounists, said to number around 80. The bagged bodies of 19 brought to Baabda hospital had remained unclaimed a week after Aoun's flight. Another 50 were stored in a small building across the highway from the hospital. This inglorious and pointless bloodletting brought an end to Lebanon's 15-year civil war, a year after an agreement to halt the conflict had been negotiated by Lakhdar Brahimi at Taif in Saudi Arabia.

A week after Aoun's defeat, Nicole drove Godfrey and me up the Damascus highway to Aley and from there southwards along the ridge of the Lebanon range towards the picturesque market town of Souk al-Gharb where the Aounists had fought for nine hours, wreaking fresh destruction on handsome 19th century stone villas. Outside the gutted Hajjar hotel, once popular with Beirutis seeking respite from the summer heat, a handful of Syrian soldiers waved us on. The Palestinian school where Marya had gone to kindergarten, was a gutted shell. After 100 metres the lower road to Chemlan melted into the hillside so we tried the upper road. But a Syrian soldier called a halt. "The road to Chemlan is gone," he said. "Yesterday a bulldozer was blown up clearing this road... without casualties."

Souk al-Gharb was deserted, Chemlan unreachable. We were fortunate we had sold *Beit al-Hindi* in February 1981 to a Lebanese doctor and his Syrian wife.

Some months after our failed try, Nicole was again prepared to try to reach Chemlan. This time we were successful only because she drove a Range Rover. The view from the road above *Beit al-Hindi* was of a battered house, blue shutters gone, and roof tiles broken. We had to fight through tall geraniums and thistles that had grown along the path on the upper terrace. The house had been hollowed out. Inside it was empty, walls scrawled with graffiti, some contributed by Fatah fighters. Marya's room and the study downstairs were pierced by mortars. Copper electrical wiring had been pulled from casings in the thick walls. But the well-built house remained solid and strong. I wondered what had happened to Umm Fawzi, our washerwoman who had insisted on sitting on a step outside the back door with her washtub on the ground in front of her instead of using the laundry room we had built on the lower floor. I assumed Umm Fawzi had died since she had been elderly at the time we left but Umm Mirhej, our cleaning woman from the same neighbouring Druze village, must have survived.

Nicosia, May 21st, 2000

Elise Elin was born in Virginia, with Brian attending Marya's delivery, while I monitored progress on long distance telephone. Elise, "Lili," conformed to the tradition of my maternal line by being a girl, first child and born on a decade thirty years after her mother. Since this event took place a continent and an ocean from Cyprus and to the west of the prime meridian, she emerged on the 20th, defining the distance between me and my family.

Southern Lebanon, May 25th, 2000

Nuha and I rose early, collected bottles of water, and descended from her flat to the street where Zein was waiting to take us to the south the day after the last Israeli soldier and the last Israeli proxy Lebanese militiaman had pulled back across the Lebanese border into Israel.

Israel and its allies had been driven from a 14-kilometre-wide "security zone" by Lebanese Hizbullah and allied Amal fighters, many from the south, who had mounted a fierce campaign to retake land initially occupied in 1978. Israel had originally seized this band of territory to counter cross-border attacks by Arafat's Fatah, following its expulsion from Jordan as a result of the Black September debacle. During its full-scale invasion of Lebanon in 1982, Israel not only drove the Palestinian resistance organisations from Lebanon but also created a new, more determined and dedicated enemy in the shape of the Shia Hizbullah, formed and fostered by Iranian Revolutionary Guards officers based in the Bekaa valley.

We drove along the empty highway to Sidon, passed through Tyre and made for Ras al-Naqura, where we paused for coffee with and quotes from Timor Goksel, spokesman for the UN force in Lebanon, which had tried but failed to keep the peace since its creation in 1978. He said before the staged Israeli pullout began in March, the UN, the Lebanese government and various political factions with men on the ground in the south had worked out who would assume control in specific areas. Christian elements were to deploy in Christian areas, Druze in Druze locations, and Shias in Shia villages. "The takeover was remarkably orderly," Goksel said. The 25th was proclaimed "Liberation Day" by the government.

From Ras al-Nakoura we proceeded through Ain Ibl to Bint Jbeil, where church bells were ringing and children were handing out sweets to local people and passers-by to celebrate liberation. A priest we met in the square said three-quarters of the inhabitants of the town had fled, many to the US where they had settled in Dearborn, a suburb of Detroit. We continued our journey along the frontier to Kafr Kila where Lebanese and Palestinians often assembled near the border fence to throw stones into Israel. After a detour to Ibl al-Saqi, to the headquarters of the Indian battalion, for a briefing and a spicy lunch, we proceeded to the pretty resort town of Marjayoun which, by mid-afternoon, was flooded by thousands of Lebanese returning to territory they had not visited for 22 years. We crawled in a traffic jam along the mountain road to Nabatiyeh and stopped at an internet cafe so I could file my story to *The Irish Times*. We finally reached Nuha's home at nine in the evening, after 15 traumatic hours on the road.

That day was Lebanon's finest. Israel had predicted a massacre once its troops abandoned the ten percent of Lebanon declared "off limits" by Israel and ruled by its officers and allies. But, tens of thousands of Lebanese had, instead, celebrated with picnics, visits to relatives and friends; taken in the scenery, paused at places near Israel's border fence, and revelled in patriotism.

Among the visitors to the south that day were Hizbullah's political organisers, security men, welfare workers, surveyors and engineers from its Jihad al-Bina construction company tasked with rebuilding the war and occupation ridden south. Iranian foreign minister Kamal Kharrazi, the first senior foreign personage to visit the liberated south, pledged financial aid for reconstruction.

Gaza, September 12th, 2005

In the early hours, the Israeli army completed the evacuation of soldiers and settlers from Gaza, occupied in 1967. In spite of bitter resistance from hard liners determined to hang onto their comfortable colonies in the north and centre of the Strip, Israeli prime minister Ariel Sharon honoured his pledge to pull out. Before departing, the settlers reduced their homes, shops, sports clubs, swimming pools, and synagogues to rubble, leaving crushed walls and splintered wood to Palestinians who had endured Israel's direct rule for 38 years.

While travelling south from Gaza City to Rafah, I saw Palestinians streaming into the settlement blocs where they stumbled over shards of glass and smashed floor and roof tiles, raised Palestinian flags, and searched for items that could be salvaged from the wreckage of settler communities. If they had been left intact, homes could have provided decent shelter for Palestinians driven by Israel from the coastal cities and the Negev, conquered and cleansed in 1948 and succeeding years.

Only settlement greenhouses were left by the Israelis. They had been bought by funds raised by the envoy for the Gaza "disengagement," former World Bank president James Wolfensohn. He had intended to turn them over to Palestinian farmers who could grow crops for export; but within 24 hours some had been looted of pumps, irrigation hoses, and plastic sheeting while Palestinian Authority police watched, powerless to intervene. The greenhouses had been seen as an engine of development for impoverished Gaza. In contrast to arrangements made by Lebanese parties and armed groups five years earlier, no serious planning had been done for filling the politico-security vacuum once Israel had withdrawn. Instead, Gaza was lawless, rogue gangs kidnapped and robbed, Fatah and Hamas were at daggers drawn.

While Gazans – like Lebanese returning to the south in 2000 – celebrated their "liberation", the atmosphere was very different from Lebanese glee on Liberation Day. Israel remained very much in control of the Strip, dominated on two sides by the army based on Israeli territory, on the coast by the Israeli navy, and overhead by the Israeli air force. Former Palestinian foreign minister Nabil Shaath, a Gazan, was not optimistic. While the soldiers and settlers had departed from the interior, he said, Gaza remained "occupied from land, sea, and air." Israel was determined to decide what happened in Gaza: whether the Strip would become a thriving Palestinian business model or continue as a coastal slum where 80 percent of the population lived below the poverty line and depended on foreign food donations.

Nabil was right. Since "disengagement", Israel has not only tightened its grip on Gaza but also conducted periodic military wrecking campaigns whenever Gazans dared oppose Israel's siege and blockade. Having "disengaged" from Gaza by pulling out 8,000 settlers, Sharon deepened Israel's engagement with the West Bank, stepping up illegal settlement expansion, planting 18,000 colonists in 18 months, building army and police bases, and declaring tracts of territory "closed military ones" free of Palestinians.

Gaza, July 2007

Gazans heaved a huge sigh of relief when Hamas fighters defeated and drove into West Bank Fatah's political cadres, security men and enforcers. Clan and factional gunmen no longer reigned. Drivers were not carjacked, kidnapped or killed while on the road. People felt safe in their homes. Gazans were given an emergency number to ring at times of trouble and, when rung, the police turned up within minutes. There were no checkpoints from Beit Hanoun in the north to Rafah in the south. Every night tens of thousands of Gazans fled their hot and stuffy homes to picnic and sleep on the beach in tents, under umbrellas, and in canvas chairs, revelling in the cool breeze from the sea.

Between June 10th and 15th, Hamas had seized control of Gaza by military means. Its well-trained, disciplined Executive Force militia, bolstered by armed supporters, had routed the more numerous but ill-trained and poorly motivated fighters of the Fatah-dominated Preventive Security agency and allied elements. Fatah had been weakened by the absence of its commanders, notably strongman Muhammad Dahlan, while Hamas' political and military leaders had been present in the Strip.

Raji Sourani, director of the Palestinian Centre for Human Rights, said both sides had violated human rights during the June clashes when 160 people had been killed, 40 of them civilians. But, he observed, "People are more relaxed, journalists and internationals do not need escorts, UNRWA's leadership is almost functioning normally." Hamas did not hold large numbers of prisoners. Collaborators with Israel and other foreign powers had fled. Hamas had the records of the Fatah-dominated security agencies as well as the serial numbers of weapons handed out to Fatah's men and criminal clans, the main sources of the violence. A secular lawyer who had done time in Israeli prisons, Sourani was highly critical of president Abbas for telling the police, attorney general, and civil courts to cease functioning, leaving Gazans without legal protections.

Hamas' takeover prompted Fatah and Abbas to carry out a full-scale political coup against Hamas by dismissing a Saudi-brokered unity government. He declared martial law, and ordered Fatah-dominated security forces to tighten Ramallah's grip in the West Bank, effectively finishing off the decade old Palestinian experiment with democracy.

Ahmad Yousef, political adviser to Gaza's de facto prime minister Ismail Haniyeh, insisted Hamas sought reconciliation with Fatah and was working with Egyptian and Saudi mediators to achieve this objective. But reconciliation and collaboration was never on Abbas' agenda while Israel and the US pressed the international community to tighten the siege and blockade of Gaza.

Cairo, November 2011

Again closed to traffic, Tahrir Square was nearly deserted, the barricades unmanned. The Second Revolution was flagging. Scraps of paper eddied in puffs of wind; vendors proffered dust-stained top hats in Egypt's black, white and red national colours and flags of all sizes. A few partially collapsed tents of families demanding the release of imprisoned loved ones remained on the grassy circle, known as the "tray," on one side of the square. A small boy jogged alongside and pressed me to buy a surgical mask to ward off tear gas. I gave him a pound and took a blue mask just as a faint wave of gas wafted over Tahrir from Muhammad Mahmoud Street where sporadic clashes continued between black-clad riot police and youths seeking to reach the ministry of interior. They protested detention of colleagues; military trials for civilians, and human rights abuses by the police and security services after the counter-revolutionary military regime had taken over from Mubarak. Four young men half carried, half dragged a wounded lad to the remaining medical tent. Fit, trim and dressed in t-shirts and jeans, the youths may have been "ultras," fans of Egypt's football teams who have a long history of scrapping with the police. A motorcycle with two riders wheeled round the wide spaces, apparently looking for someone.

As I strode purposefully past the Omar Makram Mosque at the southwest corner of the square, and behind the Semiramis and Shepherd's hotels on the Nile corniche, the odour of tear gas intensified, making my eyes water and nose run. I had to go to the US embassy to obtain a letter demanded by the Foreign Press Office stating that I was a genuine US citizen and a genuine correspondent for *The Irish Times*. The guard at the door to the consular offices sent me round the building to a second entrance. Several of Cairo's black police wagons were parked alongside the block and their black suited, armed occupants were lounging against the wall, chatting, oblivious to the gas that had blown into Garden City from Muhammad Mahmoud street. The woman at the reception desk rang the press office and told me to wait. A few minutes later, a man appeared, introduced himself and led the way through the courtyard where gas had been trapped by the high rise walls of the brooding multi-storey building. Two employees wearing blue gas masks hurried to escape the fresh odiferous consignment with its date of expiry sometime in the future, a boon provided by the US military to Egypt's military to end unrest in the streets.

Cairo, June 17th, 2012

White-suited policemen were deployed outside the arts academy in the green, affluent Zamalek neighbourhood of Cairo, but voters were few and mostly middle aged and elderly. They trickled steadily through the gates handmade for polling stations, flourishing their identity cards. Ballots carried the names, photos and symbols of the two candidates, bearded Muslim Brotherhood veteran Muhammad Morsi and clean-shaven former air force commander Ahmad Shafiq, appointed prime minister by Mubarak during the uprising in a last ditch effort to survive. Morsi's symbol was the scales of justice, Shafiq's a ladder.

Voter Amr Shaarawi explained in a few words the low turnout and lack of enthusiasm. "During the first round we preferred anyone but those two." His view was also held by a young woman voting at the Nassar preparatory school in the impoverished alleyways of the Brotherhood's stronghold near the Pyramids at Giza, half an hour's drive from Zamalek. Outside the nearby Helmiya school, there had been a shouting match between Morsi and Shafiq supporters, but voting was peaceful. Whenever Isolde, whom I partnered in polling station excursions, or I, asked why there were so few voters, officials would reply, "People will come in the evening when it is not so hot." The temperature had risen to a stunning 44 degrees Celsius by the afternoon, but in the evening it was clear that millions of Egypt's voters were "no shows".

Conspiracy-minded Egyptians held that people did not bother to cast their ballots because the election had been cooked so Shafiq, the military's man, would emerge victorious. However, they were wrong. Morsi came through.

What was interesting about this contest was the percentage of participation actually rose from the 46 percent in the first highly contested round which had taken place in May. There were a dozen candidates in that round, most of them regarded by politically savvy Egyptians as "*feloul*", remnants of the old order. Shafiq, and long-time foreign minister Amr Moussa, who was knocked out in the first round, were super-*feloul*.

In that round Hamdeen Sabahi, head of the Nasserist Dignity (*Karama*) party, was the only secular candidate who had no connections to the Mubarak regime. He had been imprisoned 17 times during the presidencies of Mubarak and his predecessor, Anwar Sadat. Sabahi had joined the protest on January 25th, 2011, the event that launched the uprising that toppled Mubarak. He had also attended demonstrations against the generals who had taken over from Mubarak. Sabahi had good "revolutionary" credentials.

He surprised many Egyptians by winning 21 percent of the vote in the first round compared to 25 percent for Morsi and 24 percent for Shafiq. By coming in third, Sabahi was unfortunately, eliminated. The fragile revolution might have had a different fate if he had run in the second round and won.

Egyptian revolutionaries were deeply disappointed and disturbed that two old regime figures – Morsi and Shafiq – stood against each other in the second round. The choice, said one commentator, was between a "theocracy" and "a police state," placing democracy activists who had mounted the 2011 uprising between a "rock and a hard place." Columnist Mona Anis boycotted the vote but her nonagenarian mother, once a communist, cast her ballot for Morsi.

He won, taking 51.7 percent of the vote against 48.3 percent for Shafiq. But only 52 percent of the electorate participated in Egypt's first relatively free, multi-candidate presidential poll.

The revolutionaries were burnt out. The Brotherhood, which had belatedly embraced the uprising, attempted to partner the military; which took power after Mubarak's fall. The movement initially promised not to field candidates for more than one-third of the seats in the people's assembly and not to run a candidate for the presidency, but had done both. The Brotherhood and allied ultra-orthodox Salafi Noor Party had secured control of both the assembly and the consultative upper house, dissolved by the military before Morsi was inaugurated.

Instead of delivering the demands of the revolutionaries, "Bread, freedom and justice", Morsi spent his year in office consolidating the Brotherhood's position at the centre of the political system and packing the already bloated bureaucracy with Brotherhood loyalists. At the end of November, he re-energised the revolutionaries by assuming full powers without judicial oversight to ensure the success of a referendum on a constitution written by a commission heavily influenced by Brotherhood supporters. He was repeatedly warned he had to share power with other political forces. He dismissed these warnings at the instigation of the Brotherhood's Guidance Council which was determined to rule without partners. It had failed to understand that power resided with the military not the Brotherhood, or even, the people.

Cairo, June 30th, 2013

As many as two million Egyptians poured into Cairo's iconic Tahrir Square, the surrounding streets, and the area around Ittihadiya palace in the Heliopolis district demanding Morsi's resignation as he marked the first anniversary of his inauguration. Chanting, "*Erhal*! *Erhal*! Leave! Leave!" Men and women of all ages and classes walked together, children skipping alongside or riding on their fathers' shoulders, youths waving Egyptian flags, carrying portraits of Morsi with an "X" across his face, brandishing red cards commanding, "Get out!"

Hebba and I squeezed into Tahrir as it filled up at about five in the afternoon and, thanks to a broad-backed friend we encountered near the Arab League headquarters, managed to cross the square to the far side. Thousands upon thousands gathered as they had in 2011: head-scarved and bare-headed girls in t-shirts and jeans, elderly women in flower print dresses, conservative women enveloped in black, only their eyes showing; men in suits and ties or caftans, boys in ubiquitous t-shirts and jeans. Hawkers sold tea, water, and fluffy ovals of pink candyfloss on sticks. Sitting with friends under an awning, Said, an activist, said they planned to stay "as long as it takes to get rid of Morsi. During the revolution, Egyptians were united. Now we are divided." He complained, "There is no fuel, electricity is cut, food is more expensive, the pound is collapsing, everything costs more."

His friend Fuad did not care who replaced Morsi. "He hijacked the revolution and has been putting the Brotherhood in power. They have to share power." The revolution has to be for "all Egyptians".

Hebba and I quickly turned round and struggled to return to Qasr al-Nil bridge to escape the throng. We only managed to cross the bridge against the flow by walking behind a horse-drawn carriage.

Cairo, July 2, 2013

Marchers carrying Egyptian flags gathered at the magical hour of five in the afternoon in the capital's diverse and widespread quarters. Egyptians tooting horns, clapping together wooden clogs, beating drums, and shouting, "*Erhal.*" Since he had refused to step down, marchers were urged to stage sit-ins at their destinations and launch a civil disobedience campaign. Morsi, ironically, took refuge in Qobba Palace, where King Farouk in 1952 and Mubarak in 2011 had taken refuge before they were toppled by the army.

The marchers were festive, convinced Morsi would be deposed as he clung to power by the fragile thread of legitimacy which, opponents claimed, had been stretched to breaking point by the Muslim Brotherhood in its drive to monopolise power.

On Gezira Island in the Nile, a ragged column of men and women of all ages and stations in society followed a battered red jeep deployed by the June 30th movement to lead chants and encourage people to flock to Tahrir Square. They danced to a popular song blaring from the speakers on the jeep, waved to people cheering from balconies overlooking the broad avenue.

Traffic halted and allowed the marchers to pass; drivers beat time on their horns. The column met and merged with another before turning the corner to cross Qasr al-Nil bridge under the gaze of the statue of Egypt's great 19th century builder, Khedive Ismail.

Nobel laureate Muhamed ElBaradei, former head of the International Atomic Energy Agency, had been named transition negotiator for the broad spectrum of secular opposition parties and factions seeking to topple Morsi. ElBaradei was to implement a roadmap to put the country back on the road to democracy. The transition plan involved the dissolution of the upper house of parliament, appointment of the head of the constitutional court as interim executive, formation of a cabinet under an independent prime minister, and presidential elections within six months.

Morsi had been given an ultimatum by the military to share power with the opposition or submit to another roadmap drawn up by the armed forces command.

Cairo, July 3rd, 2013

The Egyptian army toppled Morsi by simply imprisoning him in his quarters and turning off his phones. His ouster was announced by army chief Abdel Fattah al-Sisi, flanked by ElBaradei, Sheikh al-Azhar Ahmed al-Tayeb, and Coptic Orthodox Christian Pope Tawadros II. Sisi pledged to keep the army out of politics in an effort to assure Egyptians there would be no return to 60 years of military rule. The Brotherhood's political wing, the Freedom and Justice party, refused to attend the event and called the deposition of Morsi a "coup". Brotherhood supporters gathered in two Cairo squares and threatened to defend Egypt's "legitimately elected president" with their blood and lives.

Giza, July 5th, 2013

Having been turned away in the morning by Muslim Brotherhood security men from the massive sit-in at Rabaa al-Adawiya in the Nasr City district, I decided to go in the afternoon to Nahda Square outside Cairo University's campus in Giza. There, a smaller camp had been set up by activists; also demanding Morsi's reinstatement. The site was cordoned off by a few threads of wire, and pieces of flattened tin and string. Male volunteers in t-shirts patted down men seeking to enter, women simply passed through a narrow gap in the flimsy fence.

A scarf-less, blonde woman bearing a Morsi portrait and calling herself, "Hele", took my arm, steering me round small piles of broken paving stones, readied to repel attacks. A soiled 20-meter Egyptian flag was stretched out on the pavement. Hele pointed to a man she said was a Marxist. "I am a liberal. We are not all Brotherhood. What we want is democracy. Democracy is not a coup... We are peaceful, peaceful. You can see, peaceful."

A pretty young woman in a purple peaked hat pulled down over her headscarf told me she served as a pharmacist at Qasr al-Aini Hospital where she offered to show me the records of dead and wounded admitted to emergency. "I am not pro-Morsi. I am against the coup" that toppled him on July 3rd.

On the stage, a former minister of the Brotherhood persuasion spouted but no one paid attention. Instead, half a dozen of the thin scatterings of men and women gathered in the square drew around me, each wanting to put forward his or her views. Hanan, enveloped from head to foot in black, hands gloved, feet encased in socks within her sandals called Morsi a "national hero" who called for "justice not blood." Youssef, an English teacher, stated, "This is an Islamic revolution. The millions in the street in Mina, Zagazig, Assiut, and Alexandria make this clear." The speaker on the stage called out, "*Allahu Akbar*" and listeners replied, "*Allahu Akbar*" Another English teacher, identifying himself as Mahmoud Fawzi stated, "We want you to tell the world that we will support Morsi to the last drop of our blood."

As Hele and I made our way to the entrance to the square, she said a group would assemble shortly to march across Cairo. "Would I like to join?" It was nearing six in the evening; I had to file so I turned down the invitation, fortunately, for the armed protesters invaded Manial Island when they crossed the Nile from Giza to reach Tahrir Square, and clashed with locals and killed twelve before reaching the corniche where they fought with security forces until early morning.

Nasr City, July 8th, 2013

The Brotherhood accused the army of massacring protesters staging a sit-in outside the Republican Guard barracks, where Mosri was said to have been held. The army blamed "terrorists" for the killing of 51 demonstrators, an army officer, a soldier and a policeman. A military spokesman said at dawn a group armed with Molotov cocktails, stones, rifles and other weapons attacked the perimeter of the facility. "Shots were fired from roof tops," he stated. This was the most serious incident involving the army, which had shunned direct involvement with protesters since the uprising erupted on January 25th, 2011. The spokesman tied the attack to a violent campaign waged against the army and police by Muslim extremists in North Sinai. Leading figures and politicians across the political spectrum called for restraint while the Brotherhood urged Egyptians to rise up against "those trying to steal their revolution with tanks and deposing Morsi."

A crude barricade across the wide avenue leading to the vast Rabaa al-Adawiya encamp-ment forced vehicles and pedestrians to make a wide detour around the area where tens of thousands of Morsi supporters had settled over the previous ten days. In front of the barricade, several young men in hard hats brandished staves to fend off attacks. A woman in headscarf in charge of security at the entrance looked into my bag and peered at my Cypriot press card, unable to read either Greek or English. When she demanded to know my nationality, I replied, "*Kubrus*", Cyprus. "Welcome, welcome," she stated with a broad smile.

Camp residents lounged on mattresses and mats, gazed at passers-by, or made their way through the throng. Vendors had erected stands selling water, juice, sandwiches, bread, and other supplies. On the platform in front of the gleaming white mosque a speaker was exhorting the faithful to resist Morsi's ouster by all means. Men slipped off sandals and shoes, laid out small rugs and mats, and assembled in long lines, in preparation for the noon prayer. The speaker's voice rose and fell as he denounced the military, blaming troops for the deaths of Brotherhood supporters in the clashes early that morning. The speaker's tone sharpened as he called for martyrdom, "jihad," and "intifada," an uprising against the army. But the crowd remained peaceful, the atmosphere calm.

The people gathered at Rabaa al-Adawiya were a collection of teachers and low ranking civil servants from the provinces, farmers and manual labourers from the conservative countryside and urban slum migrants with little education and less steady employment. While Egyptians waved their national banners, Syrians displayed the flag adopted by rebels fighting the Damascus government. As we left the camp, Hussein, my driver, a dark skinned Nubian from

Upper Egypt, asked wryly, "Do you see anyone of my colour in this crowd?"

Nicosia, August 14th, 2013

A state of emergency was proclaimed in Egypt and an overnight curfew imposed after black clad riot police and plain clothes security agents stormed the two Brotherhood sit-ins where supporters continued to demand Morsi's return. Tear gas, birdshot and live fire were used to disperse protesters. Defenders replied with bricks and stones stockpiled in anticipation of attacks. Men with assault rifles and hunting guns fired at the police. The army patrolled the streets.

The Egyptian health ministry reported 638 had been killed, 595 civilians and 43 police; Human Rights Watch put the death toll at between 817 and 1,000. Fatalities during the 18-day 2011 uprising had numbered 846. Violence erupted across Egypt.

Giza, May 26, 2014

The great pyramids materialised out of the morning mist, their forms grew sharp, their rough edges clearly defined. Overhead, hung banners urging Egyptians to vote for military chief Abdel Fattah al-Sisi who was standing against Sabahi, the sole candidate who had dared enter the second presidential election race since the toppling of Mubarak in 2011. A clutch of empty tourist buses stood at the entrance to the plateau hosting the pyramids and the sphinx.

At the Ramsis school, men and women waited in separate lines to vote. The mood was festive, raucous. Women in party finery ululated as they do at weddings. "Sisi, yes! Obama, no!" chanted a woman in red with a Mad Hatter's topper on her head. Inside the polling station for women, a young judge in neat black suit and tie directed voters to teams checking identity cards and handing out ballots bearing photos of the candidates as well as their names. More than 5,000 people were slated to cast ballots at this station. In 2012, people here had voted for Morsi.

Caftan-clad taxi driver Abdel Aziz Bashar, plucked at my sleeve. “Sisi is not like Morsi. Please write that Egypt is good. Tourists can come here. Sisi will end the Brotherhood’s terrorism.”

Across from a second school, a two-storey banner bearing Sisi’s portrait hung from a balcony. Women entered the polling station, one by one. Mona, a tall handsome matron with sleek, black hair, said, “I have voted in every election since the revolution, hoping things will get better.”

The narrow alleyway was unpaved, choked with rubble and rubbish; two horses tethered to the back of a carriage moved aside as camels, their high saddles cinched over colourful tasselled kilims, loped along the potholed road. Two Japanese boarded a kneeling camel, which rose awkwardly to its flat feet. People here were desperate: without tourists there was no work and no money. Families, horses and camels went hungry.

On the pyramid highway there was a single banner portraying Sabahi, the first I saw in greater Cairo. In spite of reports that six explosive devices had been defused in Giza, women flashed the “V” Sign and trilled. They chanted, “Sisi, Sisi, Sisi!” A little girl’s face was painted with the colours of the Egyptian flag, a faint echo of Tahrir Square in its halcyon days. Men took selfies with smart phones, Joked and cheered. This was the heartland of “Sisi mania.”

Magda, a woman in a headscarf and long dress, asserted, “Sisi has the support of the Egyptian people. He will solve all the problems of the economy and work. The biggest danger in the world is religious fanaticism.” She reached out to a bareheaded woman in blue next to her.

“She is Christian, I am Muslim, she is my friend. Christians-Muslims one hand.”

The streets were nearly empty at Khan el-Khalili bazaar at the heart of Old Cairo, were Sisi was born and raised. Touts begged the few people out and about to sit down at abandoned restaurants. Behind 1,000-year-old al-Azhar Mosque stretched alleyways flanked with crumbling houses reeking of poverty. At Zahra school, teachers had covered the grimy walls of classrooms with pupils' bright art. By the time the *muezzin* announced midday prayers, 300 women had voted in one room, 500 men in the other. But there were no long lines in the alley and no "Sisi mania"on his home turf. A man in one of the small shops selling Qurans whispered, "Morsi." He was in prison awaiting trial for incitement, murder and fraud. Sisi, the officer who overthrew him, was the man of the moment.

As dusk fell, more than one-third of voters on the lists of the two polling stations at the Fine Arts College in upscale Zamalek, partially gripped by "Sisi mania", had cast their ballots. Sisi was certain to triumph but had sought a large turnout. Sisi won by a landslide – 97 percent of the votes of 47.5 percent of the electorate – although he also belonged to the "*feloul*" caste which had maintained its grip on power beyond the revolution.

11

INCARCERATION

Nicosia-Beirut, November 26th, 1998

Godfrey died of a brain haemorrhage at six in the morning. I sat beside him and held his hand once he had been moved into a ward from the emergency section at the general hospital. I notified the duty nurse before going out of the building to ring Marya who had been due to arrive before his seventy-ninth birthday on December 2nd. He had repeatedly said he did not want to be buried since he hated tight spaces, asked to be cremated and his ashes scattered in four places: near *Beit al-Hindi* in Chemlan, the Cypriot countryside, Jerusalem and Bangalore.

Since there is no cremation in Cyprus, the Indian embassy in Nicosia and friends in Beirut tackled the Lebanese authorities and the American University Hospital in Beirut to arrange for cremation there. To ensure a smooth passage for his last journey to Lebanon I took to the embassy here the certificate granting him the rank of officer in Lebanon's National Order of the Cedar which states that he should enjoy all the "rights, privileges and honours" attached to his status. It was the first time such a request had been made.

Marya and I flew to Beirut with the coffin, which was collected at the airport and delivered to the hospital. We received condolences at the AUB alumni club. When, after two days, we were returning to our hotel with the box containing his ashes, we paused at Walima restaurant to view the day's menu, and found *mugrabiyeh* was the plat de jour, the dish he and I had shared with an Indian friend the night before he had his third stroke. Nuha was sitting in a corner eating her meal and waved us over. We told her Godfrey's remains were in the parcel. She was happy to have lunch with us – all three.

Marya and I followed his instructions in Chemlan and Cyprus before she flew back to the US.

Rachel used to say Godfrey was "cherished", which he was. By me, by Marya, by friends. He could be bloody difficult when he chose but he treated everyone the same whatever their background or status in life. Children liked him because he did not look down on or talk down to them. Since he had been brought up in an Indian household where servants did for his family, had a batman when serving as an officer in the air force, and hired a maid while a diplomat and foreign correspondent, he did not drive, cook, manage his accounts, or do house-work. However, he did heat up meals prepared by me and put in the fridge while I was away from home. He volunteered in the kitchen by skinning blanched almonds when I was preparing Christmas cakes and pulling *mulokhia* leaves from their stems when I made that grand Egyptian dish. He always claimed I took the big family decisions. He was right except, when in 1988, he decided to leave *The Economist* just as Marya was entering her first term at Oxford. I was expected to agree and I did.

Gaza-Bethlehem, December 14th-15th, 1998

US president Bill Clinton landed by helicopter at Palestine's international airport to be greeted by a blustery breeze off the sea, a storm of national flags, a marching band playing somewhat off tune, and a long line of Gaza and West Bank worthies headed by Arafat, his mobile face strained to splitting point by his wide smile. Clinton's coming had conferred upon the globe-trotting Palestinian president the status of head of state even though the state was not yet in existence. The airport had begun operating a month earlier but Clinton and his wife Hillary proclaimed it officially open by cutting a red ribbon at the entrance to the elegant Moroccan-style terminal building. I had flown in from Amman ahead of their visit.

That evening Arafat addressed a capacity crowd of 700 at the Shawwa Cultural Centre in Gaza City. He accused Israel of destroying Gaza's infrastructure and crushing its population; but predicted Palestine would be resurrected. He called upon the 250 members of the Palestinian National Council present in the hall to renounce by show of hands clauses in the PLO's charter calling for the destruction of Israel, thereby recognising the existence of Israel. "I hope this will close the chapter forever," Arafat stated. Only then did Clinton, the first US president to set foot on territory controlled by the Palestinians, speak to the gathering.

Among the Palestinians I met at the time was Gaza legislator Rawya Shawwa. She had refused to attend the event at the centre, built by her father who had been mayor of Gaza for 11 years and was deposed by Israel in 1982. She dismissed the Council vote and the Clinton visit as an empty show at a time Israel had refused to carry out agreements endorsed by Clinton.

The next morning I rushed to Bethlehem to catch the Clintons' visit to the city where Jesus was born. Since I did not have a pass for this event, I was kept outside the magical circle of journalist observers by US men and women in uniform suits, ties, white shirts, and little circle pins identifying them as secret service. However, a US-trained Palestinian agent sporting the same outfit and a similar pin emblazoned with the Palestinian eagle let me through the cordon after I explained I had come from Gaza to witness this ceremony.

Jerusalem, December 16th, 1998

I climbed to the broad walkway atop the wall enclosing the Old City and, shadowed by a curious Palestinian boy, made for Lion's Gate where I released a small stream of Godfrey's ashes into the wind above the Muslim cemetery.

Later in the morning I called on Dr. Madhi Abdul Hadi, an old friend we normally visited when in the holy city. "Where is your husband?" he enquired. I told him what had happened and about my mission at Lion's Gate. Godfrey roared like a lion so I thought that was the right place to go, I said. "If you had told me, I would have gathered a few people from Jerusalem and we would have accompanied you," he replied.

When I telephoned Israel Shahak to inform him of Godfrey's death, his voice broke and he put down the phone. I did not have the occasion to speak to him again before he died in 2001.

Bangalore, January 1999

I sprinkled Godfrey's ashes in a glen in Cubbon Park before crossing Mahatma Gandhi Road to speak to Hari Kumar, editor of *The Deccan Herald*, Godfrey's home-town newspaper, about the possibility of my taking over as West Asia correspondent. The paper was the sole connection we Jansens had to India. Godfrey had been working for the paper since 1984, writing for its Foreign Panorama section.

Sudha, a friend from the paper, helped me track down Godfrey's father's overgrown grave in a corner of the large Christian cemetery and hire a man to tidy the plot, the only piece of land the Jansens retained in India.

Gaza City, October 2nd, 2009

The Strip had begun to recover after Israel's winter war. Rubble had been cleared away and some rebuilding was in progress. As usual I went to see UNRWA chief of operations John Ging, the former Irish army officer who had switched to humanitarian relief. John urged EU foreign ministers to visit and see at first hand conditions in the Strip. "There is no economy in Gaza," he said. The economy had been devastated by years of blockade and hostilities. Israel's latest war had damaged the homes of 50,000 families, destroyed water and sewage systems, and decimated the few jobs available. Only small quantities of basic humanitarian supplies were allowed into Gaza. UNRWA's warehouses were bare. The agency was operating "hand to mouth" in terms of aid distribution. "Eighty-five percent of [1.5 million Gazans] depend on handouts of food from the UN to survive," he stated, "All aspects of life are a struggle. People are losing hope. The whole society is being broken down."

He warned the attitude of Gaza's people to the outside world was being transformed. "A decent, civilised people become hostile. The most vulnerable are the children, half the population. They are susceptible to the environment which gives opportunities to extremism." In March 2007, a masked gunman had fired 14 bullets at John's armoured car as he drove through Gaza City. A second attack some months later had left one Palestinian dead and several wounded.

Southern Gaza, July 1st, 2011

Luke McBain grinned as medico international's long-awaited lorry swung out of line and made for us like a horse returning to its stable after a trying journey. On board was a cargo of cement, gravel, and iron reinforcing rods for the expansion and upgrading of a community clinic at Beit Hanoun in the north of the Strip. Luke and Ahmad Alghalban from the Palestinian Medical Relief Society shook hands.

The precious cargo, the first Israel allowed to be delivered to a non-UN organisation, had made it through Israel's Kerem Shalom crossing but still had to clear the Palestinian official checking documents in a makeshift office in a white shipping container. He demanded assurances Germany's medico and the society were not bogus outfits bringing construction materials to sell on the local market. He asked for the address of the warehouse where the cargo would be stored and warned it could not be used until the required documents were delivered to him.

It had taken three hours to reach this official while Luke checked the progress of our shipment on the Israeli side. We sat with blue-suited Palestinian policemen in the dust raised by countless lorries ferrying into Gaza plastic pipes bound for UN projects, as well as Saudi fruit juice and Italian tomato paste for the market.

During the drive to Gaza City, Luke had asked his office in Ramallah in the West Bank to speed up delivery of the documents required to clear the remaining cargo to the Israeli captain in charge of "co-ordination". A second load had clearance but the third not. Papers had gone astray.

Luke observed, "We never know what's going to happen next. I'm obliged to take delivery and supervise the process [of transferring the loads] but I can't go into the terminal. "

"Co-ordination" was the magic word. But co-ordination between Palestinians and Israelis who do not speak to each other was – and remained – a difficult business. Delivery of the materials for the joint project had taken 11 months. "We did not know if we would get permits," Luke said, referring to permission to build and to transport the materials bought in Ramallah across Israel to Gaza. After achieving numerous degrees of "co-ordination," the cargo was conveyed in trucks to the West Bank enclave's border with Israel and shifted to Jerusalem-registered Palestinian lorries with Israeli plates for the journey to the crossing on the corner of the Gaza-Egyptian border with Israel.

At Kerem Shalom, the beloved sacks of cement and gravel were unloaded by forklifts in a walled Israeli cargo bay with its Gaza gate closed. Once the Israelis had withdrawn, the Gaza gate opened and a Palestinian crew entered the bay, loaded the material onto Israeli-inspected Palestinian lorries, drove it to a second cargo area, unloaded it and reloaded it onto Gaza lorries hired by the firm in Ramallah.

After the lorry was cleared at a depot in Beit Hanoun, Luke said, "I'm obligated to send a report once the material is here and to send monthly progress reports with photos of the construction site. The warehouse is guarded by an armed guy."

Baghdad, May 2003

Iraq's most celebrated sculptor Muhammad Ghani was in his battered studio. A small man with a bald crown, white tufts of hair over his ears, he kissed me on both cheeks. His atelier had been trashed and 150 of his works in the exhibit dedicated to his work in Iraq's Modern Art Museum had been stolen during the rampage against Iraq's cultural heritage that followed the fall of Baghdad. He had organised a committee to recover stolen pieces but was unable to secure funding for the effort from the US occupation administration or any other sources.

When driving around Baghdad it was impossible to ignore his public sculptures. My favourites were the fountain in Karada depicting a woman pouring hot oil into jugs where some of *Ali Baba's 40 thieves* had hidden and the sinuous statues of story teller Sheherazade and Shahrayar on Abu Nawas Street, both inspired by the *One Thousand and One Nights*. During our first meeting in

January he had told me firmly, "I don't do Saddams," statues of the president, which had previously decorated public squares.

Muhammad Ghani had left Baghdad just before the US invasion, and returned shortly after US troops seized the city, and left again a few months later to stay with his son in the Gulf. From there he went to live in Amman but mounted forays into Baghdad, as his friend Maath said, "to litter the city with sculptures. A cylinder seal, Sinbad on an island in the river." Muhammad Ghani's longing to be in Baghdad was tempered by his desire for security and the peace of mind he needed to work.

Cairo-Dubai , February 2013

Charlie called this morning to say Ma Radi had died in Abu Dhabi. Like Muhammad Ghani, Ma had remained tethered to Baghdad – although she had lived in Beirut. She travelled to "Bags" at least once a year after Iraq's three wars – with Iran and the two Bushes. She would stay with relatives and deal with family properties, mainly the houses of Nuha, Selma and Abbad and the dying date palms on their joint property. At first she insisted on making the gruelling journey by road from Beirut via Damascus, but after entering her nineties, she conceded to fly.

During her last visit she had a stroke. Since the Iraqi capital could not provide the care Ma needed, daughter-in-law Shahoob went to Baghdad to take her to Abu Dhabi where Ma could receive proper treatment. Over lunch at Shakespeare's in Jumeira in Dubai a few weeks after her death, Abbad and Shahoob spoke to me about her life and last days. While he held her hand during her final hours, he said, "She asked for a glass of wine though she wasn't supposed to have liquids. After she died, I went home, poured two glasses and drank both." Ma treated wine as a social accessory. She never drank more than half a glass.

Known to family and friends as "Ma" for at least half a century, Su'ad was born in May 1917 as the Ottoman Empire was being carved up by London and Paris, and Iraq was swallowed up by the British empire. She lived to see the post-2003 revolt against the Shia sectarian regime imposed by Washington.

Ma was an Ottoman, a woman of Georgian, Kurdish, Turkish, and Arab blood, an Iraqi patriot. Baghdadi and Beiruti. Passports, residence permits, and visas were the banes of her peripatetic existence.

Her great uncle, Mahmud Shevket Pasha was assassinated in 1913 while serving as grand vizier of the Ottoman sultan, cousin Naji Shawkat was Iraqi prime minister between 1932-33 during the British era. Distant relative Samira Shahbandar married Saddam Hussein.

Encountering at afternoon tea, the British Empire in the person of Gertrude Bell, who drew the boundaries of modern Iraq, Ma, age five, remarked, "She's so tall."

Ma's father was an "Ottoman" disciplinarian who boasted, "My girls are not allowed to cry." Her self-control was heroic, enabling her to relegate to a compartment in her brain her deep grief over the deaths from cancer of her daughters, Nuha and Selma, my contemporaries and close friends.

Educated by French nuns and at the American school in Baghdad and Beirut College for Women, Ma married at 20. Her husband Muhammad Selim al-Radi, 17 years her senior, was in charge of Iraq's agriculture during World War II. Selma was born in 1939, Nuha in '41 and Abbad in '44. In 1947, al-Radi was posted as ambassador to Tehran and in 1949 he became Iraq's first ambassador to independent India, where Ma thrived and made firm friends.

Decades after the Radis had left India, she visited these friends on her world travels. When I chanced upon her in Connaught

Place in New Delhi in 1986, she invited the three Jansens, Diana, Sophocles, Christina and Ion who had travelled with us to an Indian high society wedding that evening where, the groom arrived on a white horse and his bride was heavily laden with gold jewellery.

Following the 1958 revolution against the monarchy, the Radis returned to Baghdad and the couple became involved in the Red Crescent Society. In the mid-60s, they moved to Beirut where he died in 1971. We met through Charlie before 1973. Selma's son Kiko and Marya, both three, became friends. During the summer months, the Radis rented a house in Abey not far from Chemlan. Whenever we went to Abey for a meal, Ma cooked a feast. I contributed spinach pie.

Marya, her light brown hair in bunches on either side of her head, and Kiko, short and stocky with wonderful black curls, ran around the house, stuffing themselves with goodies. One evening Kiko came home with us to spend the night. He and Marya shared her four- poster bed, the mosquito net fortunately tucked well under the mattress since the next morning we found each in netting hammocks on either side of the historic bed.

The black iron frame topped with brass knobs had once belonged to *Sitt* Lizzie Van Dyck, the daughter of AUB founder and medical doctor Cornelius Van Dyck. He was the most honoured and beloved by the Arabs of the missionaries who had flocked to this region during the 19th century to educate the young and translate essential texts from English into Arabic. His daughter Sitt Lizzie ended her life as a border in Chemlan in a house with a large garden. We bought the bed from *Sitt* Mariam Hitti who looked after her. The bed now resides in Nicosia.

During the Lebanese civil war, Ma continued to go back and forth between Beirut and Baghdad. I often stayed with Ma and Nuha in the flat on a hillside in Beirut. Whenever Ma would return from

"Bags" she would appear with her battered suitcase and a picnic cooler filled with Iraqi delicacies: dates, *kubbeh muslawi* or thin flat bread stuffed with herbs or meat.

Her party piece was *purdah pulao*, cooked chicken, rice and minced lamb baked in a pastry shell, which she happily taught me to make. She did not keep her recipes secret but shared them freely as she did her time and her life. She loved to entertain. Even after she had a hip operation due to a fall in Baghdad after the 2003 war.

Ma had been engaging in her daily exercise when she toppled over. This consisted of walking backwards with her eyes closed. In Beirut this was safe enough on the level back balcony of the flat, but in Baghdad she did this in the garden; which sloped down to the Tigris river. Some quack had told her if she followed his instruction regularly she would have good eyesight into old age. Whether this worked or not, in her nineties Ma donned glasses only for reading.

After the hip operation Ma returned to Beirut, armed with a stick, strode to a nearby super-market, and went out for lunch and dinner with friends. Ma and her family populated Nuha's tragic-hilarious best-seller, "*Baghdad Diaries*", about the 1991 Bush war.

Like Ma, Nuha was intimately connected to Iraq. She was tied to her country by history, culture, language, and the shapes and colours of her homeland were existential elements in her ceramics, paintings and writings. But Nu was not limited to Iraqi influences. She had also absorbed the brilliant hues and images of India as a child at the Loreto Sisters' school at Simla during her father's term of service as ambassador, and imbibed Beirut's mercurial Mediterranean moods and political absurdities.

Dressed in long swishing skirts and mismatched tops, her neck hung with necklaces, rings rounding her fingers, Nu stormed around Beirut, wild curls bouncing with each stride. Shopkeepers kept an eye out for her; taxi drivers lounging outside the Mayflower and Napoleon hotels wondered where she had gone until told of her death from a rare cancer in 2004.

Nicosia-Damascus-Beirut, February 14th – March 8th, 2005

Rafiq Hariri was slain on February 14th along with 21 members of his convoy and bystanders by a massive car bomb that targeted their vehicles as they passed the derelict St. Georges hotel on the seafront in West Beirut. Syria was instantly blamed as relations between Hariri and Damascus had been strained over the previous months. President Bashar al-Assad denied involvement and condemned the assassination. International pressure was exerted to force Syria to withdraw its troops deployed in 1976 to stabilise the country.

On the 16th, I flew to Damascus. The plan had been to spend a restful holiday with friends. Instead I pursued the Hariri story by speaking to Syrian officials about the killing. I was wheeled into the office of information minister Mahdi Dakhlallah who said Damascus had been in the process of reconciling with Hariri who was expected the evening of his assassination in the Syrian capital for a meeting with deputy foreign minister Walid Muallem. Minister of expatriates Bouthaina Shaaban told me the same thing. Some in the Lebanese press reported, without corroboration, that Hariri had refused to meet Muallem.

I returned home briefly before going to Lebanon where I tracked down Bahia Hariri, sister of the murdered politician. She said she had no information about his intention to go to Damascus; but thought it likely she would have known if he had refused an overture from Syria. This would have amounted to a rebuff at a time Hariri had still not fully committed to the anti-Syrian camp, she said. She sent me a formal statement by fax: "I'm convinced that Rafiq intended, throughout his long career, to establish a supreme relationship with Syria derived from his conviction that such a relationship should be well- balanced and for the benefit of both countries." She argued that all Lebanese wanted to know the truth about Hariri's death, "the whole truth, which is the only way the Lebanese will sustain their unity."

A non-Lebanese official, who sat with Hariri at the Etoile cafe near the parliament, minutes before he was killed, said Hariri had told him he planned to go to Damascus later in the day. After the bombing, the official, who did not wish to be identified, was presented with the chair he had occupied in the cafe by the waiter who had served the two men.

On March 8th, as Syrian troops began to pull out of Lebanon, the pro-Syria camp on the domestic political scene headed by the Shia Hizbullah movement staged a massive demonstration which packed Riyadh Solh Square at the city centre and stretched across a flyover to the base of Hamra Street in West Beirut. Nora and I stood at the centre of the flyover and observed the throng that was estimated at half a million.

The anti-Syrian camp mounted its own mass rally on March 14th; it was said to surpass the earlier demonstration in size. Many of those attending were expensively dressed women and men unused to protesting but who had come from posh neighbourhoods in East Beirut to take part. The two sides took the dates of the rival rallies, as names for their respective coalitions, constantly reminding the Lebanese public and the world of Hariri's untimely death.

While Syria's withdrawal went smoothly and troops were welcomed home with flowers and elaborately staged ceremonies, the US and its allies continued to blame Assad for Hariri's death, prompting speculation that "regime change" could be a consequence of the campaign. The release by Wikileaks of a December 13th, 2006, cable from the US ambassador in Damascus to a number of recipients appeared to show "regime change" remained on Washington minds.

Although the cable said the Assad regime was in a stronger position than at the end of 2005, the diplomat suggested a number of ways the government could be weakened and undermined, demonstrating clearly this remained a long-term objective of the US. The first recipient on the list was the Department of the Treasury, the second, Israel, Tel Aviv, indicating the defence ministry, followed by the (US) National Security Council, and the secretary of state. The order of precedence was significant.

Beirut, September 20th, 2009 - Eid al-Fitr

Beyond the black and white striped lighthouse, the sea was calm, the air soft and damp. Ramadan peace had shut down the jackhammers demolishing graceful traditional houses far below the veranda of the flat. Yellow erector-set cranes hovered idly over an eight-storey concrete shell. High-rise buildings were in fashion and flats in prosperous neighbourhoods sold for $10,000 per square metre. Buildings and banks – real estate and money – were the foundations of Lebanon's economy, growing at 6-7 percent in spite of its daunting $47 billion deficit.

But the country's political class remained imprisoned in a deadlock of its own making. The crisis began in late 2006, when the Shias, the largest community, withdrew from the government. They returned in May 2008, following street fighting and Qatari mediation. June's spectacularly corrupt parliamentary election was won by the Saudi and western-backed Sunni-Christian bloc headed by Saad, the son of the assassinated prime minister. Saad Hariri was designated prime minister but failed to form a government because the Shia-Christian bloc, backed by Iran and Syria, had refused to allow him to appoint bloc ministers. Hariri resigned. Given a second chance, a weakened Hariri, whose own bloc was divided, struggled to find a formula that would succeed. Five months after the parliamentary election, Hariri presented his "unity" government to president Michel Suleiman.

Pundits blamed international and regional intervention but sensible Lebanese argued that citizens were responsible. Squabbling politicians did not appear to care if there was a government or not. Each faction and politico was interested only in taking advantage of the deadly and divisive confessional regime imposed on Lebanon by France before independence in 1943.

While boasting about their glittering sea, high green mountains, and sparkling rivers, Beirut – Paris of the Middle East, and stupendous ancient ruins at Baalbek and Tyre, the Lebanese said, "God created this paradise on earth. But then, God created the Lebanese, to offset Lebanon's natural wealth and beauty."

Since independence, the country had been deeply shaken by two civil conflicts, the first in 1958 and the second from 1975-90, a deadly and devastating 15 years. Israel had waged two all out wars on Lebanon and staged countless raids, bombing missions and occupied a strip of land on the border. Since independence two presidents, three prime ministers, a dozen politicians, and tens of thousands of citizens were slain. After every disaster, the Lebanese tried to rebuild their lives and infrastructure. But the scars left by crises and conflict were deep and long lasting. The Lebanese had come to fear peace and good governance were out of reach.

Old friend Munir Shammaa, an octogenarian physician, remarked, "Lebanon's situation is the worst since independence. We are not a nation, we have never been a nation, we will never be a nation..."

Baghdad, July 2004

Interim Iraqi president Ibrahim al-Jaafari said the ongoing trial of toppled president Saddam Hussein would be closely monitored by

Iraqis, Arabs and the international community. "People want to see what will happen to the dictator and his cronies," he stated. The trial would show the world how to deal with "people who rule by iron and force... There is a black future for any dictator."

Speaking only a few hours after Saddam Hussein had been indicted on preliminary charges before an Iraqi tribunal, Jaafari said it was normal the ex-ruler and co-defendants should be handed over by the US occupation authorities to the Iraqi interim government, "now we have sovereignty."

Ahead of the indictment, the government had proclaimed a long-anticipated law intended to put an end to violence and restore security. Under this measure, signed by interim prime minister Ayad Allawi, martial rule would be imposed for limited periods of time and at locations where violence was rife. Jaafari expressed support for this policy but made a distinction between how Iraq would handle martial law and the way other countries in the region had dealt with unrest. He argued Iraq should not become like Egypt where martial law had been in force for 23 years.

On the issue of rebuilding the Iraqi army, then only a few thousand strong, Jaafari said there had to be a break with the past if Iraq were to have an army enjoying the respect and confidence of the majority of the people. "We cannot depend on the security system of Saddam Hussein. Before, security meant the security of the dictator, now it means the security of the people. We must have another concept, another definition of security, a new system. Rebuilding the armed forces will take time and Iraq will need the help of outside powers to maintain stability while the security forces are being recruited and trained."

A senior member of the Shia fundamentalist Dawa party and medical doctor, Jaafari had resided in exile in Tehran and London and had been appointed his party's spokesman for the Iran-backed

Supreme Council for the Islamic Revolution in Iraq. Although opposed to the US war on Iraq, he returned to the country in 2003 and played key roles in US-generated political life.

Nicosia, December 30th, 2006 – Eid al-Adha

Saddam Hussein was hanged in Baghdad at six in the morning on the first day of *Eid al-Adha* (the feast of sacrifice that ends the pilgrimage) after being tried in a special court and found guilty of committing a massacre of 148 Shias in the town of Dujail in 1982 in retaliation for an assassination attempt against him mounted by Dawa party, chosen by the US as the new rulers of Iraq.

Although official video of his appearance at the site prior to execution showed him to be collected and as dignified as could be expected, once the rope was placed around his neck his guards and some of those attending the event taunted him and he replied angrily. He was reciting the "*Shehada*", the Muslim proclamation of faith, when the trapdoor opened and his neck was broken when his body dropped through the hole.

The execution divided Iraqis. Shias celebrated, Sunnis protested, Kurds complained he had been tried only on a Dawa case: he had not been sentenced for crimes committed against the Kurdish community. Many commentators said the bench constituted a "kangaroo court" and the proceedings amounted to a "show trial." Amnesty International called it "unfair" and Human Rights Watch said the trial was "flawed" and marked "a significant step away from the rule of law in Iraq."

While the trial and execution of Saddam Hussein did, indeed, show the world how to treat dictators who "rule by iron and force," his death sentence and execution were hardly the act of a democratic regime committed to the rule of law, the type of government the Bush administration had pledged to install.

Nicosia, November 3rd, 2015

Ahmad Chalabi, chief Iraqi proponent of US-enforced regime change in Iraq, died at the age of 71 in the Kadhimiya district of Baghdad where he was born into a wealthy merchant and banking family that flourished under the British-backed monarchy. He attended Baghdad College, the elite school for boys from all confessional groups in Iraq.

The Chalabis left Iraq for Britain in 1958 after the military seized power. Ahmad Chalabi studied at Seaford College in Sussex and earned his BSc degree at the Massachusetts Institute of Technology and his PhD at the University of Chicago. He taught briefly at AUB. In 1977, Chalabi founded Petra Bank in Jordan but in 1989 he was charged with embezzlement and false accounting. The bank collapsed and Chalabi fled the country in the boot of a Mercedes. He was tried in absentia and sentenced to 22 years in prison. He was later said to have been involved in the liquidation of Lebanon's Medco Bank and its Swiss branch.

Following George H.W. Bush's war to end Iraq's occupation of Kuwait and effect regime change, Chalabi fomented rebellion in the northern Kurdish region of his country and established the Iraqi National Congress (INC) which lobbied neo-conservatives in the administration of George W. Bush and the Pentagon to invade Iraq on the false pretext that Saddam Hussein possessed an arsenal of banned weapons of mass destruction. Chalabi recruited a master fabricator dubbed "curve ball", who authenticated these claims.

Enraptured by his charm and encouraged by his commitment, the administration not only took seriously his claims but also, before the occupation, touted Chalabi as a future prime minister and INC members as senior members of Iraq's new government. By recommending that the US demobilise the Iraqi army and bar ruling Baath party members from the civil service, Chalabi bore heavy responsibility for post-occupation turmoil. Put in charge of rooting out Baathists, he dismissed experienced administrators and alienated a large section of the population. He contributed to the marginalisation of Sunnis by barring 500 from standing in the 2010 parliamentary election. Sunni exclusion and isolation led to the rise of al-Qaeda in Iraq and the founding of Jabhat al-Nusra and Islamic State, offshoots which crossed the border into Syria.

He was appointed to the interim governing council formed in May 2003, a month after the fall of Baghdad, but his credibility collapsed when no weapons of mass destruction were found and the Bush administration discovered he and the INC had no following in Iraq. Nevertheless, he served as deputy prime minister and oil minister.

He was dropped by Washington when he was found to be leaking sensitive US documents to Iran. Although charged with misappropriating and circulating currency meant for destruction, he was made chief of the Shia fundamentalist government's finance committee and had assumed charge of an anti-corruption drive.

When he returned to Kadhimiya – considered holy by Shias due to a massive shrine dedicated to two Shia imams – Chalabi found himself at home although his country was, thanks in part to his efforts, divided between Shias, Sunnis, extremists on both sides, and Kurds and its existence threatened by simmering sectarian strife.

Nicosia, June 8th, 2014

Iraq's second largest city, Mosul, fell to the radical Islamic State in Iraq and Syria (ISIS) or Islamic State (IS) after four days of clashes between the city's 30,000-strong garrison and an estimated 1,500 attacking IS fighters. IS shot, burned, crucified and hanged captured Iraqi soldiers. Entire units of the "new" US trained and equipped Iraqi army led by corrupt officers, stripped off their uniforms and fled, leaving their weapons, munitions, vehicles and armour behind. Helicopters were abandoned at Mosul's international airport. Half a million civilians fled the city of two million.

The ministry of defence ordered retreating troops to assemble at Taji, just north of Baghdad, surrendering the north of Iraq to IS just as the army had ceded parts of Ramadi and Falluja to IS early in the year. The rise of al-Qaeda in Iraq, the parent of IS, had been a direct result of the policies adopted by US-backed prime minister Nuri al-Maliki, Dawa party's head put in power in 2006. He removed Sunni officers, reconstituted the Iraqi army as a Shia sectarian force and fostered Shia militias while marginalising, persecuting and criminalising Sunnis and excluding former members of the outlawed Baath party from public institutions and political life.

Although partially trained by the US, the Iraqi army was under strength due to officer claims for pay and sustenance for "ghost soldiers" whose names were registered as recruits but did not exist. Officers unfit for command, paid for commissions or were advanced on the basis of sect or political connections.

Experienced officers who had served during the Iraq-Iran war (1980-88) were shunned, driven into exile or imprisoned. Some joined al-Qaeda to fight the US occupation and, after a decade, they and other sidelined personnel became leading IS strategists. The "new" degraded Iraqi army came up against the "old," originally fashioned as a national rather than a sectarian fighting force. The old army had been provided with well trained officers loyal to the state rather than to an ambitious prime minister determined to remain in office for as long as possible by making himself the country's politico-military overlord.

Burgenstock, March 24th, 2004

The UN drive to reunite divided Cyprus kicked off in a snow-bound mountain top resort above Lake Lucerne. UN mediator Alvaro de Soto conducted preliminary shuttles between the Greek and Turkish Cypriot teams, lodged in separate hotels, with the aim of reaching an agreement on the reunification of the island. The Cyprus republic's president Tassos Papadopoulos led the Greek Cypriot delegation; Turkish Cypriot leader Rauf Denktash had refused to travel to Switzerland because he did not want to be "put in a corner". The Turkish Cypriot delegation was headed by Mehmet Ali Talat, prime minister of the northern breakaway state recognised only by Ankara. Denktash's son, foreign minister Serdar, regarded as more pragmatic than his separatist old man, was a member of the delegation.

The latest version of the repeatedly redrafted proposed deal, dubbed the "Annan Plan", after UN Secretary General Kofi Annan, was not expected to be tabled until the end of the month and was scheduled to be submitted to the two communities in separate referenda on April 24th.

Journalists were confined to another hotel down the snow-covered mountain and had to rely for briefings on politicians from both the Greek and Turkish camps who descended from on high. Serdar Denktash was one of the first to appear and complain the UN was keeping the sides apart. Others criticised the slow pace of revisions to the plan.

In spite of the efforts by UN mediators to bridge gaps between the sides, the talks remained deadlocked. Turkish Cypriots feared they could be dominated by the more populous and prosperous Greek Cypriots, who rejected limitations on their rights to reside in and own property in the northern 36 percent of the country occupied by Turkey in 1974, which was meant to be reunited, in a proposed "Swiss-style" federation.

Annan called the 200-page Foundation Agreement the best and most balanced ever on offer and a "win-win" document for both sides. However, this was clearly not the case. When copies of the secret text were faxed to the journalists' hotel, mainland Turkish journalists uncorked bottles of champagne, prompting Turkish prime minister Recep Tayyip Erdogan, who was in Burgenstock along with Greek premier Costas Karamanlis, to warn Turkish journalists against triumphalism.

The Turkish side had every reason to celebrate. When Erdogan came down the mountain to speak to us a couple of hours after the presentation of the text, just before midnight on March 31st, he said the plan met the majority of demands of the Turkish side. The most important gain was international recognition that "two different nations and two different democracies" exist on the island, a demand Ankara had been promoting for half a century.

On the flight from Zurich to Larnaca, Claire Palley, an adviser to the Greek Cypriot delegation, said he was wrong about Turkish gains. She revealed all eleven Turkish proposals on key issues were accepted, most of them at the expense of the Greek Cypriots. They were under strong pressure from Europe and the US to agree to the deal, which it was said, could facilitate Turkey's entry into the European Union. US president George W. Bush had pressured Annan to ensure the plan would be acceptable to Turkey rather than a serious framework for the reunification of Cyprus.

Following the Burgenstock caper, Bush, his British partner in the Iraq war Tony Blair, Annan and EU enlargement commissioner Gunter Verheugen stepped up efforts to convince Greek Cypriots to say "yes" in the referendum. Pressure only strengthened the "no" camp. On the external walls of tall buildings in Nicosia huge banners proclaimed simply, "*Oxi!*" When the plan was put to the people, 76 percent of Greek Cypriots voted a resounding "no," while 64 percent of Turkish Cypriots voted "yes," as anticipated.

The powerful foreign actors had failed to understand that "no" – "*oxi*" – became an honourable option among Greeks and Greek Cypriots when, on October 28th, 1940, Greek Prime Minister John Metaxas told Italian dictator Benito Mussolini "*oxi*" when he demanded the right to occupy strategic locations in Greece. Italy responded by invading Greece from Albania, launching a Greco-Italian war that Italy lost, and compelling the Germans to occupy Greece. "Oxi Day" is celebrated every year by Greeks and Greek Cypriots, who think of Metaxas whenever they are being cornered by influential international players and foreign interests.

The republic entered the EU under a cloud on May 1st. The Turkish-occupied north was considered an area outside the control of the internationally recognised government, leaving Turkish Cypriots in the lurch and trapped in a unilaterally declared de facto entity dominated by Ankara.

Damascus, November 13th, 2011

The flight was filled with Syrians going home. Immigration was quick and the hotel taxi collected me at the exit. Traffic was easy along the airport highway but thickened when we entered the city. Mr. Ali, in suit and tie, greeted me with a saucer of jasmine flowers as I registered and collected the key to my modest room.

Agatha Christie had lodged here in March 1966 in room 107, before accompanying her archaeologist husband Max Mallowan to excavations in the north. The shell of the old British embassy, with two empty gothic arches, stands across the street, and the elegant Hijaz Railway station, built by the Ottomans before World War I, is a short walk away.

Since Syria had been gripped with unrest and conflict for eight months, the eleven million tourists expected in 2011 had stayed away. Hotels had released staff; restaurants had closed. Foreign credit cards had been barred by sanctions imposed because of the government's crackdown on protests. At Bab al-Sharqi (the Eastern Gate to the Old City), the heart of the tourist area, shops were crammed with multi-flavoured olive oil soaps, silk scarves, antiques, Iranian pottery, delicate glass bowls in emerald green and deep blue, silver jewellery, and carpets. A gallery owner urged my German colleague Karin and me to have a look at his collection of paintings by Iraqi and Syrian artists.

Dr. Muhammad Habash, a progressive Muslim cleric, member of parliament and television star, spoke frankly. "The situation is complicated, [growing] more difficult. The regime believes there is a 'foreign agenda' stirring the protests and is still using the security solution to destroy the opposition... The opposition has only one target, to destroy the regime. There are two kinds of opposition [groups]: external seeking international intervention and internal rejecting intervention.

Twenty-five percent of the people are with the regime, 15 percent with the Syrian National Council [formed by Turkey and backed by the west] and 60 percent are in the silent majority. They pray to God to stop the violence."

Mu'adamiya, February 27th, 2012

Khaled, a short man with a trim beard and moustache, and greying hair, greeted us at the door of his flat in a modest building down a narrow alley in the poor western suburb just ten minutes by minibus from upmarket Damascus. Karin and I shed our shoes in the dim corridor and followed him into the salon, taking our places on a divan across from our host's chair, a depleted pack of Lucky Strikes on the low table between us.

The room, warmed by an electric bar fire, was filled with decorative pieces in well polished brass; a sewing machine was perched on top of a vitrine displaying curios.

Sucking on his first cigarette, Khaled insisted on anonymity before he began speaking, "At the beginning of the unrest, the govern ment did not distinguish between protesters and armed elements... did not reach out to the street. [The president] said he heard their words, but now we have a disaster... Now is not the time for reforms. A man does not stop to change his shirt while his house is falling around him...

"Nothing is normal. We can't compare the situation today with last year [before the troubles]. Everything is 40-50 percent more expensive and we have less income. Some shops have closed; others stay open for a few hours. We have everything but cannot afford to buy."

Mu'adamiya had suffered curfew only once during the 11 months of unrest. "On April 23rd [2011] soldiers entered, firing their weapons in the air. But they did not attack... They had a list. They went to the homes of wanted men and took them to jail... At the beginning the soldiers were looking for people getting money from abroad [to foment trouble]. Now that the army is seeking people suspected of crimes, soldiers are more severe.

"Before people had hunting guns and no idea of using them [against other people]. Now they have weapons [of war supplied] by the Emirates and Saudi Arabia. I know the channels.

"There is a rumour war. People believe a story they hear from others and pass on an exaggerated version. There is a media war. People believe what they see on television rather than what they see with their eyes.

"There was a huge demonstration at Abbaseen [near the main bus station]. Some were shot and killed. Al-Jazeera gave the names from Mu'adamiya. So I checked with the families. Everyone was alive.

"There have been several kinds of [anti-government] protests here. Sometimes 1,000-1,500 march but mostly there are 50-150 women, youngsters and children. They chant slogans that have nothing to do with them. Women go from their father's house to their husband's house. They are at home all the time, they never have contact with the regime... They don't understand what they are protesting about. Demonstrating is a new thing, a fashion.

"If I am to go to a demonstration, I must know what it's about, what's its objective. I tell them I will walk to the security headquarters across town to ask for the release of prisoners. But they don't call for such things.

"Political people have to have a programme... I cannot identify a movement that has a plan to get us back to normal life, establish a new government, create a new society, and provide for the future.

"The government, the opposition, the street, none of the three has a plan and no influence on each other. Exiles don't agree with the street... Every opposition group has its own agenda, nominees for ministries, and a foreign paymaster with its own interests."

His daughter, 13, entered shyly, shook hands, went to the balcony to pat a small white dog scratching at the door. The girl was Khaled's youngest. A daughter, 20, has married; his son, 17, is at school. Khaled, 44, a became a barber at 17-18 and prospered but closed his shop when copycats drove down prices. "Now I trade," he shrugged. "I love my profession but only cut the hair of my friends."

He said as long as external powers back competing factions, there can be no agreement on ending the conflict in Syria. "We have to stop the killing and hold a dialogue. Outsiders don't care for any

Syrian's life. People are starving while exiles offer men weapons. Sixty-seventy percent of the people in the street are absolutely against weapons.

"To reach a solution we must end outside interference... start by agreeing on a small step. We must take charge of our own affairs. Our main problem is that we are not working for ourselves while the outsiders are working for themselves. Shame on all those who have power over Syria.

"The solution is not for tomorrow, or next week. There will be many more deaths, much more destruction."

In my article on the interview I dubbed Khaled, "The sage of Mu'adamiya."

Damascus, November 26th, 2013

A random mortar fired from the countryside by insurgents punched a hole in the glowing mosaic, depicting a city of colonnaded buildings and trees, on the outer wall of the vast prayer hall of the eighth century Omayyad mosque, regarded as the fourth holiest place in the Muslim world. Fragments from a second round pierced windows and wounded the fabric of the building.

Syria's director of antiquities Maamoun Abdulkarim was furious and frightened. "What if mortars set fire to the wood and the carpets? The destruction of the mosque in Aleppo is a loss for all eternity. We must ask all sides not to fire into the Old City," he stated.

It would have been a tragedy for mankind if the National Museum, a rich repository of Syria's historical treasures, was hit, he stated. "We have evacuated everything but large stone items from the provincial museums and hid artefacts in safe places."

Mortars and bombs were not the only dangers the war posed to Syria's 12,000 year-old cultural heritage. Fighters sheltered in monuments, putting them at risk, while opportunistic and professional looters pillaged excavations. "There are 10,000 sites in Syria, so it is impossible to protect all of them," Dr. Maamoun stated.

In Dura, a third century BC town on the ancient trade routes, "there is a mafia at work," and 400 thieves "arrive each day" to strip away treasures. Fifth-millennium BC Mari in Deir el-Zor province and the "Dead Cities" of Idlib were being ravaged. The Omari mosque in Deraa in the south was excavated illegally. The Crusader fort of Krac des Chevaliers "has been occupied by the [rebel] Free Army for a year."

He continued, "Turkey opened the door for [looting] mafias as well as [foreign fundamentalists]. Turkey robbed entire factories from Aleppo. Turkey behaves as an enemy of Syria."

His department depended on local communities to protect sites. "Our message is: 'Don't put politics above our patrimony... Our cultural heritage is for all.' Local guards and functionaries play the role of intermediaries between us and their communities."

The looting of Iraq after the 2003 US invasion preoccupied him. "We are trying to raise public consciousness so the Iraqi experience is not repeated. We may not be able to eliminate losses but we can reduce losses."

He was sharply critical of the international community. "Sanctions form a block between us and [foreign archaeologists]. We receive personal e-mails [from colleagues] saying, 'Hello.' This is how we are treated after a century of scientific co-operation with Europe and the US. We need expertise to reduce losses." He dismissed claims sanctions did not target Syria's heritage. "Employees and guards hired by foreign missions are not being paid because of sanctions [against Syrian banks]. Some missions have brought cash from Beirut to pay [staff]. "

Nicosia, August 31st, 2015

On the phone from Damascus, Dr. Maamoun initially said he did not know the extent of the damage inflicted by Islamic State fanatics on the 2,000-year-old Temple of Bel in the ancient city of Palmyra. But satellite images revealed, tragically, that the temple had been brought down by massive explosions that had shaken the city. The radicals regarded the temples at Palmyra – which had been used as churches and mosques in the past – as sites of idolatrous worship. The cult had previously destroyed ancient temples, churches, and mosques in both Syria and Iraq.

The destruction of the Bel temple followed a similar assault on the smaller Baal Shamim temple constructed about the same time.

Islamic State fighters had overrun Palmyra and the adjacent modern city of Tadmor on May 21st after several days of clashes with Syrian troops. During August, the Syrian army took up positions about five kilometres from Palmyra but did not launch the planned operation to retake the area because the chief buildings in Palmyra had been mined.

Nicosia, September 2, 2015

Satellite images revealed the destruction of the Bel temple shortly before US president Barack Obama was due to receive Saudi King Salman, a key player in the conflict in Syria. The Saudi religious establishment, the monarchy's partner, preaches strict adherence to the 18th century ideology of Muhammad ibn Abdel Wahhab, who launched a puritan revivalist movement in the central region of the Arabian peninsula and formed an alliance with tribal leader Muhammad ibn Saud. His successors not only maintained, but, deepened the relationship and proclaimed "Wahhabism" the official version of Islam.

Since the 1970s, Saudi Arabia spent more than $100 billion exporting Wahhabism to the worldwide Muslim *Umma* by funding mosques and madrasses, providing preachers and indoctrinating Muslims working in Saudi Arabia and the Gulf countries. The campaign had been highly successful. Wahhabism has spread across the Muslim world and has fostered the rise of al-Qaeda type movements and affiliates in the Middle East.

Islamic State takes its cue from the Saudis who behead those convicted of capital crimes and have not only destroyed pre-Islamic sites but also those associated with the early days of Islam, practices of the Islamic State cult has followed in Syria and Iraq.

Homs, June 4th, 2014

For a few weeks in 2011, Homs was the "crucible of the revolution," inspired by the glorious uprising in Egypt's Tahrir Square, but revolutionaries and their slogans were soon eclipsed by armed men who were overtaken by radical jihadis with their own agendas. When I was last here on Palm Sunday, the Old City was still in the hands of a mix of insurgents buttressed by elements of al-Qaeda's Jabhat al-Nusra. They had been persuaded to evacuate and after weeks of three-sided dickering involving the UN, the insurgents, and the government and were ferried out on buses to a town held by anti-government forces north of Homs. The jihadis and their colleagues left behind a wasteland.

Nevertheless, a few short weeks after their evacuation, the Old City was preparing for the ground for reconstruction. The Old Clock Tower, a landmark consisting of clock faces fixed to a lamppost, had the clocks replaced. They were keeping track of hours, days and weeks until the Old City was rebuilt. The black and white New Clock Tower, battered but standing, had survived in a wide square surrounded by ruins. The hot air bore the heavy smell of scorched concrete.

A team of municipal workers was trying to repair an electricity transformer serving the area. Engineer Farouk Hishmeh, hat planted firmly on his head to ward off the sun, said, "Twenty percent is restored. We have ten teams and ten workshops here. It will take a year to do the job."

Rubble had been piled on the right side of the narrow streets so cars could drive on the left. Soldiers and national guardsmen kept watch. Few people were about, some assessing damage to their homes and shops. Others just curious. Churches and mosques had received equal treatment by the fighters holed up in the Old City. Father Zahari Khazal clad in a spotless black soutane, supervised workers repairing the vengeful damage inflicted on May 7th on one of the oldest churches in Christendom, the church of the Belt of the Virgin Mary, built 59 years after the crucifixion of Jesus. Fortunately, the precious relic had been hidden by parishioners.

Departing fighters had burnt bibles and furniture, blackening the interior walls of the church and cracking marble floor tiles. "A Syrian commander burned the churches, on orders from outside," Father Zahari said. "No outsiders will help restore the church. The Syriac community will do it." He was a member of the committee that negotiated the withdrawal of the fighters from the Old City and escorted 900 fighters to their destination when they had departed a month earlier.

The 19th century Khaled Ibn Walid mosque, built by Ottoman Sultan Abdel Hamid on the site of a 7th century mosque had been sandbagged and used by jihads as a firing position. Battle scarred, looted even to the taps on the marble fountain providing water for washing before prayers, the mosque remained closed, its congregation driven from the Old City.

12

SANCTUARY

Baghdad, January or February 1992

Godfrey and I went to see our old friend Jabra at his house on Princess Street in the Mansour diplomatic quarter. It was a small house full of books and papers that crowded in on visitors. A house where Jabra wrote reviews of Arab poetry, novels, films, music and art, and where he had translated Shakespeare and T.S. Eliot into Arabic. A house furnished with the paintings of Shaker Hassan, one of Iraq's greatest and most innovative artists, and sculptures of Muhammad Ghani. A house where Jabra and his wife Lamiya raised their two boys.

Jabra was someone we had known forever. He used to come to Lebanon during Baghdad's long hot summers, to spend time in Beirut or in Souk al-Gharb, the town next to Chemlan, our mountain village. He invited me for tea during my first visit to Baghdad in February 1967 when I was scouting for contributors for *Middle East Forum*. Jabra and Lamiya met me at the Mansour club where she complained repeatedly that it was not the more snobbish Alwiyah Club located in the city centre. She also quizzed me closely about Jabra's friends in Beirut: Walid, Tawfiq, the two Yusifs, and others. What were they like? A large woman in a shapeless dress, Lamiya had never been to Beirut. During Jabra's frequent travels, she remained in Baghdad, the city that had given him asylum and anchored him.

When I returned to Beirut, Jabra's friends interrogated me about the mysterious Lamiya. She eventually paid a visit to Beirut, satisfying both sides' curiosity.

Theirs had been a great romance. He was a Cambridge graduate, teacher of English, a Christian, a Palestinian from Bethlehem; she a Muslim, daughter of a distinguished family that opposed the match. Jabra became a Muslim, married Lamiya and made his name as an artist while making his living working for the glossy Iraq Petroleum magazine; Lamiya briefly taught English at the university but reverted to bridge, her vocation.

Jabra was worn down by sanctions, the war and power outages. One of his sons had been in a foxhole on the Kuwait frontier when heavy US bombing took place during the 1991 war. Out of the storm of dust thrown up by the explosions, pages from Jabra's writings blew into the young man's sand sanctuary, falling on his face. "He knew then he would survive," Jabra said, seeing this as a sign or, perhaps, convinced of the magical power of literature. Many in his son's unit had been killed. He and other survivors walked back into Iraq. Jabra took us to an exhibition of young Iraqi painters at an atelier in Mansour. The new generation was, we could see, well on the way to proving, once again, Iraqis were the best of the Arabs in arts.

Nicosia, June 27th, 1993-December 11th, 1994

Iraqi painter Leila al-Attar, her husband and their housekeeper were killed and their daughter blinded in one eye by a US missile strike on their home across the street from Jabra's house.

I rang Jabra to make certain he had survived. He was in shock, his voice almost a whisper. "Why hit here? Why hit here?" he asked repeatedly. Leila, who was also director of the Iraqi National

Art Museum, had been a close friend and colleague in Iraq's still flourishing art world.

Bill Clinton had unleashed 23 cruise missiles at Baghdad in retaliation for an alleged mid-April Iraqi plot to kill former US president George H.W. Bush during a visit to Kuwait. The US claimed the missile that hit Mansour had been meant for an Iraqi intelligence headquarters; the nine innocent civilians killed were dispensable, "collateral" victims. The missile had, reportedly, been incorrectly programmed.

Jabra died after a car crash 18 months after the missile strike on Princess Street. On April 4th, 2010, a car bomb destroyed Jabra's house, burned and shredded his collections of books and paintings, smashed his sculptures, and killed 17 people. The nearby Egyptian embassy was thought to be the target this time.

Gaza, September 2003 and August 2005

Hassan had not left Gaza for more than a decade. In 1995 he applied to the Israelis for a pass to make the Hajj, but was refused. He kept to Gaza City, busy with his work and his garden. "I find gardening very satisfying," he said over lunch of *maqluba* – lamb, cauliflower and rice – at his family's top floor flat in a tall building on Omar Mukhtar Street.

I found their second son, Karim, in bed, cheerful, cosseted by his family. He had been seriously wounded in an Israeli strike targeting Hamas militants travelling in a car near their building. A shrapnel fragment had lodged at the base of his skull two millimetres from his spine, a larger piece had broken a finger and another had sliced a piece of bone from his leg.

When I visited the Strip nearly two years later, Hassan took me to his garden, a walled enclosure planted with fruit trees and grape vines, marrows, eggplant and melons. His wife, Maha, seven children, and her parents were already there, sitting on chairs in the shelter of a massive vine. While Maha brewed coffee, Hassan washed a bowl of freshly picked grapes in sweet well water. He said he had given up discussing politics - "too dangerous."

He was fortunate. He had a profession and a plot of land. By focusing on the garden, he found some respite from the constant pressures building up in the pressure cooker that was – and is – Gaza. Unable to sit at home doing nothing, many Gazans have revived small family plots that had lain fallow for years. These gardens feed large Palestinian families and provide some income for those who sell their produce.

Sayafa, January 26th, 2009

Salah al-Ghoul had dreamt of living peacefully on a farm on the Gaza Strip's northern border with Israel after the 2005 withdrawal of its settlers and soldiers. He began building a modern duplex mansion that September, investing his life's savings of $770,000 in the house and nearby farm buildings. He felt safe, secure on home ground among clansmen. When the Israeli onslaught began at the end of December 2008, 120 members of his extended family were confined to their homes.

Salah's wife, two sons and five daughters had gone to stay in Gaza City but his son, Muhammad, 17, and a cousin, Akram, had remained at the Sayafa house to help tend the cattle, camels, and poultry. At four fifteen on the afternoon of January 3rd, Salah and a labourer were in a shed feeding the calves when the house disappeared in a cloud of smoke and dust. The two men covered their faces and hurried towards the house but found only rubble and the dismembered bodies of the two youths.

"We had coordination with the Israeli military. My cousin was in constant contact with the local commander. The Israelis watch everything that goes on in this area. They even know which birds are nesting in which trees. They also know us and are aware there were no fighters here."

En route to his farm, we had driven through a devastated landscape. Roads had been erased, land had been ploughed by tanks, houses facing the sea had been levelled to clear the route taken by Israeli armour and troops moving north. The American International School had been flattened. Million dollar villas belonging to Fatah officials had been reduced to rubble.

As we stepped out of Salah's battered vehicle, he pointed out an Israeli watchtower 500 metres from his front gate. In the distance was the smoking chimney of the power plant in the Israeli coastal city of Ashkelon. We climbed over the gate, lying across the entrance to the garden, scrambled over chunks of concrete and broken tiles, glanced at the shallow crater next to a blue tiled ornamental pool. The sweet smell of death hung in the air. In the shed lay six bloated corpses of cows and the ragged form of a baby camel, the bones of its front legs exposed. Feathers from two dead ducks were scattered on the ground.

When Salah's cousin heard the explosion and seen the smoke, he rang an Israeli Druze officer to ask for clearance for a rescue mission. The jeep, driven by the cousin's son, was hit by two shells, breaking the young man's leg and puncturing his body with shrapnel. A Red Cross ambulance was fired upon when it tried to reach him.

A few hours later, Israeli television showed photographs of the F-16 strike on the house taken by cameras in the nose of the plane. Salah planned to lodge legal proceedings against Israel.

Jerusalem, April 15th, 2012

Khan al-Zeit street was packed with people, festooned with fairy lights and bunting. Shops offered glowing oranges and apples and light delicate pastries stuffed with nuts and dates nestling in plastic boxes. We brushed past silk scarves and delicately embroidered Palestinian dresses hanging on wooden doors of shops and glimpsed gleaming golden necklaces in a window display designed to entice wealthy pilgrims to make generous presents during the season of rebirth and renewal.

We shouldered through the crowd making for the Greek Orthodox service in the body of the Church of the Holy Sepulchre, shared by this denomination with Roman Catholics, Armenian Orthodox, Copts and Syriacs. Just beyond the entrance to the Via Dolorosa, where Jesus bore his cross to Calvary, we ascended to the roof of the vast church up a flight of steps and a ramp in a tight press of patient, quiet Ethiopians. Abi caged a slender candle off a neighbour and handed it to me. "For later". No one minded he had invited three all too obvious Europeans to attend the mass. The Greeks and Armenians required impossible-to-obtain tickets to attend their services but not the Ethiopians.

On the other side of a metal fence erected by the Israeli police to divide the narrow passage, young men, who had made an *acte de presence* at the mass, were descending to cafes to while away the solemn hours before the joyful resurrection ceremonies.

As Ethiopian priests conducted the service in a rectangular tent made of clear flowered plastic erected on the roof we followed Michael, a tall fair German Lutheran pastor, up a rough flight of stairs to a plateau dubbed the "garden". Between the trunks of spare, spiky pines we had a panoramic view of the scene. Directly across from where we stood was the dome over the central hall of the vast church, lamps glowing behind windows framed in stained glass.

Below was a shifting, swaying mass of standing pilgrims, many wrapped in white gauze shawls. Women with their heads covered wore gowns edged in bright strips of cloth. Others sat on carpets laid against the wall of the small chapel in the centre of the courtyard, or perched on folding chairs. The priest sang the interactive service in Amharic, the congregation replied with required phrases. Cameras flashed, people spoke on mobile phones to relatives in Ethiopia, Canada and Germany. "Guess where I am", was a common question.

As midnight approached, the throng bowed and held its breath until the bells began to clash and clang, filling the city with their raucous voices. We descended to the courtyard where a brocade umbrella bobbed out of the tent, sheltering a priest carrying a large, flat, Abi said, handwritten Bible which pilgrims flocked to touch lip and chin. The devout that entered the tent to take communion exited with their mouths covered with their hands to seal in the sacrament. Young men hustled in tables and planted bowls of steaming sauces and plates of food for pilgrims who had fasted since Good Friday.

Wearied by the long spectacle, we departed at two in the morning, before the dancing began. On the wick of my candle I caught a flame from a neighbour before we reached the steps to the street. We bought chilled bottled of water from a Palestinian youth before making our way along Khan al-Zeit, its shops sung in sleep, to Damascus Gate where an intrepid hawker stood guard over his stock of white sports shoes.

Rada, June 2005

Archaeologists, diplomats, and journalists converged on this dour, dusty town in central Yemen to celebrate the restoration of one of the country's most splendid monuments, the 16thcentury Amiriya palace and its unique painted mosque. The three-storey princely palace, crowned with domes and graced by Arab arches, shimmered like a great white wedding cake amid Rada's chocolate brown mud-brick buildings. Built by Sultan Amir ibn Abdel Wahhab, the final ruler of the Tahirid dynasty that ruled between 1454 and 1517, the Amiriya is one of the largest of Yemen's many monuments and the most ornate.

The foundation stone, which bears the sultan's name, was laid in September 1504. The construction took five years, said Selma, who took 23 years to "bring it back to what it was".

Selma had fallen in love with the Amiriya 25 years earlier while working for a Dutch aid project involving the creation of a national museum in Sanaa, Yemen's capital. She convinced the Dutch – also engaged in urban and agricultural development in Rada – to preserve the long neglected Amiriya, then in an appalling state.

In need of financial aid and technical expertise to rescue the palace, the Yemeni government appealed to UNESCO which dispatched experts who estimated that the bill would be $5 million. This estimation was too high, argued senior Yemeni politician Abdel Karim Iriyani. "We can do it the Yemeni way," he contended, by using traditional materials and craftsmen. The Dutch agreed and signed a joint-financing agreement in April 1982. The gentle and gentlemanly Iriyani commanded Selma, an Iraqi woman who did not take kindly to commands, "Go to Rada and become a builder."

She began by recruiting the Rada region's foremost stonemason, *Usta* (Master) 'Izzi Muhammad Gas'a, a devout man in his late sixties who accepted half pay because the Amiriya contained a mosque and had served as a *madrassa* (religious school). Work began that November with the clearing out of decades of rubbish inside and around the Amiriya. In March 1983, Gas'a began shoring up the foundations and the buckled and crumbling outer walls. A second *usta*, his cousin, Abdullah Rizk, worked on the interior of the first floor where Selma believed she had discovered the world's first shower stalls.

Although the workers were from Rada, providing employment in this poor town of the region's poorest country, deeply conservative townspeople resented what they considered to be external intervention in their affairs and, in particular, the leading role played by a "foreign" woman. Selma wore ankle length skirts, shirts with long sleeves, and a small Omani-style turban, but she refused to submit to a face veil or agree to remain in the background. Selma behaved as Selma had always behaved: assertively and in-charge.

Once the consolidation of the fabric of the building was done, Selma and her Yemeni counterpart Yehya Nasiri, had to recreate *qadad*, a water-proofing plaster used from the eighth century BC in Yemen to clad the exteriors of grand houses and monuments. The effort was successful only because *qadad* had been employed until the 1970s, before being gradually replaced by cement. *Usta* 'Izzi managed by trial and error to replicate the specialised *qadad* mixtures required by every stage of the reconstruction process.

Qadad is a versatile substance made of freshly fired lime soaked in water and mixed with fine sand, pebbles, or volcanic ash. Applied to stone or baked brick surfaces, *qadad* hardens into cladding as fine as polished marble; thinned *qadad* can be used to fill cracks and fissures. Since the *qadad* used by the Amiriya's original builders had lasted for 500 years, Selma quipped, "We hope our *qadad* will last another 500 years."

Selma spent 15 years cleaning and restoring the stucco decorating the prayer niche and walls of the small mosque. She began scraping away accumulated bird droppings and dirt with dental tools but found metal instruments too harsh. She decided to get help. One day in 1998, she strode unannounced into the office in Rome of the *Centro de Conservazione Archeologica* and proposed its highly qualified experts restore the mosque's badly damaged painted surfaces. Roberto Nardi and his colleagues – who had worked on the Roman forum and Capitoline Museum – not only agreed but also trained Yemenis to maintain the Amiriya and carry out such work elsewhere.

While she showed off the miracle of the tiny mosque, Selma pointed to the flowing floral patterns overhead. The 16th century craftsmen, she said, "Used Indian motifs, probably taken from Kashmir shawls. The workers who built the Amiriya put all of their skills into this building. It's a record of their art. They knew the Tahirid era was coming to an end. Tribesmen were attacking."

One Yemeni worker told Selma, "I can remember when you came to Yemen, Rada was a ruin and you were very young." Another Yemeni said to Ma Radi, "Selma has only one defect. She's not a man." When Ma asked if Selma were a man, he responded, "She'd be our president."

Washington-New York City, May 2006

War and Cultural Heritage, Cyprus After the 1976 Turkish Invasion, published by the Modern Greek Studies Programme at the University of Minnesota in late 2005, took me to the US capital to speak at the National Press Club and to Congressional aides at a lunch meeting in the offices of the House of Representatives. Afterwards I went by train to New York City, where I addressed a gathering sponsored by the Onassis Foundation.

In New York I stayed with Selma and her husband Qais in their Columbia University flat. On the afternoon I arrived, the Aga Khan's son Hussein turned up unexpectedly. The topic of conversation was the presumed site of the 2007 Aga Khan Award for Architecture. Selma's Amiriya was expected to be one of the winners. Kuala Lumpur had, apparently, been chosen, Hussein said. None of us were enthusiastic.

The next morning, Selma and I went for a walk round her neighbourhood, pausing at the outset at a newspaper kiosk to reserve a copy of the *International Herald Tribune*, which Selma said was usually sold out before she claimed one. While we followed Selma's normal 45-minute route past shops, cafes, and office blocks, she kept fussing about the paper, complaining that we would not find it on our way back to the flat. I had noticed in Yemen, nearly a year earlier that her short-term memory was failing. There had been considerable deterioration since then and Qais and her friends worried that her memory could go before the award ceremony. Somehow Selma's mind hung on.

Kuala Lumpur, September 2007

Many Radis and friends flew across the world to see Selma receive the award. Sonny and Gita from New York, Ma Radi from Beirut, Abdel Karim al-Iriyani from Yemen, Hamida (nicknamed "Handybags" by the Radis) and her husband from Pakistan. Contrary to our prejudiced prediction, Kuala Lumpur was grand, a relief from politics, work stress, a balm to the spirit.

Ma and I went on a bus tour of the city, shunned by Selma, Qais and the rest of our group as too touristy. Our guide was one of Malaysia's most prominent architects who took us to the city's main sites and described their unique features. Intrepid Ma, nearing ninety, was determined to miss nothing. With her stick in a firm grip, she climbed the formidable steps to the plaza of Majed Negara, the National Mosque, where the policewoman inside the door of the prayer hall tried to put us off. "Only Muslims," she said. "I'm a hajji," I replied and Ma chimed in, "I'm an *Omari*," a person who has made the "little pilgrimage" to Mecca out of Hajj season. We later drove through the Chinese residential quarter marvelling at elegant 19th century homes, each with distinctive doors and trim.

That night Selma's friends dined at a fantastic open air Hakka restaurant not far from our hotel and finished off our busy day by repairing to its roof terrace to sip red wine as fine mist curtained the nearby banded silver Petronas Towers.

Women in saris and long silk dresses and men in dark suits skirted the green park, made their way past the twin towers, mall, and convention centre to the philharmonic hall, ascended the curving staircase and took seats in the auditorium to attend the Aga Khan Award ceremonies. The Silk Road Ensemble, a group formed by the Aga Khan to revive traditional music of Central Asia, opened the gathering with a lilting, then lolloping composition for strings and drum.

Nine projects in eight Asian, African and European countries had been chosen for the highly coveted award, conferred by the Aga Khan, Karim al-Husseini, descendant of the Prophet Muhammad and 49th imam of the Shia Ismaili sect who was celebrating the golden jubilee of his imamate.

On the stage sat architects, engineers, sociologists, patrons and clients, a mud-brick master builder, past and present mayors of the divided Cypriot capital, Nicosia, and Selma and her Yemeni colleague Yehya. Yemen's Amiriya and the medieval high-rise mud-brick city of Shibam, represented the rescue of past glories from collapse due to neglect and oblivion.

Samir Kassir Square in central Beirut, the main market in Koudougou, Burkina Faso, and a school in Rudrapur, Bangladesh, embodied the present. The University of Technology Petronas, 300 kilometres from Kuala Lumpur, the Moulmein Rise Residential Tower in Singapore, and the Dutch embassy in Addis Ababa were chosen to stand for the future. Rehabilitation of the Old City of Nicosia under a master plan implemented by Greek and Turkish Cypriots was the final choice.

After the presentations in the hall outside the auditorium, Selma glowed with pleasure while receiving congratulations, her mind free of Alzheimer doubt and confusion as she hugged the Aga Khan.

Nicosia, Christmas 2013

I delivered my usual homemade Christmas cake and potted plant, a cyclamen this time, to Nitsa in remembrance of Kyria Olympia, who had cleaned my house for 30 years, retired at 82 and died in her nineties. She was a "lady" in every sense of the word, upright, dignified, respected.

Nitsa sent me home with a plate filled with traditional Cypriot Christmas biscuits and a long leaf cactus in a narrow, cut glass vase. When I tried to resist the plant, Nitsa pressed. "You must take it, in honour of Olympia. I will put your plant on her grave." Cyclamen is Cyprus' national flower.

Kyria Olympia had worked as a home help in my neighbourhood for years before we arrived. By some miracle she and her shepherd husband, Michalis Michael, a tiny bent man who wore traditional Cypriot "*vrakas*," knee length baggy trousers, and boots, had succeeded in building dowry houses for her daughters before constructing a home for themselves in the village of Yerolakkos, just north of Nicosia.

In addition to being a "lady," Olympia was a survivor. One day over coffee in my sitting room, Olympia, short rotund, a scarf round her head, told me and another of her clients the story of her family's escape when Turkish paratroops landed early on the morning of July 20th, 1974. Explosions woke the villagers who saw armed men floating from the sky on parachutes. Michalis persuaded his wife and children to get onto the back of a lorry and drive to the mountain village of Kakopetria, where he thought they would be safe. He stayed behind to gather some of his goats and sheep and, riding a horse or donkey, herded the animals to the village of Kokkinotrimithia where he awaited developments. Determined to go home, he sat for 20 years on the dividing line with his livestock, his only capital. He and Olympia lived in a chicken coop in the village, half an hour's bus ride from Nicosia's centre.

After the 1977 meeting between president Makarios and Turkish Cypriot leader Rauf Denktash, Olympia packed her bags believing she would go home soon. Talks between the two leaders did not produce a breakthrough. Olympia unpacked. Whenever there was a hopeful sign on the political front, Olympia would ask us, "Should I pack?" The journey home never came.

She moved from the chicken coop to a decent house next to her son Costas and his family in a refugee estate on the edge of Nicosia. Her husband stayed put, with his dwindling flock. Family members drove to the village to provide him with food and clean clothing until they decided enough was enough. They sold the animals and shifted him to the house. But he was restless, unemployed. After some time, he fell and died at a great age, still yearning for his native village. Longing even for his place on the line where he could just about see the village on a clear day. The massive church near the family's new home was packed for his funeral with refugees who honoured his tenacity, his determination to defeat de facto partition of his homeland.

Kyria Olympia attended Marya's wedding; I the weddings of two of her grandsons, Michalis and Melios. During Melios' reception, guests bent and kissed her hand while she sat just inside the entrance to the hall. Olympia introduced me to her family and friends, proud of her job as a cleaner.

As I said, Olympia was a lady, her labour did not define or demean her. After she retired, I used to visit her every Christmas and Easter, exchange family news, show her photos of Marya, Brian and their daughter, Elise. In hospital after giving birth to Elise, Marya had a call from Olympia. I was travelling when she died and missed her funeral but called on the family to condole. The cactus is not an apt representative. Olympia was a soft, gentle person as well as a lady.

13

LIBERATION

Baghdad-al-Qaqa, January 18th, 2003

My driver and I collected Andre Brie, a German socialist member of the European Parliament, early in the morning and proceeded to UN headquarters at the Canal hotel on Palestine Street. We paused on the roadside, engine gunning, until a dozen white four-wheel drive vehicles shot out of the parking lot, followed by a posse of press ignorant of the destination. We sped through traffic, dodging over-loaded lorries, family cars, and battered jeeps, until we turned off the highway to Hillah and zoomed through moonscape where salt lay on the surface of the dead land. Our destination was al-Qaqa's sprawling munitions and explosives factory. The team of inspectors, 32-strong I later learned, were ushered into the walled complex while the media were told to stay outside. We waited for six tedious hours while the inspectors meticulously examined the entire site and collected samples, the liaison officer told journalists who had hung on until the bitter end. This was the inspectors' fourteenth visit to the site.

We had a good opportunity to form a sense of the place while we stood in front of its massive yellow brick gates, fashioned in the style of ancient Babylon. There was almost no security. Vehicles came and went. When the shift changed, employees' identities were cursorily checked. Some carried bags of food into the facility.

Reddish yellow smoke poured from a plant within the grounds throughout our stay. We were diverted by range-firing of flares at the centre of the vast complex. A previous visitor to nuclear plants elsewhere, Brie remarked this was certainly not a nuclear facility – or one manufacturing weapons of mass destruction. Iraq's alleged possession of such weaponry was cited as the US pretext for waging war on the country.

Once the inspectors had left, we were given a brief tour. Facilities in use stood beside those bombed during the 1991 US-led war and a December 1998 US attack. We were taken to a field of bombs – small red bombs, medium-sized green bombs, and large silver bombs. "All empty, these have been here since 1989," stated the plant director. "These are bombs meant to be dropped from planes. We make all kinds of munitions here. We make sulphuric and nitric acid, nitro glycerine and other explosives. "

Baghdad, January 19th, 2003

The chiefs of the UN inspection effort, Hans Blix and Muhammad ElBaradei arrived at noon and left 24 hours later after reaching a 10-point agreement with the Iraqi government on facilitating and expediting operations. Iraq had accepted their requirements but balked over fresh demands imposed on the UN by the Bush administration, such as spy plane over-flights and sending Iraqi scientists for interviews outside the country. Blix in New York and ElBaradei in Vienna revealed they had the feeling that the US and Britain were determined to go to war, pretext or no pretext. A source within the inspectorate said in an e-mail made available to me that the inspectors had "seen a lot, resolved many issues, and [obtained] reasonably good cooperation" from the Iraqi government. He denied US allegations the Iraqis had been uncooperative. He said the technical report on Iraq's nuclear capabilities, which he had written, had been finished in mid-January and transmitted to Blix and ElBaradei. The report said Iraq was not involved in any prohibited nuclear weapons activities but he took the view that his assessment would be ignored by the hawks in Washington and London.

Baghdad, January 25th, 2003

Baghdadis went about their normal daily routines while they waited for another war they did not want. They had suffered bombing during the Iraq-Iran war of 1980-88 and privation since the punitive US-imposed sanctions regime following Saddam Hussein's 1990 occupation of Kuwait as well as the destruction wreaked by George H.W.Bush's 1991 war to drive Iraq from the emirate.

Beit al-Iraqi had survived the last turbulent years of the 20th century. The mansion had been built on the mudflats along the Tigris river during the waning years of the Ottoman Empire, withstood British rule, World War II, the 1958 revolution and subsequent upheavals. Amal Khedeiry who grew up in a similar house two doors down the street, was afraid *Beit al-Iraqi* would not survive fresh conflict.

Beit al-Iraqi means the "Iraqi House", but the house was not typical of all Baghdad. Its architecture and style belonged to the Rasafa quarter on the eastern side of the river and to its bank.

Built by Amal's uncle, the house followed Arab tradition by presenting a blank face to the world. Her father and three brothers had constructed four spacious houses here so their families could move out of their closely built town houses and enjoy the cool breeze from the river during Baghdad's stifling summer months. "They didn't have architects then. The owners of the land told the masons and carpenters what to do and the houses went up."

For generations, the Khedeirys had lived near the 12th century mosque erected by the jurist Shaikh Abdel Qadir Gailani and renovated and expanded in the 16th century by the Ottoman Caliph Suleiman the Magnificent. Like so many other Iraqi families, the Khedeirys and their homes were intimately tied to the glories of their country's past. Baghdadis spoke of the Abbasid caliphs, who made the city the centre of the civilised world, as if they had ruled yesterday. Furthermore, Iraqis felt themselves to be Iraqi, like Amal whose paternal grandmother was Kurdish and maternal grandmother Turkish.

The city's buildings and their embellishments were a blend of Mesopotamian and Islamic. Bronze tableaux in the squares enacted Assyrian conquests and the *Tales of the Thousand and One Nights.*

"My father moved here permanently after he married my mother." Her mother was Syrian. He married late. "He fought the British and was condemned to death by General Maude," she said, but was sent into exile in India for two years. He didn't interfere in politics but he didn't like foreigners stepping into his country." She made a clear distinction between shunning domestic politics and resisting foreign occupation. One did not argue with an Iraqi *hala* (beauty). Iraqi beauties do not suffer opposition, whether westernised, like Amal, or traditional, enfolded in black abayas. Covered women are not cowed women.

Beit al-Iraqi began to play a key role in the creative life of Iraq, the most artistic of all Arab countries, during World War II when British archaeologist Seton Lloyd lived there. "He helped to establish the Iraq Museum. His wife was a sculptress who taught our greatest sculptors, Jawad Selim and Muhammad Ghani," stated Amal.

She studied in England and Switzerland, married and lived for some years in Lebanon. In the mid-1980s she decided to renovate *Beit al-Iraqi's* rooms with Rashid street frontage. "When the work was done they were so beautiful I couldn't rent them. Since I always loved crafts I decided to make a centre. I opened *Beit al-Iraqi* in

1987. I used to travel all over the country and go to people's homes where they did their work. There was no society for craftsmen and women, their skills were deteriorating. I set up a loom and invited someone to weave. I asked people to come and bring their work.

"We also established a cultural centre here. We began courses in calligraphy and painting on glass. We had summer classes in painting for children and lectures throughout the year. We established societies for architects interested in restoration of old buildings and collectors of stamps and old currencies."

But Amal's boundless creative energies were stymied and sapped by the 1991 war. During its first days, *Beit al-Iraqi* was badly damaged when US warplanes bombed the Jumhurriyah bridge. The outer wall was blown in, the roof of one room collapsed and the second storey was destroyed. "By the time we finished rebuilding this floor, we could do no more. Everything was so difficult... Every time we try to do something, we are threatened, so we stop," she said.

Her house in north Baghdad was also damaged badly. "I spent a whole year without glass in my windows and doors. It was so cold at night that I went to Nuha because she has a chimney. During the time we didn't have glass for the windows, cats and dogs came in the house, but there was no stealing. Things are different now. People are very poor because of sanctions. We're not afraid of bombs, we're afraid that there will be no one to keep order [after a new war]. This government has a hold on the country, the people who may come here to rule [may] not understand how to control Iraq."

Amal had made no preparations for war. "I haven't packed up anything, rolled the rugs or bought supplies. Last time I got ready ahead of time. But there's no one to help now. Many houses near mine are empty. People have died or gone abroad." She still clung to the hope that there would be no war.

Baghdad, January 27th, 2003

As opposition to the war grew, international figures came to Baghdad to consult with the government on how best to ward off Bush's military adventure, many rightly predicted would have disastrous results. Among the visitors were Irish Labour party spokesman Michael D. Higgins, Senator Michael Kitt, and Foreign Affairs Committee secretary Padraig Allen, who had arrived in Baghdad on the 23rd.

The Irish delegation met Iraq's deputy prime minister Tareq Aziz in his sumptuous office in a monumental building in Baghdad. The Irish radio correspondent and I were permitted to tag along on the understanding that if Aziz asked us to leave we would comply. He not only allowed us to stay; but offered us coffee and the opportunity to ask questions at the end of the meeting. Michael D. urged Iraq to agree to a mission of eminent persons – perhaps including Nelson Mandela and Jimmy Carter – which would attempt to avert war. He said since the US and Britain were "losing ground in the public mind," this could be built upon. Priority must be given to preventing war and achieving disarmament, stated Michael D. Tareq Aziz said such a mission would be welcome in Baghdad. Unfortunately, it was not attempted.

I was fortunate. During my ten-day stay in Baghdad I was one of the few people who could both send and receive e-mails. Following a flurry of e-mails sent in December by Western officials to Iraqi military officers, urging them to turn against or overthrow Saddam Hussein, Baghdad had shut down incoming e-mails. My *Irish Times* e-mail was one of those affected but not my Cypriot Orthodox Church e-mail. It had been overlooked by the censors. This was considered a blessing by a Christian technician at the internet centre at the Rashid hotel. The person who passed on to me the e-mail from the man in the inspectorate was Imad Khadduri, an Iraqi scientist who had worked in the nuclear programme until the summer of 1991 when Saddam Hussein had ordered it to be dismantled.

New York, February 5th, 2003

US Secretary of State Colin Powell told the Security Council the inspectors' effort to avert was a forlorn hope. Pre-empting reports to the Council by the UN weapons teams, he falsely claimed Iraq possessed prohibited weapons of mass destruction and harboured a terrorist group headed by Abu Musab al-Zarqawi, an al-Qaeda operative. Although France, Germany, and Russia were sceptical, Bush had not massed troops in the region to pull them out without a fight.

Powell later expressed regret over that speech but by then it was too late.

Amman, March 2003

I did not go to Iraq during the war. While I was in Baghdad, a colleague was in Amman getting a visa for Iraq. I was dispatched to Amman where I spent five weeks waiting for the expected flood of refugees to pour across the border. When they did not come I reported on daily briefings by UN humanitarian agencies based in Jordan but constantly kept up to date on the course of the war in Iraq.

Amman-Baghdad, May 7th-10th, 2003

Not knowing what we would find in Baghdad, Selma and I went shopping for essentials at a supermarket in Amman. Crackers, biscuits, peanut butter, juice, instant coffee, water, powdered milk. Back at the hotel we put on our bathers and went for a swim in the chill Intercontinental pool. I did a few lengths but Selma kept distracting me with comments about the journey we were about to make.

We rose early the next morning. The cars came at six but we left late. Midnight flights bringing the rest of the mission from Stony Brook University and *National Geographic* were delayed. Bleary-eyed archaeologists and photographers wanted a shower before climbing into the big four-by-fours. I sat in the front with the driver in one car while Selma and Mac, suffering from jet lag, slept in the back seats. We breakfasted as always at the cafe in Ruwaished favoured by drivers. At the border a listless US soldier glimpsed at our passports and waved us through. Iraq was open to all comers. The route took us through the desert to Rutba and eventually Ramadi with detours round collapsed bridges and flyovers. Ramadi was always a welcome sight: it is only an hour's drive from "Bags", the Radis' nickname for Baghdad. Ma Radi and Nuha were waiting.

The Orient Palace in Karada was a small, shabby hotel favoured by UN personnel on tight budgets. But the rooms were clean and had working fridges, and the dining room, furnished in the 1950s and never updated, boasted a pianist at dinner-time and served chilled Turkish Efes beer.

Our job was to find out what had happened in the Iraq Museum following the fall of Baghdad on April 9th. We relied for the full story on Donny George, head of research for the Department of Antiquities. He and other museum staff had stayed in the museum from the start of the war until April 8th, but when fighting became intense in the neighbourhood, the staff went home and the guards fled. The next day, two US armoured vehicles entered the museum grounds and spent two hours before departing. Looting began on the 10th while US tanks took up positions on the broad avenue in front of the museum. Small groups of thieves entered the building from the back and carried away television sets, computers, and equipment from offices.

The rampaging gangs did not arrive until late in the day and began stealing and breaking artefacts, which had not been removed from the galleries and consigned to protected bunkers for safekeeping. The watchman, the only person left in the museum, appealed to US troops in the tanks to halt the pillage. They did nothing. US Central Command had not processed orders to protect the museum and transmitted them to officers in the capital. Looting continued for two more days and was halted only when Donny and his colleagues returned on the 13th. But even after they had imposed a certain amount of control, determined thieves continued to find ways to enter the building and snatch treasures.

Forty-two unique items were initially reported to have been stolen from the galleries, and thousands more from three of the five vast storerooms that were breached and trashed by the mob. Tens of thousands of the 170,000 identified and labelled objects from excavations were cast about, stolen or destroyed. Most looters were ignorant people on a spree, but there were among them professionals who knew what they were about. This was suggested by the targeting of three of the museum's most culturally and historically important artefacts. The first two were 5,000 year-old Sumerian pieces from Uruk, the marble head of a woman, known as the "Warka head," and the tall, delicately carved limestone "Warka vase." The head, which closely resembled Nuha, was believed to be the first, or a very early sculpture of a living person. The third piece was a 300 kilogram copper statue of a seated youth, which was dragged through the main door of the galleries, breaking the steps to the ground floor.

Bush and his entourage had been warned in the months before the conflict by leading US archaeologists and historians about the dangers of waging war on Iraq's thousands year-old cultural heritage. But the White House, the State Department, and the Pentagon had done nothing. Defence secretary Donald Rumsfeld, a principal advocate of the war, had responded to damning reports in the media by saying, "Stuff happens."

"Stuff" would not have happened if the Bush administration had refrained from going to war or if Rumsfeld had taken the advice of army chief-of-staff Eric Shinseki who had told the civilian war camp several hundred thousand troops would be needed to keep order in Iraq after its occupation, a figure far higher than the deployment proposed by Rumsfeld and his deputy Paul Wolfowitz.

At the museum we also met US marine colonel Matthew Bogdanos, an assistant district attorney from Manhattan with a degree in classics, who had been put in charge of the investigation into the thefts and the effort to recover artefacts. He held court in a long room with a long table covered in items either returned by Iraqis or recovered. A good many were from the museum's substantial collection of fakes. He was both cocky and defensive when confronted with criticism of the US military's failure to protect the museum, the repository of the relics of ancient Mesopotamia and the powerful Semitic, Christian and Muslim empires that had ruled this part of the world. He later turned out to be a devoted champion of the cause of recovering Iraq's lost treasures and became Selma's close friend.

The brief bout of chaos in the museum was matched by anarchy in the streets of Baghdad. Neighbourhood telephone exchanges were targeted by arsonists who also set fire to the main telecommunications centre. We stopped and stood on the side of the street watching the building smoulder while the culprits, two I think, could be seen climbing upwards from floor to floor to escape the flames and smoke. Iraqis in the crowd blamed "Kuwaitis" seeking revenge for Iraq's 1990 occupation of the emirate but no one really knew who was responsible. The iconic building designed by Iraq's leading architect Rifat Chadirji had been hollowed out by US bombs during the 1991 war and reconstructed by teams of workers. The fire was a major disaster.

Looting was rife in Baghdad and across the country. The Modern Art Museum was pillaged. The National Library and Archives, containing materials collected over centuries, was trashed, pillaged and burned. Factories, police stations, government offices, and water treatment plants were cleared. Gangs ransacked Basra University and carried off chairs and desks. Electricity pylons were toppled by explosives, planted by saboteurs. Robberies, rapes and muggings were commonplace.

Baghdad, May 14th, 2003

I declined to join a bus trip organised by Ahmed Chalabi's outfit to Mahawil some 90 kilometres south of Baghdad to witness the unearthing of a mass grave said to contain the bodies of hundreds of Shias slain by the fallen regime. Instead I attended the press conference given by Maj. Gen. David McKiernan and Maj. Gen. Buford Blount who were harshly castigated by the international press for failing to provide security in Iraq. The briefing took place in the sweltering main hall of the international conference centre in Baghdad. Asked why US troops did not shoot looters, Blount replied that they were not threatening US personnel but "just stealing something", reminding journalists of the pillage at the museum and Rumsfeld's "stuff happens" remark.

McKiernan said 200 looters had been arrested over the previous 48 hours and announced first offenders would be held for 20 days rather than two. He insisted the US military had been increasing the number of troops, military police and Iraqi police on patrol.

The lights suddenly died, plunging us into darkness until television teams at the back of the auditorium switched on their battery powered lights. The generals, who had claimed conditions had improved since the beginning of the occupation, stumbled, then with good humour, resumed answering uncomfortable questions.

The next day, Iraq's US viceroy L. Paul Bremer gave his inaugural press briefing at the centre. The conference had been originally been scheduled earlier but was postponed with no reason given. Dressed in a light suit, tie and beige desert boots he strode confidently onto the stage and made a brief statement, promising to take questions.

He said he had come to Iraq to rebuild the country after years of "depravity" and oppression. He claimed the US occupation had already freed Shias to conduct religious events in accordance with their traditions, town councils had begun to meet, water quality in Basra was better and more Iraqis had electricity than before the fall of the regime. He admitted, however, law and order was a problem in Baghdad and pledged to "extirpate" the ousted Baath party and its members from all positions of power. The electricity was cut before he had time to reply to mainly hostile questions. When television teams again offered to light up the scene, he stalked off the stage.

Over a dinner of pepper steak and Efes with Mac, I asked if he had been acquainted with Sami Said al-Ahmad in Chicago and explained that he had "made" my life by introducing me to the Arab world. Mac had known Sami well, said he had taken a job teaching in the west, Colorado, perhaps.

I had been told by someone at the museum that Sami had returned to Baghdad, and was teaching at the university. "Well, then," said Mac, "let's go and look for him tomorrow." "Where?" I asked. "In the souk, his father had a shop selling silk." Mac and I set off on foot. Since it was Friday, the souk was closed, shuttered and darkly threatening, so we walked on through empty streets until we reached al-Mutanabbi street where the weekly market in second hand books was in progress. Mac asked a bookseller if he knew Sami. The man did but had not seen him for some time. Among the books arranged on a dusty sheet on the pavement was an all too familiar copy of *The United States and the Palestinian People*, my first book published in Beirut by the Institute for Palestinian Studies. I had seen the book when visiting the book market in January but had resisted buying it. "It's fate," said Mac. "You have to take it now." On the fly leaf, I wrote the date, May 16th, 2003.

Baghdad, May 17th, 2003

Nuha invited us to a party at the handsome house in Adhamiya she shared with Selma. My driver and I scoured Karada for bottles of Ferida beer, certain to disappear from the market thanks to bans on alcohol consumption demanded by religious conservatives. The invitation was for five, tea-time, because it was too dangerous to drive around the city after eight. Ma Radi had cooked one of the ducks that had grazed in the garden, plank-grilled a huge fish (*masgouf*), and prepared a collection of salads. Among the guests were correspondent Jane Arraf, then working for *CNN*, and the owners of Ferida. It was a curious party, both happy and sorrowful because Iraq was in such turmoil. Ma, who spent most of her time in Beirut, had consistently argued against both Bush wars.

When Selma, Mac and I got in the car to return to the Orient Palace, Nuha came out of the house with a dish of water and tossed the water onto the back of the car. "This is traditional here," Selma remarked. "We must return soon."

Early the next morning Selma and I rode back to Amman with a Russian journalist and the following day went our separate ways.

Nuha was in Beirut during my subsequent visits to Baghdad, and died of a rare cancer on August 31st, 2004; I never saw her after the party.

Abu Ghraib, August 4th, 2003

A tour of Baghdad's notorious Abu Ghraib prison – built in the 1950s by British contractors, was the main media event of the day. The complex, reputed for brutality under Saddam Hussein was closed in 2002 but re-opened under the US occupation administration. Situated at the edge of Abu Ghraib's agricultural area, the vast dun-coloured walled compound blended into the desert landscape. Outside the sandbagged gate flanked by armoured scout cars, detainees' relatives waited. Just inside the gate was an enclosure constructed of stacked rolls of razor wire where there were tents for temporary accommodation of prisoners.

The press was briefed by General Janice Karpinski, commander of the US 800 Military Brigade based in Long Island, New York. In June 2003 she had been placed in charge of US-run prisons in Iraq. She said her troops, both regulars and reservists, were manning facilities, which had been made serviceable after the war.

Some 5,000 Iraqis were being held, 75 percent for criminal activities. Only 200 were prisoners of war, the US claimed. The majority of the latter had been released on parole after swearing not to carry out offenses against occupying US and allied troops, she stated.

Political detainees included civilians picked up in random sweeps, irregulars who fought US and British forces and high ranking officials held for interrogation and investigation to determine whether they had committed crimes while in power.

We were taken to see rooms used for torture, complete with implements, before the previous November when Saddam Hussein had released all inmates and closed the prison. The prison had been looted during the US war and records destroyed.

As we left the compound, a small group of prisoners approached the wire holding up a sign written in English on a flattened cardboard box: "We want freedom".

In January 2004, Karpinski was reprimanded, relieved of duties in Iraq and rotated home. In April, *CBS* television's *60 Minutes* broadcast photos of Iraqi corpses covered in blood and hooded, naked prisoners piled on one another being taunted by a US female soldier. On May 10th, Seymour Hersh, writing in *The New Yorker*, leaked a secret US army report compiled months earlier on sadistic prisoner abuse and torture by US soldiers, military police and contractors.

Baghdad, August 10th, 2003

Baghdad zoo was a peaceful place where a few men and women, families and groups of youths came to walk without worry. An island of security in a city beset by bombers, arsonists, Ali Babas, and kidnappers. Foreign soldiers who could not protect people just about managed to protect the zoo's surviving animals.

At the gate I met Ahmed Abdel Razzak, a caretaker doing the rounds with food for vegetarian residents. Ahmed and his assistant had a barrow of apples, pears, plums, grapes, greens and bread. Our first stop was at the cage of a pair of northern Iraqi brown bears with dusty fur. They were stretched flat on the floor, prostrated by the heat. We strolled past cages holding happily wagging stray dogs, some with puppies, taken in by the zoo. "They'd starve if we don't look after them," Ahmed remarked, offering me a charming white puppy with tufted ears. I had to refuse. Taking an undocumented Iraqi puppy to Jordan and Cyprus would have tied me in red tape for months and the puppy would have ended up in quarantine in Nicosia.

There was a pointy-nosed coyote and a slim wolf, which had rubbed off patches of fur on the bars of his cage. The cages were clean, the animals had a fresh supply of water, and appeared to be well fed and in good health.

After the city had fallen to US forces, the zoo had become a target of looters who took water pumps, cages, animals and birds and smashed items they could not carry away. "We lost nearly all the animals and all the birds," Ahmed said, regretfully. Rockets broke open the lions' enclosure, freeing three of the big cats, later shot by US troops.

We crossed a patch of grass to a set of cages housing three baboons, one an old lady who adored the spicy bunch of greens Ahmad pushed through the bars. In another cage, an elegant cheetah was coiled near the door leading to a run which she shared with her mate. "She was Uday's house pet," remarked Ahmed. "You can go into the cage and stroke her." Uday was Saddam Hussein's erratic and cruel eldest son, killed in a shoot-out with US troops in Mosul three weeks earlier.

The African porcupines rattled their long white quills in greeting as Ahmed tossed fruit into their enclosure. Four lions were inside their cages in the lion house, two teenage females, fur sleek and shiny, were patting each other in play. They had come from one of Saddam Hussein's palaces.

A middle-aged lion couple was dozing. Outside, in a moated enclosure, were five more lions, stretched out in the shade. Pacing her private quarters, one lioness, Sugar, an elderly pensioner with large tawny eyes, had been brought to the zoo in a car in 1995.

A Bengal tiger, who clearly thought highly of himself, stalked back and forth along the bars of his cage to show off his fine coat. The meat-eaters dined on defrosted buffalo meat imported from Bombay and bought in the local market.

Ahmed, who had been a keeper for 13 years, made a beeline for the ostriches. He was especially attached to a haughty grey female who looked down her beak at us, panting slightly in the heat. She and the two males had been found in Uday's garden.

"I took off my belt, looped it around her neck and then ran five kilometres across Baghdad with her. When we came through the gate, everybody clapped."

He pointed to the empty enclosure built for elephants. "There has never been an elephant in the Baghdad zoo. I have never seen one. Only in photos. We can't afford an elephant. It eats hundreds of kilos of grass every day." For him, the problem was between man and man. "The war destroyed everything in Iraq."

Before the war, the zoo was the largest in the region, with 600 animals. In 2001, it had 1.5 million visitors. In 2002 it closed for a $50 million upgrade. In May 2003, there were only 50 animal residents, some rescued from abandoned gardens belonging to members of the toppled regime.

Baghdad, September 20th, 2003

During a party after the zoo had closed for the night, a US soldier killed Mamdouh, one of the two Bengal tigers after the arm of a sergeant was mauled by the big cat when the man breached the outer fence of the animal's pen. Mamdouh, a zoo-born 14 year-old survivor of the 1980-88 Iraq-Iran war and the 1991 and 2003 US wars on Iraq, was shot to death by a US occupation soldier in a country attacked on the false pretence that Saddam Hussein possessed weapons of mass destruction. A keeper called the tiger "the most precious animal in the zoo."

The incident inspired Indo-US playwright Rajiv Joseph to write *Bengal Tiger at the Baghdad Zoo*, a 2011 Broadway play about the shooting at a time Iraq was descending into chaos and blood-letting. The work was a finalist for the Pulitzer Prize.

Baghdad, December 14th, 2003

I found Lamia in her temporary office at the Iraq Museum where staff and experts from abroad were still struggling to discover what was missing after the museum was raided and pillaged following the fall of the Iraqi capital to invading US forces. Lamia was cheerful; "You're coming with us to the Gailani Mosque this morning. We brought an *abaya* for you." She held up a black cloak edged with delicate gold thread embroidery.

We were welcomed as royalty at the magnificent 700-year old mosque. Lamia and her daughters are descendants of the 10th-11th century Islamic scholar and mystic Abdel Qadir al-Gailani. who belonged to the line of the Prophet Muhammad on both paternal and maternal sides. He taught at his own *madrassa* in Baghdad and when he died at 89, his body was entombed at the site in a shrine beneath a beautiful Persianate tile dome. As our guide led us through the wide courtyard, Lamia paused to comment on the inscriptions written high on the wall above the arches of the pilgrims' hostel. "They used to include Shia as well as Sunni sayings and verses from the Quran. But after 1991, when Saddam succumbed to Saudi influence, the inscriptions were changed. They are solely Sunni now. Shias and Sunnis used to come together in this mosque. It was a local meeting place. There was a soup kitchen across the street where poor people were fed."

The tomb of the shaikh, founder of the earliest Sufi order, is surrounded by a rectangular sliver cage, similar to the shrine of John the Baptist's severed head in the Omayyad Mosque in Damascus. Abdel Qadir's tomb has more of the feel of a resting place of a Shia saint rather than a Sunni pundit. But then, Sunni Abdel Qadir was a descendant of both Hassan and Hussein, the grandsons of the Prophet revered by Shias.

In the library we were shown illuminated copies of the Quran that had been thrown into the Tigris in 1258 when the Mongol warrior Hulagu conquered and laid waste to Bagdad. It is said the Tigris went black from the ink of all the books Hulagu's fighters had consigned to the river.

As we walked by an enclosure where her forbearers lie, Lamia quipped, "There're my family graves."

Lamia returned to the museum while I went to Mansour to an internet cafe where I was set to write and send a story before meeting Yaqthan and going to lunch at the house of Lamia's sister, Asmah. At that time filing had to be done at cafes because there were no household connections or wireless. As Yaqthan and I made our way across Baghdad in noontide traffic, he received a call on his mobile from his brother Nasir, a member of the US-appointed "governing" council. "I won't be coming because I'm going to see Saddam Hussein. He was captured yesterday. They want us to confirm his identity."

Asmah's grand house, designed by Rifaat Chadirji, the splendid fare, and the conversation of clever and informed guests were forgotten when the *BBC* began broadcasting images of the fallen Iraqi president onto the flat television screen mounted on the wall near the dining table. The Iraqis were insulted and infuriated by the way he was exposed, humbled, his hair and beard unruly and matted, his head pulled round so his captors could take a DNA swab from his inner cheek. "He may have been a bastard," said someone, "but he was our bastard. He was president of Iraq, after all." We watched his humiliation over and over, listened to the commentators, and heard how he had been found in a hole at a farm not far from his natal village of Awja near Tikrit, the city that gave its name to his ruling clan.

I returned in the late afternoon to the internet cafe in Mansour and wrote story after story covering the news and local and Arab reaction. It was after 11 at night when my driver conveyed me to Karada through the dark, empty streets of Baghdad past Firdos Square, where the statue of Saddam Hussein had been pulled down on April 9th. The dimly lit lobby of my small, modest hotel was a beacon in the gloom.

Baghdad, June 23rd, 2004

Karin and I went shopping in a Karada supermarket for food and essentials for the flat she had rented, as she had planned to reside most of the year in Baghdad. We bought sheets and towels from Syria, well known for good quality, kitchen implements, and food – tinned olives from Turkey, instant coffee, powdered milk, frozen items, and fresh vegetables and fruit. Halloumi cheese from Cyprus: I could not make out how the cheese had reached Baghdad. The furnished two-bedroom flat was on the fourth floor of a building with a view of the polished steel surface of the Tigris. When I opened the fridge door to put in our purchases, I found a shelf filled with tins of Red Bull energy drinks belonging to the Austrian photographer invited by Karin to share the flat and the rent. Once our purchases had been stored, I began to fill up empty plastic bottles with water in case of water and power cuts. I had been well trained by Lebanon's civil war.

Christian Peacemakers, all from North America, who had settled into a flat on a lower floor not only invited us to dinner but also had a great deal to say about their mission. Followers of Mahatma Gandhi and Badshah Khan, the Afghan "Frontier Gandhi", they distributed leaflets to Iraqis to inform them of their rights under the occupation, joined Iraqi protests, and visited US prisons to try to track down "disappeared" Iraqis whose whereabouts were not known to their kin. Tracking down "blacklisted" Iraqis was particularly difficult.

Maxine said the summer before they had taken part in a protest against unemployment outside the compound housing the occupation administration. But after sitting and standing for weeks in the heat and dust both Iraqis and Peacemakers went home, discouraged. In January, well before the eruption of the Abu Ghraib scandal, the Peacemakers team had reported to the occupation authorities about abuses and mistreatment of detainees. The Peacemakers had raised the cases of 72 prisoners and said harsh treatment was routine rather than exceptional. A few "bad" soldiers were not the problem.

Sheila observed that US soldiers who had received English language Peacemaker leaflets had simply accepted them without comment before the Abu Ghraib storm broke but became negative afterwards. Greg, who had served in Palestine earlier, said the situations here and there were similar. "There are house raids where Iraqis have their men seized and valuables stolen, people are arrested without reason, without being charged, and released without reason. There are collective punishments and targeted assassinations. The US has learnt a lot from Israel." He dismissed the Bush administration's claim that Iraq had constituted a threat to Israel.

Sister Anne, who had been in and out of Iraq since 1991, was proud of the team's success in securing pay for teachers, freeing detainees, and joining the bereaved in prayer at grave sites.

Baghdad, June 28th-July 4th, 2004

Forty-eight hours early, fearing a violent response, the US occupation authority handed over sovereignty to the Iraqi interim government.

In the run-up to the announced event, insurgents had slain scores of Iraqis and abducted at least one US soldier.

The secret transfer took place in the heavily fortified "Green Zone" the US had constructed around the Rashid hotel, the convention centre and Republican Palace. Bremer, at the end of his destructive term as viceroy, shook hands with interim president Ghazi al-Yawar and prime minister Ayad Allawi. Since the transfer was not broadcast live on television, Iraqis did not know it had taken place until news leaked out. In spite of the hand-over, 160,000 mainly US troops remained in occupation and laws made by the US regime continued in force, unless and until abrogated by the new government.

Two days later, on the morning when the hand-over had been scheduled, two mortars whizzed over our building, prompting us and the Peacemakers downstairs to rush to the roof to see a couple more land in the Green Zone, to cheers from people in walking on the Tigris corniche. A huge red, white and black Iraqi flag, folding and unfolding gracefully in the wind, revealed that Bremer and his team had retreated from their plan to impose a new flag, featuring blue and yellow stripes and a blue crescent on a white background, a banner the majority of Iraqis hated.

There was no safe place in Iraq – or Baghdad. Even the "Green Zone" was a dangerous place. Iraqis warned about the risk of mortar and suicide bomber attacks at the zone's checkpoint at eight in the morning when people were travelling to work or lining up to present petitions to the authorities. Karin and I took such warnings seriously when going there for press handouts or appointments with occupation officials.

Insurgents had begun to take hostages that April. Scores of foreigners and hundreds of Iraqis were seized, some ransomed, some released and others beheaded. Among the abductees were three Indians, two Kenyans, and an Egyptian, all lorry drivers who had been snatched just before I arrived in the Iraqi capital. The group claiming the operation called itself the "Bearers of the Black Banners" and demanded that the drivers' home countries pull their citizens out of Iraq, threatening to kill the hostages if this was not done within 72 hours. Drivers of lorries transporting food to US troops from suppliers in Kuwait were common victims. *The Deccan Herald* was, naturally, eager to have coverage of this story but there was no news. A day before the kidnapping, a warning against collaborating with the occupation forces had been issued by the *Khaled Ibn al-Walid* brigade, the military wing of *Jamaat al-Tawhid wal Jihad*, the Unity and Holy War group, led by Abu Musab al-Zarqawi, dispatched by al-Qaeda to Iraq after Bush's war to launch resistance operations.

Karin took me to an elegant home filled with paintings and books to meet her German friend Helma, wife of Amer al-Saadi, the former minister of industry and defence industry, who had served as Iraq's contact with UN inspectors before the war. Three days after the fall of Baghdad, he had handed himself in to the occupation authorities who classified him as an "enemy prisoner of war", a person who could be held indefinitely without recourse to a lawyer or family visits. Helma had not seen him since that day.

Compelled to wear an orange jump suit, he was confined to a narrow cell, with an hour out for exercise and no books or writing materials, nothing to occupy his mind except the one-page Red Cross letter he was allowed to write to Helma every month. She was not permitted to give him any news in her letter so he was cut off from the outside world. "He used to lie on his bed and compose poetry," she said, "or do cross-words." All in his head for he had no pencil or paper. Six months after he was detained, he was given a plastic chair and other simple amenities, Helma said as we sat down to a vegetarian dinner.

Helma had been discussing her husband's case with a UN official at the Canal hotel on August 19th, the previous summer, when a suicide bomber driving a cement mixer brought down the building, killing UN envoy Sergio de Mello and 21 others and wounding scores, including Helma. She was unconscious for two days before waking up in a military hospital. Helma was still shaken by the experience of near death.

We went several times to see Helma. Karin, who was writing her biography had become close friends. Godfrey and I had interviewed Amer the morning after the US had sent cruise missiles into Baghdad in 1993.

Trained as an English teacher, Helma had met Amer in Britain where he had been sent on a government scholarship to study physical chemistry. He had played a key role in providing the missiles Iraq deployed against Iran during the 1980-88 Iraq-Iran war. He retired from the military as a lieutenant general in 1994, and took up ministerial and advisory posts. While serving as liaison with the UN weapons inspectors, Amer had said Iraq had no weapons of mass destruction at the time the US went to war, an assertion that apparently peeved his US interrogators. He was number 32 on the US list of most wanted members of the ousted regime.

While we were waiting for an appointment with Iraqi Governing Council member Adnan Pachachi, a former foreign minister, Saifi, an aide, suggested that Karin and I visit an art dealer whose home was nearby. This tidy, detached house on a quiet street in the Mansour diplomatic quarter was a treasure trove of Iraqi art. Ranged around the sitting room were works by the country's pioneers, as well as the second generation of painters. All were covered in a thick layer of grime. Fearing bombs and looters would ravage his shop in the commercial area during the first Bush war, the art dealer, Basim stated, "I brought them here in 1991 and told my wife not to clean the salon." I peered at the works of Faik Hassan and Jawad Selim, dusty, sorrowful, and neglected. The founding fathers of Iraqi art. I was familiar with their names but their paintings were new to me. Basim was asking high prices.

A large, particularly grubby painting leaning against the wall caught my attention: a neighbourhood scene in Baghdad during a festival with children on a hand-propelled ferris wheel, a slide and a swing, an impressionist painting still on the stretcher painted by Akram Shukri, the first Iraqi to secure a scholarship to study art abroad. The price was a bit steep. Nevertheless I asked if Basim could remove the stretcher and roll it into a tube. "No problem," was the reply. I did not have the cash to buy it then, but promised to return in August.

14

INCARCERATION

Ramallah, November, 12th, 2004

Arafat came home to his ruined *muqataa* to a chaotic welcome from tens of thousands of Palestinians who poured in from all corners of the Israeli-occupied West Bank, filled the streets, clambered over the compound's walls and swarmed onto the wide parking lot. Ramallah residents crowded onto the flat rooftops of apartment buildings surrounding the *muqataa*. Palestinian flags and the yellow banner of his Fatah movement hung limply from balconies.

He arrived late in death as he had almost always done in life. I waited impatiently with other journalists – television teams, radio broadcasters, and pencil press – on an upper floor of an unfinished building with a view into the heart of the *muqataa*, listening to the *BBC* on my transistor radio, my computer bag slung over my shoulder, as always. The throng sighed and crowed as two helicopters circled overhead. Arafat borne in one, and escorted by the second. They had flown from el-Arish in Sinai.

Arafat's aircraft landed on the tarmac to raking gunfire, ululations from women and shouts of "Welcome Abu Ammar," "Welcome Old Man," "*Allahu Akbar*!" from tearful men. The throng pressed so closely to the helicopter that the door could be opened only a crack, forcing those inside to plead for mourners to move back. The coffin, draped in a Palestinian flag, emerged after twenty-five minutes once a police jeep had forced its way through the crowd and the men aboard had taken charge. The coffin was hefted onto the shoulders of young men in uniform, green berets on their heads.

The flag was dragged off as mourners reached out to touch the coffin. Palestinians chanted, "With our blood and our soul we will redeem you, O Abu Ammar." A formal laying in was cancelled and he was buried quickly at the corner of the parking lot in a freshly prepared grave of marble slabs under a copse of straggly trees and newly planted olives, brutally trampled by the throng. As I crossed the tarmac towards the area where condolences were being received, Palestinians began to pile the grave with tributes of flowers, portraits of Arafat, and black-and-white headscarves that had become the emblem not only of Palestinian resistance to Israeli occupation but of the global struggle for justice.

That morning Arab and other dignitaries had taken part in a carefully orchestrated state funeral service near Cairo's international airport. It had been attended by Egyptian president Hosni Mubarak, Saudi Crown Prince Abdullah, Jordan's King Abdullah, Syrian president Bashar al-Assad, Lebanese president Emile Lahoud, British foreign secretary Jack Straw, Irish foreign minister Dermot Ahern, and US assistant secretary of state William Burns. Arafat's coffin was carried on a gun carriage to an airbase from where he was flown to Sinai and thence to Ramallah.

Arafat had died on November 11th from a mysterious illness that had begun a month earlier with nausea, vomiting, abdominal pain, and diarrhoea. His health deteriorated gradually, specialists were summoned. After doctors from Tunisia, Jordan and Palestine could not discover the cause of his illness; he was flown by Jordanian military helicopter to Amman from where he was transported by military plane to a hospital in a Paris suburb. On November 3rd he lapsed into a coma from which he never regained consciousness.

I had taken the road to Ramallah and walked round the *muqataa* for three days before his arrival, waiting for news from Paris and canvassing Palestinian opinion on his passing. Many I queried thought he had been poisoned by Israel, a view shared by some of his entourage and doctors. I was not certain. When I had last met him in May 2002, he was not a well man. I had accompanied Irish Red Cross president David Andrews and Isolde on a visit to the "Old Man" shortly after Israel had concluded its reinvasion of Palestinian towns and cities and pulled out its troops. At the end of the meeting, Arafat, shrunken and pale, shook hands with all of us. His hand, exhibiting a slight tremor, was cold, bloodless, the skin almost transparent, his smile slightly crooked, but his eyes were bright as he bid us goodbye.

After his 1992 plane crash in a sandstorm in the Libyan desert, Arafat was not as sharp or tough as he had been. He was fragile, his English, learnt late in life, had deteriorated. Godfrey and I had met him in Tunis in 1985 on the sidelines of an Arab League seminar where I had given a paper on the development of the Israeli peace camp following Israel's 1982 war on Lebanon. Although the encounter was well after midnight, Arafat was alert and commented in fluent English (with a slight Egyptian accent) on the topic I had addressed. He pulled out of his breast pocket a clipping of an article from an Israeli paper discussing Peace Now and other Israeli groups lobbying for withdrawal of Israeli forces from Lebanon and negotiations with the Palestinians. He was optimistic and cheerful, fully in control, and ready for negotiations. But Israel, the US, and Europe were not ready to talk to Arafat. It took them three years to engage and talks began seriously in 1988 only after he had secured the adoption of the Palestinian Declaration of Independence and capitulated to key demands put forward by Israel and the US.

Arafat seemed diminished when I met him again in Tunis a few days after the deeply flawed 1993 Oslo agreement had been initialled and shortly before it was signed with great pomp and ceremony on the White House lawn. The failure of Oslo to achieve an end to the occupation and the violence of the second intifada gradually destroyed Arafat, his dream of Palestine, his hopes for his people. The Palestinian Authority, which he had founded and ruled, was corrupt and widely accused of mismanagement.

Nicosia, April 2004

Having assassinated Hamas founder Shaikh Ahmad Yassin on March 22nd and Abdel Aziz al-Rantisi on April 17th, Ariel Sharon had publicly threatened to kill Arafat on April 23rd. Sharon said, "I told [US president George Bush the following during a meeting with him on April 14th]... in our first meeting about three years ago I accepted your request not to harm Arafat physically. I told [Bush] I understand the problems surrounding the situation, but I am released from that pledge. I release myself from this commitment regarding Arafat." While the White House did not react, national security adviser Condoleezza Rice telephoned Dove Weisglass in Sharon's office to state US opposition to "any move" and secretary of state Colin Powell said Sharon's commitment stood.

Arafat's detention in the *muqataa* during the final two and a half years of his life had sapped his strength and undermined his health. The leader who had put Palestine back on the world map and reclaimed the right of Palestinians to exist, died disappointed, and broken. Israel denied him burial in the Haram al-Sharif mosque compound in Jerusalem so he was laid to rest in a cement sarcophagus in Ramallah in a tomb said by the Authority to be temporary. At the insistence of Muslim clerics and family members who argued such a burial was a violation of Islamic tradition and practice, Arafat's body was, the next day, wrapped in a shroud and buried in the earth of captive Ramallah.

Occupied East Jerusalem-the West Bank, January 2005

Ahead of the presidential election on January 9th, I attended a lukewarm rally near Ramallah for Mahmoud Abbas staged by Fatah and a more spirited gathering addressed by his chief rival Mustafa Barghouti, who said he had been arrested and roughed up on several occasions and one of his Gaza campaign workers slain by Israeli army snipers. Other West Bank candidates also suffered Israeli harassment while Gaza hopefuls were unable to campaign in the West Bank.

The choice of Israel, the US, Europe and the Arab rulers, Abbas was expected to win by a large margin. The godfather of the misbegotten Oslo accords, he rejected armed resistance and remained totally committed to negotiations as the sole means of securing a Palestinian state alongside Israel. He ignored Israel's refusal to negotiate seriously while it colonised East Jerusalem, the West Bank and Gaza and slew Palestinians. Five days before the vote, three brothers aged between10-17 were killed as they worked in their fields in northern Gaza. Israel permitted just over 5,000 Palestinian residents of East Jerusalem to cast ballots in post offices in the city; the remainder of its eligible voters had, once again, to travel to centres outside the municipal borders of the holy city, annexed by Israel in 1967 and claimed as its exclusive capital.

Abbas won 62 percent of the vote with a turnout of 50 percent, a result Hamas claimed as a victory for its call for abstention. Many Palestinians were simply unable to cast ballots due to confusion over where they should vote; others refused to participate in an election Fatah had done its best to manipulate.

Back in Nicosia, I hung on a hook in my front hall the badge obtained from the Palestinian election commission allowing me to enter polling booths. This badge joined a fat bunch of plastic covered identity cards suspended on coloured ribbons. A curious dossier of events I had covered over the years: elections, international conferences, a fair in Irbil in northern Iraq, and the visit of Indian prime minister Indira Gandhi to Cyprus.

Jerusalem-Bethlehem, late January 2006

As the election campaign for the Palestinian parliament wound down, I drove to Umm Tuba, a village on the edge of Jerusalem, with Scandinavian colleagues to interview jailbird Muhammad Abu Tir. He was number two on Hamas' Change and Reform list, after the movement's chief Ismail Haniyeh. Abu Tir, who dyes his beard bright orange with henna, was literally the most colourful character standing for the legislative assembly. Although dubbed a "terrorist" by Israel and considered an ultra-conservative fundamentalist by many, he had adopted the moderate line Hamas had decided to follow. He refuted claims his party would impose Muslin canon law, Sharia, on Palestinians if Change and Reform won a majority in the council. Sharia, he said, could be a source of legislation. Alcohol would not be banned and women would not be compelled to wear the headscarf, or *hijab*, although he favoured separation of males and females at school.

The ruling party, Fatah had a hard sell. The Fatah-run Palestinian Authority was widely accused of nepotism, graft and mismanagement while Hamas had not been tarnished by years in power. Sitting in his office in Jerusalem, Bernard Sabella, a Christian Fatah legislator from Jerusalem, warned there were multiple Fatah candidates, one official, others "independents," in every constituency, risking division of the vote, while Hamas had nominated a single candidate for each constituency.

During the first legislative election, boycotted by Hamas, Fatah had won 66 of the 88 seats, but its term had long expired when Abbas, under pressure from the US and other western countries, agreed to hold a second parliamentary poll. The campaign had been hard fought and bitter between Fatah, the unacceptable status quo party, and Hamas' Change and Reform, its name amounting to a promise to the electorate.

On election day, I made the rounds of polling stations in East Jerusalem and Bethlehem. Lines were long and cheerful: Palestinians were eager to cast their ballots. Unlike 1996, this was a real contest. During his tour of polling stations with members of his observer team, former US president Jimmy Carter paused at the post office on Salah ed-Din street in East Jerusalem to wave to Palestinians gathered in the street to discuss the vote.

The test of Palestinian democracy began when the counting began after the polls closed and the efficient central election commission began to release results. Hamas won 74 seats out of 132 in the expanded council, Fatah 45, although the difference in the number of votes between the two main parties was only 30,000. Nationalists, leftists and independents won 13 seats. As the results were posted on the election commission's website, I carefully went through the list, constituency-by-constituency, and found that Hamas had taken 44.45 percent of the vote, Fatah 41.43.

As Sabella had warned, Hamas' votes were for a single candidate while Fatah's votes were shared by several. Opinion surveys had predicted a Fatah victory. In Ramallah, the Palestinian administrative capital, Hamas took all the seats except two reserved for Christians. Seventy-seven percent of voters in the Palestinian territories had taken part, 82 percent in Gaza. On the day after the election, poll monitors Carter, ex-Swedish prime minister Carl Bildt, former Spanish foreign minister Ana Palacio, and ex-Albanian president Rexhep Meidani held a press conference. Carter reported that the election, the third he had observed in the Palestinian territories, was honest, free, fair and non-violent.

I arrived early at the press conference and took a seat in the front row, determined to query Carter on his attitude to the result. In the run-up to polling day, the press had reported he and the US government had suggested it would be unfortunate if Hamas was victorious. The first to ask a question, I reminded him of this report and asked if it was "fair" to intervene in this way. He brushed my question aside but after the conference concluded and we were filing out of the hall, one of his aides tapped me on the shoulder, "Would you like to meet the president in a room next door?" We were three, a Canadian, a European and I. As we took our seats across the table from Carter, he greeted me by saying I was right. It was not fair.

Keen to ensure the results of the election were observed, Carter went the next day to Ramallah where he found the Fatah-dominated cabinet had resigned. Abbas had decided to reject Hamas' proposal to form a national unity government and had adopted a policy of non-cooperation. Carter also learned Hamas legislators would be denied passes needed to travel around the occupied territories, making it impossible for the council to meet.

The international community backed Abbas' rejection of Palestinian democracy. The Quartet – comprised of the US, UN, European Union and Russia – argued Hamas could not take part in government unless it renounced violence, recognised Israel and accepted agreements reached between the PLO and Israel. These three demands and Abbas' policy of non-cooperation destroyed Palestinian unity while Israel continued to expand colonies, conduct incursions into the West Bank and wage war on Gaza.

Larnaca, August 22nd, 2008

Just before ten in the morning two frail wooden boats backed away from the quay at Larnaca's port, rounded the breakwater and put to sea bound for Gaza to breach the Israeli siege and blockade of the coastal strip. Flags of the 17 home countries of the 44 activists on board fluttered from the rigging of "Free Gaza", a retired Greek island-hopping ferry, and "Liberty", a clapped-out Greek fishing boat. The vessels had been cleared to depart only after their hulls had been examined by a police diver to ensure no limpet bombs had been attached. In February 1988, a ferry chartered by the PLO to carry Palestinian deportees to Gaza had been damaged by a bomb while moored at Limassol. Three Palestinian officials had been killed by the blast.

Free Gaza movement organisers of the voyage of the two tiny, unseaworthy boats had arrived in Cyprus at the end of July, expecting to set sail after a few days. But the boats limped from Greek port to Greek port, engines broke down and had to be overhauled and navigational and communications equipment had required repair. Everything that could go wrong seemed to go wrong. Temperatures soared to 38-40 degrees Celsius in Nicosia while the activists trained in non-violent resistance techniques, in case the boats were boarded by Israeli naval commandos. Their rooms at the hostel of Cyprus University in Nicosia were not air conditioned so heat exhausted the activists. Octogenarian Holocaust survivor, Hedy Epstein, one of the stars of the mission, suffered from the heat. Yvonne Ridley, a British journalist held for 10 days by the Taliban in Afghanistan; Anne Montgomery, a Catholic nun from the US, who had been with Christian Peacemakers teams working in Iraq and Palestine; and British journalist and broadcaster Lauren Booth, Tony Blair's sister-in-law, were also taking part.

Bil'in, Israeli-occupied West Bank, August 2005

I had met Hedy on a protest Friday in the Palestinian village of Bil'in in the West Bank. I had just arrived to cover the event when I saw a little lady, dressed in an elegant suit, comfortable heels, a hand-bag over her shoulder, standing in the shadow of a door across from the mosque waiting for the march against Israel's wall to begin. She was togged out for a bridge afternoon, I in jeans and t-shirt for a rout. Hailing from St. Louis, she said she was a member of Women in Black, an Israeli-international group seeking peace and justice for Palestinians.

Inside the Abu Rahma house, the base of operations, Quaker veterans of the weekly demonstration handed me slices of onion to counter tear gas Israeli troops routinely used against protesters. A woman who had spent the night was packing clothing into her rucksack. Like Hedy, she had come from the US to take part. From a town near Detroit, she said. "I grew up in Michigan", I remarked. "Where?" she asked. "Bay City," I replied. "So did I," she responded, asking, "Central or Handy?" It turned out that she had been in Central High School with my brother, Jon, whom she said she had fancied for a time. A third activist had been to Smith College, not far from Mount Holyoke, and a fourth had an *Irish Times* connection. I found it curious I should meet these women in the small, obscure West Bank village of Bil'in where they were taking part in a weekly protest that had begun in January.

The walk to the location where the wall was set to be built began after midday prayers. In the vanguard were Israeli peaceniks deployed to absorb any violence inflicted by Israeli troops already installed in the olive grove at the bottom of the slope from the village. Their job was to prevent marchers from reaching villagers' land slated to be behind the wall and cut off from its owners. "Internationals" came next and then Palestinians. Carrying flags and placards denouncing the wall, the activists, more than 150-strong, walked in good order until they were halted by heavily armed Israeli soldiers, garbed in helmets with wide visors and webbing and flak jackets. I kept to the sidelines as a journalist covering the protest rather than a participant.

After a few minutes of discussion between Israeli officers and protesters, tear gas canisters were fired around and into the gathering, followed by percussion grenades meant to clear the way for the advance of the soldiers into the village. Palestinian youths picked up stones from the hillside and hurled them at the troops. More gas, more grenades forced the protesters to retreat to the top of Bil'in. This had become a regular dance, occasionally fatal for Palestinians, choreographed by both sides. I was grateful for the slice of onion I had slipped into my pocket.

The dogged determination of the protesters was not in vain. After only a few months of Friday demonstrations, the Israeli high court ordered the demolition of sections of the eight-metre high concrete slab wall.

Nicosia, August 15th, 2008

Nora, a Palestinian whose family hails from Gaza, invited Free Gaza to celebrate Hedy's birthday, a cheerful occasion that lifted the spirits of the frustrated, weary sailors still without ships.

In the days before the party, I had taped a long interview with Hedy whose life story could have been very different if her parents had taken the opportunity to leave Germany for Palestine in 1938.

Hedy was born in 1924 in the Black Forest village of Kippenheim near Freiburg. When Hitler rose to power, she was eight years old. Her parents quickly understood the risks of remaining in Germany and tried to get out. They were prepared to go "anywhere in the world" but Palestine, she told me. They opposed the Zionist project. "I really didn't understand fully at the time what it means to be a

Zionist or an anti-Zionist. But if my parents were anti-Zionist, I am an anti-Zionist. In the village there was a Zionist youth group and all the Jewish children participated, but not I because my parents did not allow me to participate."

Although her parents had packed three suitcases with the hope of escaping across the nearby Swiss border, they failed and after some time the suitcases were unpacked. They continued to believe the family could leave together until the night of November 10th, 1938, *Kristallnacht*, when Hitler's thugs smashed Jewish shops and businesses and attacked Jews in Germany and Austria. Hedy's father was arrested and taken to the Dachau concentration camp. When he was released, her parents decided she should leave on the Kinder transport which took Jewish children to Britain. Her parents told her they would meet soon. Her parents did not survive.

On May 18th, 1939, Hedy departed with 500 children; the youngest was six months, the oldest 17 years. "My number was 5,480," she said. England took in 10,000 in the nine months before the outbreak of war." Some were placed in foster homes, others in institutions, the eldest went to war."

Hedy stayed with foster families for short periods before quitting school, getting a job and moving into a home for young refugee women. Fluent in German and English, she travelled to Germany in 1945 where she censored outgoing and incoming mail and eventually assembled documentary evidence for trials of doctors accused of experimenting on prisoners. She emigrated to the US where an uncle and his wife had settled in 1938, found a job in New York City, then decided to go to university in Minneapolis where she met her husband. They eventually made their home in Missouri where they raised their children. Israel's 1982 war on Lebanon and the Sabra-Chatila massacre of Palestinians transformed Hedy into an activist. She made her first visit to Israel/Palestine in 2003 and in 2006, during Israel's next onslaught on Lebanon, she took part in protests in Israel itself, attracting considerable abuse. As a requirement for joining the boat journey to Gaza, Hedy had to learn to swim. Unfortunately, she fell ill with heatstroke and did not make the voyage.

Gaza, August 23rd, 2008

The Greek-flagged ferry and fishing boat received a tumultuous welcome in Gaza after breaking Israel's siege and blockade. Millions around the world watched real time satellite images of thousands of Palestinians gathered at Gaza's little fishing port, some taking to boats in a happy flotilla, boys swimming alongside. Car horns honked and Palestinian flags snapped in the breeze as the freedom sailors disembarked and were greeted by a delegation of Gaza worthies.

Although their navigational and communications equipment had been disrupted and Israeli naval vessels had shadowed the little boats until they approached the Gaza coast, Free Gaza had run the blockade. The movement proclaimed the voyage had forced Israel to make a policy change since its foreign ministry had announced, "humanitarian and human rights missions to Gaza will no longer be threatened or stopped by Israel."

Larnaca, August 30th, 2008

The Free Gaza and the Liberty sailed into port after dark. On board were 31 activists and seven Palestinians. As the sailors stepped off the boats onto the quay, they were handed red roses, embraced by the Free Gaza shore team, and surrounded by journalists seeking interviews. The Palestinian who caught everyone's attention was Saed Mosleh, a teenager who had lost a leg to an Israeli tank shell in 2006 and was seeking a custom-made prosthesis. He and his farmer father, Khaled, had been denied visas to exit the Strip. The other five Palestinians on board were Maha Darwish and her four children who had come to Cyprus to visit her brother who lived in Limassol and had not seen his sister for a decade. Her husband was in Egypt.

Nicosia, August 18th, 2014

While surfing for material for *The Deccan Herald*'s school paper on the shooting by a white police officer of black teenager Michael Brown in Ferguson, Missouri, I discovered that three days after celebrating her 90th birthday with her family, Hedy had been arrested and handcuffed in St. Louis outside the state governor's office and charged with "failure to disperse" during a protest. On May 26th, 2016, Hedy died at her home in St. Louis.

Damascus, February 2012

Damascus was not quite its normal self: there was a whiff of gunpowder in the jasmine- scented air. Syrians dodged traffic jams, parked on sidewalks, basked in sunlit parks, sat in cafes where they smoked water pipes and drank tea, hoping the conflict – not yet a full-scale war – would soon end. Damascenes still greeted foreign visitors met on the streets with, "Welcome to Syria" and "How are you?" But they had stopped trusting the world outside their ancient oasis. They believed Turkey, the Arabs and the west, which had courted president Bashar al-Assad for the previous five years, were conspiring to overthrow him and install a government subservient to the west. They compared the expatriate Syrian National Council (SNC), founded by Turkey and based in Istanbul, to the US Central Intelligence Agency-funded Iraqi National Congress (INC). This group had promoted Washington's 2003 war on Iraq by falsely claiming Saddam Hussein had weapons of mass destruction.

No one was winning the 11-month old Syrian conflict. While most of the country remained under government control, entire districts of cities, towns and villages in the north, south and east had fallen to armed groups which had sidelined diminishing popular protests. Regime hawks responded to the challenge by escalating the crackdown on dissent and mounting operations against rebel gunmen with the aim of imposing a "military solution." Arms flowed in and rebel factions proliferated. The SNC refused negotiations with the regime while opposition factions in Damascus called for dialogue. The death toll stood at 6,000-7,000.

Nicosia, September 21st, 2012

Abdel Aziz al-Khair and two colleagues disappeared while driving along the Damascus airport boulevard on their return from a visit to China. Khair, a medical doctor, founder of the domestic opposition National Coordination Board and former communist, had served long years in prison where he had built up a good practice and compelled the authorities to establish a clinic for inmates. He was the true face of the Syrian uprising-revolution, a secular democrat, a man of peace in a country headed for multiple wars, civil and proxy.

Damascus, March 15th, 2015

Passengers exhausted by their long journey sat on the kerb or lounged against the buses that brought them from the north central city of Raqqa, conquered by Islamic State in 2013 and proclaimed the capital of its caliphate in 2014.

Some of the arrivals were from Raqqa itself, others from further north. Men predominated: tribesmen wearing red-and-white checked head cloths and fleece jackets and farmers in coats and jeans. There were, however, a few elderly Bedouin women with small facial tattoos and young mothers with babies and lumpy bundles.

Men who came alone to Syria's capital consulted doctors, renewed identity documents, and registered births, marriages, and deaths before returning to Raqqa while those with families sought refuge.

The weary throng waited patiently for identity cards to be checked by besieged soldiers seeking to detain wanted persons and insurgents dispatched to plant bombs.

At a cafe over glasses of sweet tea, seven farmers described Raqqa under Islamic State. The men, five in coats or sweaters and trousers, two in caftans, were eager to speak and offered their full names, which I did not record since the internet was monitored by the radicals. The conversation flowed seamlessly, one clarifying, another elaborating.

"Only buses come from Raqqa. *Daesh* does not allow us to carry anything. The trip is 13 hours. But it took three hours to pass from Raqqa. It is controlled only by *Daesh*. It holds 20,000 acres [Raqqa city and countryside]. *Daesh* drove out other groups."

When I asked about crops, a solid man with thinning, swept-back hair replied, "This year has been good for cotton, wheat, maize and vegetables. We have rain and irrigation." Seeds were provided b y the World Food Programme and delivered by the Syrian Arab Red Crescent (Sarc).

"Raqqa has no government, no law, no courts, no schools. *Daesh* arrests many people and puts them in prison. Sometimes for practicing different Islam," the man continued.

"You must pray five times a day. They fine people who smoke $10 and even put them in prison for a few days. Fighters use drugs that come from Afghanistan and Turkey."

"US planes attack near the border, in the countryside, but not in the town. The Turkish bor-der is open," stated a serious man, his arms thrown wide. "The Turks control the economy in Raqqa. They bring poor quality, second rate goods." There is no security. Everybody has to be careful... A lot of armed *Daesh* are in the streets. Sixty percent are foreigners – Afghans, Chechens, French, Italians, Turks, Germans, Chinese, Danes, and Australians. Forty percent are

Arabs – Moroccans, Tunisians, Libyans, Saudis, Iraqis and Syrians. The Tunisians and the Saudis are the worst. The Saudis have lots of money. *Daesh* does everything by force... The common language is bad Arabic. Fifteen thousand control Raqqa.

"They have tanks and heavy weapons they brought from Iraq [since the fall of Mosul last June] but no air force." Several of the men said they had seen beheaded corpses in the city centre.

Another man added, "Foreign fighters bring viruses and microbes but the Syrian health ministry sends doctors with medicine and vaccines." The Sarc clinic had closed but some volunteers remained.

"It's like living in a prison. When we finish work, there's nothing to do. There are no cafes, no restaurants, no television, no books, no reading. You cannot open the radio. No mobile phones: the government stopped coverage. Only satellite phones with *Daesh* that cost 50 Syrian pounds ($0.30) a minute, too expensive. We can have computers in our houses and there is foreign internet but not Syrian. *Daesh* publishes a newspaper.

"*Daesh* collects taxes. 30 percent of earnings, in US dollars. Food is available at high prices. We get three hours of electricity every 24 hours from private companies. We are going back 800 years."

He pointed out Raqqa was once the summer capital of Harun al-Rashid, the great Arab caliph who ruled from 789-806. His cultivation of learning made his reign the Golden Age of Islam. *Daesh* "destroyed his statue and the statues of lions in the park and looted items in the museum. The archaeologists moved most things to Damascus."

Civil servants continue to receive their salaries but "they have to go to Homs to collect their pay. *Daesh* allows this so it does not have to aid their families.

"Sixty percent of the people still live in Raqqa because they do not have the money to leave or they want to keep their homes and land. *Daesh* takes over the houses of people who leave. Before [*Daesh*], there were many refugees in Raqqa, from Homs, Hama, and Aleppo. It was a safe area. They fled."

"No one knows where [*Daesh* commander] Abu Bakr al-Baghadadi is. No one sees him. He is like a swallow," said a smiling farmer with sparkling eyes, lifting and plunging his hand to imitate the flight of a swallow. *Daesh* will leave Raqqa. People do not accept this kind of treatment."

Damascus, July 26th, 2015

The Damascus Declaration issued at the close of a two-day conference on combating terrorism urged the international community to place all terrorists on lists, brand them a common enemy, compel countries to cut off support for such organisations and prosecute violators under international law.

By holding the conference and promulgating the declaration, the Syrian government and its allies – Iran, Russia, and Lebanon's Hizbullah – sought to convince the US-led coalition to make common cause against Islamic State, al-Qaeda affiliate Jabhat al-Nusra, and other Sunni extremist groups which had been wreaking havoc in Syria since they took control from rebel factions branded "moderates" sheltering under the umbrella of the Free Syrian Army created by Turkey and recognised by western and Arab powers.

While the US and its partners seemed to be moving glacially toward coordination as a first step, they still were reluctant to join the battle against IS and Nusra because they enjoyed the patronage of Saudi Arabia, Qatar, and, of course, Turkey, regional powers meant to be members of the US-recruited coalition. Cooperation was a long leap away even though Syrian fatalities had, it was estimated, risen to nearly a quarter of a million. Ten million Syrians had been driven from their homes and lands by the four and a half year conflict, four million forced to take refuge in neighbouring countries and hundreds of thousands of compelled to board rickety boats and rubber rafts to reach sanctuary in Europe.

Beirut, January 23rd, 2016

The Syrian crisis might never have become a war if US president Barack Obama had not declared on August 18th, 2011, Assad has to "step aside," Ali, an independent Syrian opposition source said. The regime was ready to make a deal on limited reforms in order "to survive". Assad did not have a free hand. He had to balance pro-and anti-reform forces within the regime. But, Ali observed, a deal could have provided space for reformists to secure the adoption of at least portions of their agenda.

Former US defence secretary Chuck Hagel had stated ten days earlier, "We have allowed ourselves to get caught and paralyzed on our Syrian policy by the statement that 'Assad must go.'"

In August 2011, the opposition was weak, consisting mainly of the Muslim Brotherhood-dominated SNC and the Free Syrian Army, made up of defected army officers and men. A deal with Damascus would have left them high and dry.

But Obama's call for Assad to resign finished off an early accommodation with the government that led to the take-over of the armed opposition by radical fundamentalists, drew in regional and international players and transformed the Syrian uprising into multiple proxy wars involving the US, Europe, Turkey, Saudi Arabia, and Qatar on one side and Russia, Iran, Iraq, and Hizbullah on the other.

Damascus, June 1st, 2014

In spite of a peppering of insurgent mortars and loud reports from army artillery pieces lobbing shells in response, Damascus was calm, busy and bustling. The city was festooned with banners, posters and placards bearing Assad's Image. Two and three storey-long Syrian flags hung from commercial and residential blocks in the modern city. Tiny triangular flags fluttered on cords strung across broad streets in both upscale neighbourhoods and ancient alleyways where little boys wheeled round and round on bicycles.

Billboards were plastered with portraits of Assad flashing a small smile at Damascenes walking round the Seven Fountains Square in front of the Central Bank. Down the avenue, the windows of Syria's most famous chocolatier, Ghraoui, displayed boxes for its delicious wares decorated in the colours of the Syrian flag and commanding buyers to vote.

Other placards and posters called on voters to cast their ballots for former minister Hassan al-Nouri, one of Assad's two rivals for the job. Nouri was a wealthy man who financed his own campaign. The third contender, Maher al-Hajjar, a member of the communist party, did not seem to have resources to finance his campaign. Both were critical of the government's failure to deal with the country's economy and social problems but not of Assad for his handling of the unrest and insurgency that had killed 100,000-150,000 people and driven over nine million Syrians from their homes.

Although in theory and form Syria's first multi-candidate contest, the election was a one horse race won by the incumbent, granting him another seven years in office with the possibility of running, under a new constitution, for another term. As the final result was announced on Syrian television, celebratory fire erupted across the city, shooters forgetting that bullets shot in the air come down, wound and sometimes kill innocent civilians. The security man in my hotel went out on his balcony and loosed off a burst from his machine gun and a mortar struck in front of the bakery across the street. The explosion, and the screams of victims, could be heard by Evelyn Bracken in Dublin while I was giving her the final election results on my mobile phone. When I told her what was happening, she demanded, "Why are you speaking to *The Irish Times*. You should be under your bed." A Spanish colleague had been downstairs in the entrance of the hotel on his way to buy a snack at the bakery when the mortar hit, killing one customer and wounding another.

15

SANCTUARY

Amman, April 9th, 2009

On the sixth anniversary of the fall of Baghdad to US forces, Iraq remained a country riven by conflict. Bombers had slain 45 people and wounded scores in Shia quarters of the capital earlier in the week. Only Mosul and Kirkuk in the north were free of sectarian strife.

Baghdad's Sunni bombers had escalated their onslaught because the ethnic cleansing of the city's mixed quarters had been completed. Before the 2003 US war, the population of the central districts of the city had been roughly 50 percent Sunni, 50 percent Shia. Following the US occupation Sunnis fled; their numbers were said to have fallen dramatically, leaving a solid Shia majority. Vengeful Sunni men who had suffered family members killed or abducted, homes demolished, and livelihoods destroyed, had joined al-Qaeda factions determined to wreak revenge on hapless Shias.

An expert on Iraqi security said the refusal of the Shia-fundamentalist dominated government to induct into the armed forces fighters from the Sunni Awakening Councils, which had partnered US troops in containing al-Qaeda, or to provide fighters with security or civil service jobs had prompted them to join their former enemy or other armed groups. Awakening fighters who were well informed about al-Qaeda elements in their localities had ceased cooperating with the police, preventing them from identifying and neutralising them.

Iraqi media reported military officers from the outlawed Baath party had regrouped and may have been responsible for deadly bombings, which coincided with the anniversary of the fall of Saddam Hussein's regime.

An Iraqi friend fresh from Baghdad said "criminality" was rising due to the dismissal of hundreds of policemen and soldiers accused of corruption or membership in al-Qaeda. Many had formed or been recruited by gangs preying on civilians. Trained only in working with weapons, "these people resort to kidnapping for money and robbery," he stated.

"Iraqis still do not know if they will return home safely once they leave their homes," an Iraqi woman resident in Amman observed. "We Iraqis don't know what we are doing, what our future will be. We want a normal standard of life. We want schooling and medical care... clean water and electricity all day. People have to programme their days by when they have electricity [8-12 hours in 24]. Using generators or buying from neighbourhood providers can cost $600 a month. Everything is expensive," she stated.

Following the 1991 US-led war that drove Iraq from Kuwait, she continued, "The government put mobile generators on the streets and fixed the infrastructure in no time. The politicians who returned to Baghdad with US forces in 2003 are interested only in enriching themselves."

Iraqis did not want to be named when discussing conditions in their country. This was true during the reign of Saddam Hussein and remained true after his fall. Even Iraqis living in Amman.

Jordan was the main refuge for Iraqis. In the run-up to the US war, the UN had erected a tent city at Ruweished near the border where tens of thousands could be received and provided with shelter and sustenance. Iraqis did not come. The tents folded, the camps were abandoned. Iraqis arrived later in waves, particularly after the bombing of the Shia shrine at Samarra at the end of February 2006, an attack that unleashed two years of sectarian conflict and the rise of al-Qaeda.

Eventually the refugees numbered 750,000, about 300,000 registered with the government or the UN. Many of the rest were illegals. Early arrivals did not need visas, but, alarmed by the steady flow of long-term refugees, the Jordanian authorities limited entry by imposing strict conditions and insisting on a financial guarantee of $25,000 for a couple and each child over 18. Middle class Iraqis were forced to sell their homes, furniture and cars to finance their exile. When the money ran out they returned to Iraq and, often, moved in with relatives.

Refugees were from all classes, sects and ethnicities. Wealthy businessmen built grand villas in upmarket neighbourhoods of the Jordanian capital, upper middle class Iraqis managed quite well but middle class families struggled. The poor, the majority of them illegals, lived eight to ten to a room in slum flats they rarely left for fear of being caught by the police and deported. Iraqis formed national subcultures. They patronised Iraqi-owned shops and restaurants and congregated at Iraqi weddings and funerals.

Amman, May 2006

A master brewer, Yaqthan was reduced to making non-alcoholic beer in the original flavour as well as strawberry, lemon, apple and peach when he left increasingly violent Baghdad. "It's much more difficult to make non-alcoholic beer," he said. "It's necessary to compensate for the taste and smell of alcohol. Non-alcoholic beer is very delicate; it's sensitive to infection by bacteria. Beer is just not the same without alcohol."

After studying biology at university in Britain, Yaqthan was sent to Germany by Iraq's Ferida firm to learn beer making, an ancient craft traceable to the Sumerian civilisation of Iraq. The most ancient depiction of beer drinking is on a 6,000-year-old clay tablet showing people sipping the beverage through straws from a communal bowl. A 3,900-year-old poem honouring Ninkasi, the goddess of brewing, contains the oldest known beer recipe. Beer is mentioned in the epic of Gilgamesh and the Old Testament. Noah packed beer for his journey on the arc. In the 1790s BC Hammurabi, the law-giving king of Babylon, laid down the first regulations for taverns. At that time there were 20 varieties of beer in Mesopotamia. Until fundamentalist sectarianism was planted by the US in Iraq, modern breweries had done well in spite of 60 years of political turbulence and warfare.

The first Western-style beer was produced during the period of British colonial rule by a wealthy Shia businessman called Madhaf Khedeiry, who had purchased a small brewery from a British naval vessel after World War II, Yaqthan said. "He started doing stout. But it was not profitable so he invested more money and made lager."

In 1954, Khadduri Khadduri, a Christian originally from Mosul, established the Eastern Brewery, which made Ferida. Both firms flourished due to the unquenchable thirst of British troops and administrators and the emerging class of prosperous local businessmen who gathered for pre-prandial beer at the elegant teak bar of the Alwiya Club.

The 1958 revolution that ousted the British-backed monarchy did not diminish the Iraqi taste for beer, although the officers who took over were suspicious of the Alwiya Club clique.

Beer was so popular that the Baath party, which seized power in 1968, nationalised the Khedeiry firm and the government established two breweries, one in the mixed Christian-Muslim city of Mosul and the other at Amara, a strict Muslim city where locals refused to work in a brewery and Chinese workers were imported to run the facility.

Ferida reached peak production of 30 million bottles a year during the 1980-88 Iraq-Iran war. The beer was sold "always bottled, never in tins," stated Yaqthan proudly.

When sanctions were imposed after Iraq's invasion of Kuwait in 1990, the government ordered a 50 percent cut in production and banned external financial transfers. Ferida survived by bartering malt and hops with a supplier adept at getting round the rules. "How he paid was not our concern. He gave us 100 tons of malt for 30,000 cases of beer."

In 1998, Ferida concluded a deal with a Jordanian company for the production of beer in Amman. "In tins," remarked Yaqthan, disapprovingly.

Ferida remained a family firm until 2001 when Saddam Hussein's eldest son, Uday, and his friends acquired partial control and made soft drinks as well as beer.

In the aftermath of the US occupation, imported Turkish and Dutch beer competed with Ferida and in 2004 Shia fundamentalists began burning shops selling alcoholic drinks. Clandestine vendors hawking beer in buckets of ice appeared beneath Baghdad's Jadriya bridge alongside heroin and hash pedlars. The rise of both Shia and Sunni fundamentalist factions, banned during the republican and Baathist eras, ended public beer drinking in Baghdad and Basra. Kidnappers, bombers and shooters closed down hotels and restaurants, people stayed at home rather than risking violence in the streets.

Yaqthan held on in Amman for as long as he could, hoping things would get better in Baghdad and he could return home, but he joined the Iraqi migration to Toronto where his wife and sons had settled in the expectation of becoming Canadian citizens. Iraqi passports were problematic during both the Baathist and US occupation regimes.

Beirut, September 25th, 2014

The stench of raw sewage mixed with the perfume of spent aircraft fuel and the salty scent of the Mediterranean greeted visitors exiting Lebanon's international airport. Traffic along the airport boulevard was slowed by trundling water lorries that created bottlenecks when they entered the city's narrow streets. The rumble of huge neighbourhood generators and the clack of small private generators competed with hooting horns of impatient drivers stuck in jams. Both generators and vehicles spewed fumes and soot. Drifts of rubbish mounting on street corners were swept into the maws of roaring garbage lorries. Beirut had become a nightmare city.

A report issued by the Lebanese environment ministry revealed how the influx of refugees from the Syrian conflict had placed a "heavy burden on Lebanon's fragile environment." The document showed the figure of 1.087 million Syrian refugees who had registered by May became 1.4 million, or 28.9 percent of the population, if unregistered Syrians, Palestinians from Syria and Lebanese returning from residence in Syria were counted. By the end of the year, this figure was set to rise to 1.8 million. The influx had boosted Lebanon's population density by 37 percent, from 400 to 520 persons per square kilometre.

Lebanon was overwhelmed by solid waste, which was either dumped or burned. Environment minister Muhammad Mashnouk said, "There are dumping grounds on the outskirts of every village and city and some are as large as football fields." Smouldering rubbish polluted the land, ground water and atmosphere and created serious health hazards.

Air pollution had increased by rising levels of gases emitted by refugee vehicles, residential heating plants, and electricity production. Lebanon bought 589 megawatts of electricity from war-torn Syria at a cost of $150 million but this barely alleviated the shortage. Large areas of the country received only four hours of government supplied electricity daily – two in the morning and two in the evening and depended on generators.

Water resources were being depleted at an accelerating rate and the quality of water was deteriorating. While Beirut and its environs suffered from a serious shortage, other regions managed. Springs and wells tapped by firms selling water were being drained and polluted by exploitation.

The influx of refugees only contributed to Lebanon's environmental catastrophe. Decades of governmental neglect and corruption were the main reasons for the dire state of affairs, which the arrival of hundreds of thousands of refugees had made worse. Lebanese of all social backgrounds and persuasions argued the country's system of governance was broken and must be replaced by new political, economic, and social institutions, but this did not happen. Powerful vested interests in the status quo reigned. While Lebanon suffered from human and violent spillover from Syria's civil conflict, neither local politicians nor regional and international powers fighting proxy wars on Syrian soil worried about Lebanon.

Damascus, March 18, 2015

Four years of warfare, destruction, displacement and sanctions had shattered the Syrian economy. The value of its currency had fallen dramatically, inflation stood at 30 percent, and unemployment had reached 60 percent. Nevertheless, Souk al-Hamadiyeh was packed with men, women and children shopping or window-shopping. Vendors hawked cheap toys in the centre of the cobbled route;

porters with carts of goods drove dangerously through the crowd. About half way down the 18th century souk there seemed to be a riot, a protest, or some sort of ruckus.

Instead, I found scores of people clamouring for ice cream while others peacefully spooned their precious ration into their smiling mouths. Small children in tasselled knitted hats dribbled melted ice cream down coat fronts. Elegant matrons carried plastic dishes away from the scrum in order to eat in peace. For Syrians, this parlour, founded by the Bakdash family, is synonymous with ice cream, and ice cream is a small boon at time of war.

Mwaffaq Bakdash invited me to sit down at a table in the crowded shop. "We serve 15,000 customers a day," he said. Ottoman pashas and officials attended the opening of the shop in 1895 by his grandfather, Muhammad Hamdi Bakdash, who died in 1966 at the age of 100.

He invented the recipe and method Bakdash still follows for its pistachio-clad "*bouza*", an elastic confection made of milk and heavy cream; mastic, an aromatic resin collected from the resin tree; and *sahlab*, flour ground from a tuber belonging to the orchid family. Fresh fruit and rose essence flavours are also made along with a range of milk puddings, the same menu the founder adopted in this very shop.

Bouza was originally frozen in a metal container sunk in a wooden barrel filled with ice and salt. The mixture was then pounded with a long-handled mallet. "Since there was no electricity, we went to collect ice from Jebal al-Shaikh [the nearest high mountain occupied by Israel in 1967] and stored it in 20 caves. Donkeys and horses ferried ice to the shop" until electricity came in 1922. Today, stainless steel containers are fixed in a refrigeration unit. Pounding continues with special wooden tools, crafted by Bakdash.

"We did not close when the Turkish period ended [with the collapse of the Ottoman empire] and the french colonial period began after the First World War. King Faisal of Syria and Iraq came in 1918." He was deposed by the French in 1920 and installed as king of Iraq in 1921.

"Lawrence of Arabia visited us in 1927-28," he said. The shop stayed open during the struggle for independence, achieved in April 1946, and has continued to trade ever since, receiving Arab and foreign leaders and personalities. Their black and white photos adorn the walls of the inner rooms.

The missionary founder – whose two sons and four grandsons now run the business – began exporting workers to make *bouza* to Turkey in 1897, France in 1903, and England in 1905. Others were sent to Russia and the US, where the name Bakdash survives. A branch has been established in Jordan, where more than a million Syrians have settled since the outbreak of war.

Maaloula, July 27th, 2015

The 14th century Christian town of Maaloula had cleared away rubble from the streets and repaired the worst of the damage to the two revered convents trashed and sacked by insurgents led by al-Qaeda's *Jabhat al-Nusra* during eight months of occupation. A French organisation had pledged to rebuild the institute dedicated to the preservation and teaching of Aramaic, the language spoken at the time of Jesus, which had survived in Maaloula and nearby villages. A few shops selling cold drinks and wrinkled fruit had resumed business at the town centre; an occasional car made its way through the largely empty streets. Once an open town, a place of pilgrimage for all comers, visits to Maaloula were limited. Outsiders, including Syrians had to secure army permission to enter. The townspeople and government do not want a repeat of al-Qaeda's occupation.

Municipal counsellor Joseph Saadeh, a dentist, said 1,000 of the town's 3,000 permanent residents had returned. Before the insurgent occupation, there would have been 12,000 in summer, largely families from Damascus escaping the heat of the capital. Maaloula was decidedly cooler than Damascus, even at midday. The breeze was fresh and dry, the air unpolluted. Most of those who had returned were old folk eager to escape from exile. Among them were 50 Muslim families, despite betrayal by some of their number.

As we stood in a narrow alleyway in the shade of rough stone-walls of the houses on either side, Joseph related what had taken place in early September 2013. "Maaloula was attacked by the Free Army backed up by [al-Qaeda's] *Jabhat al-Nusra.*" They came from the top of the mountain and quickly overpowered 50 local defenders. The attackers knew exactly about our weak points, who our leaders were. They had supporters among Muslims in the village," who at the time constituted about a quarter of the population.

"In the 1980s, the Muslim Brotherhood began to convert some local Muslims to its ideology and Saudi Wahhabis came with their puritan teachings," he continued. "Before that time, Maaloula's Christians and Muslims lived together peacefully. Muslims helped us prepare for the feast of the Holy Cross on September 14th. Things began to change in 2011."

Betrayed by fellow villagers and attacked by fundamentalist fighters in 2013, the people of Maaloula fled to the neighbouring Muslim village of Ain al-Tineh where they were welcomed. Many went elsewhere to join family members. Maaloula's guardian and tour guide, Joseph stayed in Ain al-Tineh.

The Safir hotel had remained frozen in the liberation day scenario, blasted and burned, its floor strewn with shards of glass and chunks from the ceiling but the Catholic St. Sergius and Bacchus convent next door had been cleared of rubbish and rubble. Large stones that had been blasted from the vault had been replaced and heavily cemented. The convent's centuries old icons and books had either been destroyed or looted and exported.

Rubble had also been removed from the Greek Orthodox St. Takla convent, half way up the rugged gorge where Maaloula was built, and an electrician had installed new tubing for electrical wiring in the walls. Fresh paint had been applied to the reception room where Karin and I met the mother superior in the spring of 2012. Wooden icons, split down the middle by iconoclastic fundamentalists, had been set against a wall. Orphans who had lived here were installed in a convent near *Crac des Chevalier*, Syria's monumental Crusader fort.

I had last visited Maaloula on April 15th, 2014, with six other journalists convoyed by Syrian army officers to the crest of the mountain where the Safir hotel and the Catholic convent are located. The day before this visit, three Lebanese journalists from Hizbullah's Manar television station had been killed when they entered the town. Our Syrian army minders were not taking any chances with us. Before we entered, they made us wait on the roadside with a troop of soldiers until they checked out the situation.

On that occasion we had skated over the very same broken glass, tiles and plaster to reach the hotel terrace where Syrian soldiers and Lebanese Hizbullah fighters were waiting for their snipers to finish off die hard Nusra fighters left behind after the insurgents had been routed. A ripple of machine gun fire and the thud of explosions rose from below as one of the Syrian officers sat under the palm leaf covered pergola and smoked his water pipe. Waiting, waiting until the shooting and explosions stopped before ordering his men to descend the slope to mop up residual defenders.

Sarajevo, July 2014

Bullet pocked walls flashed by the window of the taxi carrying me through the dark city from the airport. Since my normal destinations are battle scarred Gaza, Baghdad and Damascus, I felt quite at home here, attending a brain-storming session on management of southern European cultural heritage during wartime and under post-war conditions. While Israel bombed Gaza, ten "experts" finalised a list of recommendations on destroyed and damaged heritage to be presented to the Parliamentary Assembly of the Council of Europe. While Cyprus marked the 40th anniversary of the devastating Turkish invasion of the north of the island, Turkish Cypriot Ali Tuncay and I provided information on the joint effort of the Greek and Turkish Cypriot communities to rescue and preserve their common cultural heritage. Before leaving for Sarajevo, I had been briefed by Takis Hadjidemetriou, the prime mover on the republic's side.

At the end of the first day of discussions, we visited Sarajevo's town hall, built during the rule of the Austro-Hungarian empire and inaugurated in 1894. In August 1992, Serbian shelling completely destroyed the building, then the national library containing 1.5 million volumes, 155,000 rare books, and 700 unique manuscripts. Restoration by Austria began in 1996, and completion was celebrated in May with a concert by the Sarajevo Symphony Orchestra. We were led into the Moorish-style building through a side door, ushered into the grand lobby to the strains of the Blue Danube Waltz, and taken on a tour of elegant rooms perfumed by paint. Their walls so bright as to be gaudy.

That evening four of us strolled through the market near our hotel and dined at a restaurant where beer and wine were served at the same time devout Bosnians were breaking the Ramadan fast with tall glasses of lemonade and plates of seasonal specialities.

After our final session, we were taken to Mostar in Herzegovina to see the reconstructed old bridge built by the Ottomans in the 16th century and destroyed by Croats in 1993. An icon of the war that tore apart Tito's Yugoslavia, the footbridge arches over the Naretva River, connecting the two sides of the town. Crossing on the day we visited meant dodging thousands of tourists whose visits to the town provide funds for the upkeep of the bridge.

South of Mostar, at the 15th century town of Pocitelj, we climbed the steep slope to a ruined fort and were offered tea at the home of an engraver, a member of the resident artists' colony dwelling in beautifully restored stone built houses roofed with dark stone slates.

Back on my journalistic beat, the death toll in Gaza was 76 Palestinians and five Israelis and a Thai. The Islamic State systematically blew to bits Muslim shrines in northern Iraq, beginning with the tomb of Jonah, the Biblical figure who, according to tradition, survived being swallowed by a whale. The tomb of Daniel, who had been imprisoned with a lion, and the shrine of Seth, said to be the third son of Adam and Eve, were also destroyed.

Palmyra, April 6th, 2016

The road to Palmyra was long, the journey paused by checkpoints, but traffic was light. At the first checkpoint our three-car convoy was greeted by the general in charge of military media relations for the province of Homs. He provided us with an escort of four armed soldiers in a yellow taxi. After some time, this group peeled off and was replaced by another taxi carrying armed troops. Further on, a pick-up with a mounted machine-gun became our escort, and was replaced by an armoured pick-up with a machine gun.

We were told *Daesh* fighters lingered in the desert near Palmyra, but 60 kilometres from the city, our final armed escort turned back leaving us on our own and wondering why the army did not accompany us all the way to the city with its ancient ruins, recaptured from *Daesh* on March 27th. The only sign of the ongoing war was a charcoaled corpse in boots lying on the roadside near Palmyra.

Ancient Palmyra, the "City of Palms," is a Neolithic site, which entered the history books 4,000 years ago. Palmyra was a regional commercial hub, a transit point for Silk Road caravans travelling to and from China and India to the Mediterranean. The city-state was a wealthy, autonomous area in the Roman empire when, Palmyra's beautiful warrior Queen Zenobia, a descendant of Egypt's Queen Cleopatra, seized territory from Rome. Between 269-72 AD, she conquered Anatolia, Lebanon, Palestine and Egypt. Rome responded by taking back its lands, capturing Zenobia, and transporting her to Rome, where she, apparently, married a provincial governor and gained recognition as a philosopher.

Palmyra was a city of ghosts. Ghosts of its illustrious ancient past as well as its precarious present. The new city had been emptied of its 750,000 citizens as well as of the 250,000 refugees settled there in the belief that *Daesh* would not be permitted to capture this city and its splendid Greco-Roman ruins. Islamic State fighters arrived in convoys from Deir al-Zor to the north on May 21st, 2015. Neither the Syrian air force nor the warplanes of the US-led anti-Islamic State coalition took notice.

The cult came, saw and conquered. Murdered and destroyed. The new city was empty, its blasted and bludgeoned buildings offered rough shelter to the Syrian soldiers who had returned after a bloody battle, victory determined by Russian airpower. Islamic State gunmen fled with their families, hostages and slaves.

The ruins of the 2,000 year-old trading city no longer hosted the radicals but the shades of previous conquerors, none of them eager to lay waste to monuments that had stood the test of time. Defined by the mauled municipality building on one side and the battered museum on the other, the square was the site of atrocities against monument and man.

At the entrance to the museum, one of the first victims, the Lion of Lat, a first century BC statue of a lion gripping a crouching gazelle, had been crushed. Fortunately, the museum had been cleared of its moveable treasures two days before the fighters arrived. The roof had been holed by shells. The first floor was littered with splintered wood, fallen chunks of plaster, and stones. Funerary monuments depicting persons and the statue of Athena in graceful flowing robes had been beheaded.

As was Palmyra's living monument, Khaled al-Asaad, the 82-year old curator and protector of the ruins for more than half a century. After Islamic State seized Palmyra, he hid in a nearby village but was found, tortured and decapitated in the dusty square in front of the museum. His body, his head between his feet, glasses poised on his nose, was displayed on a stumpy metal structure on the traffic circle.

Beyond the killing ground was a post commanded by a Russian army officer in full uniform, flanked by armed and tanned young soldiers with bare torsos. The officer forbade photos of Russians but told us we could walk safely through the white and gold limestone ruins, the entrance guarded by a pair of Russian soldiers in black, automatic weapons to hand.

A photographic drone brought by a colleague soared, circled and buzzed like a hive of angry bees over the sentinel columns basking in the hot spring sun. The 2,000 year-old Bel Shamim temple was the first monument Islamic State had imploded; in its place was an empty arch and rubble. The Victory Arch consisted of two stumps and a pile of stone blocks. The amphitheatre, which used to host concerts and plays, remained intact. On the stage victorious Islamic

State commanders had lined up 25 Syrian soldiers on the stage and ordered teenage recruits to execute them.

Grafitti on the gate to the compound housing the Bel Temple, dating to 32 AD, warned "citizens and brothers", the latter cult members, entry is "forbidden". The temple, rival to Lebanon's Baalbek, had been reduced to a single arch sitting on top of a mound of whole and broken limestone blocks, some massive, bleached white over the centuries.

The wind picked up as we walked along the colonnade of Straight Street, the main avenue of Greco-Roman Palmyra. Joseph, a former tour guide who currently conveys journalists, pointed to small shelves toward the top of each column. "There were statues of generals on these shelves. They were put so high so they could be seen by Zenobia and her retinue as they rode by on their camels."

Palmyra glowed golden as the late afternoon sun began to sink. The voices of the Antiquities Department team sent to survey the damage to the site echoed among Palmyra's 1,300 columns. The flat, metallic reports of near and far explosions rolled over the vast site while invisible Russian sappers blew up mines, sending up puffs of smoke frittered away by the breeze.

I strolled out of the ruins with Wael al-Hafian, chief engineer of the Homs branch of the Antiquities Department. "It will take a month to clear the mines before we can begin the technical work [on the broken monuments]... Palmyra was ruled for 1,400 years by Muslims, who did not seek to destroy it. Only these [puritan] Wahhabis have tried. They want to take away our history, culture and identity so we will accept them."

Damascus, April 7th, 2016

Although fears over his security had paused the visit of Syria's Director of Antiquities Maamoun Abdulkarim, he was delighted and excited over the liberation of Palmyra. When we met in his office at the National Museum, he urged me to have a look at images of the site captured by the drone on the day I had walked around the ruins. "All the stones are there, we can rebuild. We can reconstruct the two temples and the Triumphal Arch from materials in place on the sites," he stated.

"We are preparing a plan to reconstruct. We have photos of the state of the buildings before *Daesh* and after *Daesh*. We will respect the authenticity of the buildings and not add foreign material to the facade. We have the expertise. The foundations of the Bel Temple and Bel Shamim are solid, the stones are not broken. We can quarry stone from Palmyra if we need to." The same was true of the broken Triumphal Arch.

He had detailed architectural drawings of the two temples prepared by French archaeologists Robert Ami in the 1930s and Paul Collar from 1953-56. "We have a team of 30 persons - architects, archaeologists and engineers." From drone surveys of the site, he concluded 80 percent of Palmyra had survived.

His department was preparing plans for UNESCO and its partners and consulting inter-national experts who can help raise funds. "I can give you a promise that we can finish the maximum of the work within five years. The monuments will not be the same as before *Daesh*. I hope the international community understands that the restoration of Palmyra is for the whole world and the issue will not be politicised." He feared sanctions imposed on the Syrian government could hinder the work. "Palmyra is our common heritage."

Rawabi, April 28th, 2015

Ghazi and I set off early for our appointment with Asmah Salamah who was set to take us on a tour of Rawabi, the first new Palestinian town to be built in the West Bank for as long as anyone could remember. A stout, balding former taxi driver, Ghazi and his brother had inherited their deceased father's business selling and installing tyres for West Bank customers. Ghazi, whom I had known for 20 years, was interested in Rawabi as a place where he might be able to retire and escape Jerusalem's tensions and complications.

Driving through Ramallah and Bir Zeit we saw signs directing motorists to Rawabi but after entering the spare countryside beyond the university town, we became hopelessly lost and had to ring Asmah to ask for guidance. She collected us at a roundabout we had gone round at least three times while hunting for Rawabi.

We followed her Mercedes up the road to Rawabi, situated on two limestone ridges in the Judean mountains. We started our visit in what could be called the "construction area", where huge golden, cream and grey stone blocks excavated from the hillside were cut and shaped and cement was mixed. Men in bright vests and hardhats were going about their tasks. Asmah said Palestinian blacksmiths and carpenters came from all corners of the West Bank to work on Rawabi. "The labour force works three shifts and we have enough material on site so that if the road is closed, construction can continue." Israeli settlers occasionally harassed workers and stole Palestinian flags flying from Rawabi's public buildings.

Rawabi was built to house 25,000 people in the initial stage and to expand to 40,000, if there was demand for flats. When completed it was to have 23 neighbourhoods, three schools at all levels, a mosque, a church, shops, a commercial centre, restaurants and cafes, cinemas, and a golden stone amphitheatre where audiences could attend plays and music performed against the backdrop of the purple-green hills. Streets are paved with red, black and grey bricks and each neighbourhood has its own parking arrangements, which Ghazi said, *sotto voce*, were inadequate. Furnished model apartments were spacious and comfortable but similar. Buyers could choose from a limited range of floor tiles, kitchens and other built-in fittings.

The project, the brainchild of Bashar al-Masri, a wealthy dual-US-Palestinian citizen, was funded from his private fortune and by the Qatar Investment Authority. The Palestinian Authority was unable to raise the $140 million it had pledged to pay for Rawabi's external infrastructure. Money was tight at times. Deputy manager Amir Dajani said, "Apartments cost between $80,000-$220,000, depending on size and location." Much cheaper than in East Jerusalem, where Ghazi lives, or in Ramallah, a jungle of costly high rises. Civil servants and academics were expected to choose Rawabi.

Dajani continued, "We were delayed for 18 months" due to Israel's refusal to allow the laying of a 1.1 kilometre pipe to Rawabi across "Area C," the 62 percent of the West Bank under full Israeli control.

Ghazi sighed in disappointment as we departed and were driving toward Bir Zeit. Rawabi was not a dream town providing an escape for life as a Palestinian.

Settler violence, access roads and water were major issues for families seeking to live in Rawabi, a town that could, ultimately, become just another Palestinian islet in the Israeli military sea the West Bank had become. Under the overly optimistic Oslo Accord, Palestinians had expected Israel to withdraw from the West Bank which would have become the heartland of an often promised Palestinian state that had never emerged.

Homs, December 15th, 2015

At the Palmyra Square entrance to the city, the red, white and black Syrian flag flew over an empty firing position made of rusting metal barrels wedged between two ancient columns. Syria's former manufacturing hub and third largest city was once again fully under the rule of Damascus.

The green, white and black flag of the rebellion, launched in 2011, had been struck and the guns had fallen silent in al-Waer district, the last to remain a hotbed of the insurgency. A UN-brokered ceasefire and the December 9th evacuation of 719 fighters and their families had signalled an end to the war with al-Waer. The remaining 2,000 fighters and their families were due to be relocated to insurgent-held locations in the north and west in February. Before the crisis, al-Waer had 300,000 residents, 75,000 were said to remain, many displaced from other areas.

The sole entrance to al-Waer was a passage at the edge of a large Syrian army camp on the western outskirts of Homs. Civilians crossed in both directions. Arrivals' parcels were checked by soldiers sitting at a table beneath a simple shelter. A pick-up piled high with crates of eggs and two small lorries carrying defrosting meat were waiting for permission to move into the town.

Dr. Zacharia al-Shaar stepped back from his van as it was being loaded with boxes of medical supplies, including ones for kidney dialysis, for al-Birr hospital, run by a charitable organisation. The hospital offered free treatment for all, he stated, including fighters. "The situation is better now but foreign fighters remain. They don't want reconciliation, they take orders from outside." Among the foreign militants were Chechens, Saudis, Afghans, Tunisians, and Libyans who had entered al-Waer through tunnels, which had eventually been destroyed by the army. "Water is ok, we have 9-10 hours of power," the doctor stated.

At the checkpoint, marked by a few strands of wire and rubbish, boys of nine and ten waited for bags of freshly baked bread from the vast mechanised bakery nearby. Each family received eight flat round loaves a day for about $0.16 a parcel. Fresh food brought in by merchants was expensive but basic supplies – rice, sugar, and lentils – were provided by humanitarian agencies granted infrequent access.

Opponents of the truce in al-Waer responded on December 13th with triple bombings killing 22 and wounding 104 in the eastern Homs neighbourhood of Zahra, a loyalist stronghold.

The Old City, evacuated by fighters in May 2014, was calm. Rubble had been cleared from the streets and electricity restored although current was rationed. Some damaged homes had been repaired, families were returning, drawn back by reopening schools. Shops and restaurants had revived. A decorated Christmas tree gleamed in the window of al-Bustan, a popular restaurant displaying seasonal menus.

16

LIBERATION

Nicosia, March 24th, 2017

The popular unrest of the Arab Spring crushed and Cairo's Tahir Square once again a busy traffic hub, Egypt's ousted president Hosni Mubarak became a free man when released from custody at a military hospital in Cairo's Maadi suburb and returned to his villa in the wealthy Heliopolis district. His lawyer, Farid al-Deeb said Mubarak, 88, had breakfasted with family and friends, indicating the authorities had spirited him through the capital's streets early on the Friday holiday to avoid attracting attention, gridlock in the streets and enemies. Around the time he left hospital, a man died and his wife and two children were injured by an explosion not far from the hospital.

Mubarak had been acquitted by Egypt's highest court from the charge of failing to prevent the deaths of 846 protesters in clashes with riot police and plainclothes security agents during the 18-day uprising that ended his 30-year rule in 2011. Following his fall on February 11th, Mubarak had fled Cairo for his mansion at the Red Sea resort of Sharm el-Sheikh. Two months later he was detained with his two sons, Gamal and Alaa, for questioning on allegations of abuse of power and corruption. He was ordered to stand trial before a special court in Cairo that August at a time Egyptians were protesting in the streets and squares against the successor military regime for failing to carry out the demands of the revolution – "Bread, freedom and justice."

Aware that public opinion insisted on accountability for the misdeeds and repression of the Mubarak era, he and his sons were held in prison and treated as criminals when they were compelled to appear in the cage which serves as a dock in Egyptian courts. The proceedings were televised in Egypt and round the world in a show of compliance with the demands of volatile crowds.

In June 2012 he was convicted on the charge of involvement in the deaths of protesters and sentenced to 20 years in prison. Retrials began in 2013, ending with his acquittal on March 2nd this year. The court not only declared him innocent but also rejected further calls for retrials and demands from victims' families to renew civil cases.

In January, the high court had upheld a three-year prison sentence for Mubarak and his sons on corruption charges. The sons were released as they had served the allotted time but Mubarak remained at the military hospital until the authorities felt it was safe to free him. The Mubaraks still face prosecution for allegedly receiving gifts worth hundreds of thousands of dollars from *al-Ahram*, the state-owned daily. Mubarak is also banned from leaving Egypt due to investigations by the Illicit Gains Authority for increases in his personal fortune after his ouster.

Egypt had come full circle since his removal. As Mubarak's post before becoming vice-president had been air chief marshal, the military was determined to look after its own. Thousands of Muslim Brotherhood supporters and dissidents had been imprisoned while Mubarak and his entourage were gradually freed by the courts. Protests were few and muted as Egyptians sought an end to the instability, violence, and economic upheaval that had followed liberation.

Nicosia, April 23rd, 2003

Shortly after seven in the morning, Hanum Fikrit Ahmad Mavroupa, an elderly woman from Potamia, one of the rare remaining Turkish Cypriot villages in the republic, showed her identity card to Greek Cypriot police at the Ledra Palace hotel crossing office, and walked past the barrier through the buffer zone to the Turkish Cypriot checkpoint. The police ignored her. She sat down on a bench under a tree and waited. A Greek Cypriot couple turned up and were told, "Not today," although the Turkish Cypriot authorities had announced the opening of the crossing would take place that morning. More people from both communities arrived and hung round until a high ranking Turkish Cypriot official turned up and gave the order to let them through. The first Turkish Cypriot, Hasan Pala, an artist, crossed at nine thirty and made his way into the south. The old lady going north waited until eleven. News that the Green Line crossing was open had spread like wildfire. By noon hundreds of people had gathered on both sides of the line, clamouring to cross. Greek Cypriots were allowed to drive their cars into the north if they bought insurance from Turkish Cypriot vendors who normally dealt with tourists. Turkish Cypriots had to come on foot. The republic, taken by surprise by the decision to open the crossing, had to make arrangements for insuring vehicles.

At the end of the day, nearly 3,000 Turkish Cypriots and 1,700 Greek Cypriots had crossed and returned to their own sides. The atmosphere was cheerful and relaxed. At least 150 Turkish Cypriots, including a lad on a bicycle in the first wave, went to the Nicosia district office and applied for passports from the republic. Turkish Cypriot documents were recognised only by Turkey.

Over the next few days the Ledra Palace crossing was mobbed. In the south, Greek Cypriot cars parked along the sides of roads nearby. Some people slept overnight in their vehicles; others went home, leaving their cars in line to make the journey the next day. Thousands of Greek Cypriots took advantage of the four-day Easter holiday to visit former homes in the north, the walled city of Famagusta, and the collapsing monastery of Saint Andreas at the tip of the Karpass peninsula. Turkish Cypriots crossing on Easter Sunday were offered coloured eggs and braided bread, a holiday delicacy. For the first time in three decades, Cypriot accented Greek conversation was heard in Kyrenia's tiny harbour.

For Cypriots breaching the Green Line was an event comparable to the fall of the Berlin wall and proof the two communities could get on and live together. Opposition Turkish Cypriot politician Osker Ozgur said at an Easter gathering in the republic, "The people have proved that the division of our country is artificial."

Pundits said Cyprus' scheduled 2004 entry into the EU had put pressure on Turkey, the occupying power in the north, to open the gates to show that Ankara was prepared to resolve the Cyprus problem by ending division of the island and separation of its communities. As a member of the EU, Cyprus would have a veto on Turkey's accession to the bloc.

Baghdad, August 2004

The situation had gone from bad to worse. Tahrir (another Liberation) Square at the centre of the capital was a sweltering traffic jam. Famous fish restaurants along the Tigris were closed. US armoured scout cars, weapons trained on advancing vehicles, parked on the islands separating the tides of traffic along Karrada's broad avenues. Resistance fighters determined to attack US troops and Ali Baba primed to prey on civilians lurked in the shadows. Electricity was fitful, phones worked within but not between districts.

I went to the Alwiya club, founded in 1924 by the British, for a meeting with Dhari Khamis Dhari, a municipal councillor from

Abu Ghraib, the urban and agricultural area west of Baghdad, an area made infamous by its prison. A descendant of a leading figure in the 1920 rebellion against Britain, Dhari was very proud of Abu Ghraib's council, the first to be founded after the US war. It ran the police, 135 schools, the local irrigation system, and other key services.

Over tankards of beer, Dhari, a German-trained engineer and tribal elder, said, "Security is much better in Abu Ghraib than Baghdad, perhaps because Abu Ghraib's inhabitants are tribal. I told the Americans just after the war to protect [essential infrastructure] but they failed. They came without a plan and did not know what to do. They could not cope.

"I have repeatedly asked the Americans to fix security – theirs and ours. But they reply that if they spend more time on their security, they will have to give up time to work on our security, electricity and water. I recommended that they handover [our] security to our police. They know the place. They know who the criminals are and where they live. Our police need cars and radios to operate."

Dhari was in despair, "Things are going too slowly." One of his friends, whom he met at the club bar every Friday at noon, said, "The British knew how to be occupiers, the Americans don't."

Baghdadis found the lack of communications particularly galling. Shortly before my arrival, Iraqis and visitors who had mobile phones with roaming applications suddenly discovered they could switch on to two providers, one Bahraini, the other Kuwaiti, which had set up networks in the capital. People were liberated from irksome satellite phones that worked only outside buildings when they worked at all. But after a few days, the occupation regime closed down the companies and prohibited mobile services operating without approval by the authorities. They were in the process of issuing tenders for a nationwide network, which would not be ready before November. Until then Iraqis seeking to contact family, friends, and business associates had to rely on internet cafes that had sprung up all over Baghdad and other cities and towns.

Dhari and his friends were not the only Iraqis impatient with the US authorities. Over a biryani lunch at the White Palace across the street from my hotel two Iraqi businessmen complained they and their countrymen were being excluded from reconstruction and development contracts. "US officials ask us to submit detailed tenders for projects and then handover our specifications to foreign firms which get the contracts," said one. When I took up this accusation with the young woman handling relations with Iraqi businessmen, she shrugged. She was a China specialist with no experience in the Middle East.

Shortly before I was set to leave Baghdad, *The Irish Times* asked me to go on a mission with a US military unit. When I asked to see the person in charge of "embeds" at the press office located in the convention hall, an officer appeared from the inner office. I apologised for the lateness of my application but wondered if it would be possible to fix something for the next day. She was doubtful. It normally took several days to organise "embeds." In friendly fashion I asked where she was from. "Virginia," she replied. Where in Virginia? I persisted, well aware that making a personal connection might magic an arrangement. "Ashland," she responded. Ah, my daughter lives in Beaverdam. "My mother goes to church in Beaverdam."

Early the next morning Abu Ammar drove me to a military camp on the edge of the city where I was supposed to meet a team conducting tankers delivering water to a poor district. The guard at the gate sent us to the British-built Iraqi military academy some distance away. I waited impatiently while another guard processed several people in line, afraid I would miss my "embed" which was supposed to be at ten o'clock.

After he had phoned someone inside the base on behalf of another person, I used the "where-are-you-from" ploy; this time, Michigan," the state of my birth, worked. He soon ushered both Abu Ammar and me through the outer gate into the security line to be searched. I passed inspection easily but Abu Ammar, a tough middle aged Shia with a bristly chin and a grubby caftan, squirmed in embarrassment when he was patted down by a young female officer. The US had put women on security duty to check both men and women without thinking that Iraqi men, unused to handling by women other than their wives and mothers, would object to this procedure.

Once inside the academy, we were told to go back to the base we had first visited. When we got there I managed to find an officer who had been informed of my "embed". But we did not depart right away. We had to wait for the water tankers. Two of the soldiers on the mission took me to their quarters, an air-conditioned barrack room with two sets of bunk beds, its walls decorated with family photos. The soldiers, both from the south, offered me a ration bar dubbed "meals ready to eat." I asked if they had proper chow sometime during the day. They replied in the affirmative but said that everything they consumed came from Kuwait. Can you eat anything from here? I demanded. No. I had noticed there were lovely watermelons and other fruit on a stand just outside the base gate. My hotel served steaks, chops, pastas, fish and a wide range of vegetables.

I was kitted out for the mission in helmet and flak jacket, which I put on over my white Indian *kurta* and cotton trousers and was given two bottles of water. Our pair of humvees were basic. No windows or doors, broken seat belts, sagging bucket seats, a hole through the canvas roof to allow the machine gunner to stand and survey the scene around us. The temperature was 55 degrees Celsius, making it impossible to touch the frame of the vehicle. Only one battered tanker turned up. The other had broken down. As we pulled out of the base into traffic, I found huge lorry tyres, their treads worn thin, rolling just outside my window.

We proceeded to the outskirts of Baghdad to twin towns – one shaped like a triangle, the other rectangular. Our translator directed us along a lightly etched track in the sand past people who shouted in menacing tones, "Where is the electricity, where is the electricity?" At triangle town we stopped at a make-shift square surrounded by tumbledown mud brick houses and tents where men, women and children crowded round with buckets, tins, and even tea pots to collect water from the gushing hose at the back of the lorry. Here, water not electricity was priority.

When we returned to base and I took off my flak jacket, my sweat soaked *kurta* and trousers clung to my body.

On the afternoon before my departure, Karin and I returned to Basim's house in Mansour, to his salon filled with paintings by Iraqi pioneer masters worth a fortune to him and his family. Selling just one would keep them for a year he said. I had to pay and collect my painting. I had dreamed of the painting during my absence from Baghdad. I don't know why. It is not a joyful painting although of a festival. The mood is more solemn than cheerful. He had rolled the canvas, pushed it into a tube and bound it securely. When I passed the tube through the x-ray machine at the airport, the man on duty asked the age of the painting. "Seventy-six," I said. "The year is written on the painting." He did not bother to check.

Living with this impressionist painting is a curious experience: it is never the same. It changes colour and shading throughout the day. In the afternoon, yellow makes it bright; in the evening purple transforms the scene into the dusk shut down of the little amusement park.

A few months after I bought the painting, Basim's ill-disposed neighbour told a US officer his children were fighting against the occupation. Soldiers arrived, trashed the house and arrested his grown Down's syndrome children. They knew nothing of politics or resistance. By buying the Shukri I had saved it from destruction.

I was very happy. My friends the Radis were not in Baghdad during my last visit to the city.

After well-known Irish-born aid worker Margaret Hassan, whom I had met earlier, was kidnapped that October and killed a few weeks later I decided to stay away until there was a semblance of security.

Doha, March 2007

The scrum at airport immigration was generated by undisciplined Asian labourers brandishing letters awarding visas. Cool men in white thobes and head coverings behind a bank of desks processed each case efficiently, quickly and waved all comers through. Helma met me at the exit and we waited for Amer to make a round of the packed parking lot and pick us up. Since it was the eve of the Friday holiday, the streets in town were packed with cars. Although I had seen Helma often in Baghdad during the long hot summer of 2004, I had met Amer only once, in his office in January 1993, the morning after Bill Clinton made his first cruise missile strikes on industrial targets in central Baghdad.

Detained a decade later by the US occupation regime, Amer did not emerge until 2005 from the US prison for leading figures in the ousted government. He was working as research adviser at the Qatar Foundation. Helma and Amer drove me to the handy service flat she had found for me at the centre of town.

The next morning I rang Imad. "We're going to the beach. We'll pick you up in 15 minutes." Although I had never met him, I recognised Imad immediately. He closely resembled his brother Walid who had been a good friend for decades. After collecting the rest of the picnic party – two Iraqi families and two Filipino maids in two large vehicles, we convoyed to a crusty beach on the Gulf of Bahrain.

A US and British-trained nuclear scientist, Imad, also employed at the Qatar Foundation, offered me a tin of Guinness before setting up his apparatus to broil slabs of fish over charcoal. "Qataris like Iraqis," Imad observed. "They welcome us and even thank us for working to build their country." About 1,000 Iraqis had already taken up jobs in Qatar where they felt at home with blue skies, desert landscape, and blistering heat in summer.

While Imad seasoned the coals before laying the fish on the grill, he prepared his water pipe before telling me how he left Iraq. Since his wife Niran and their children had left and settled along with many Iraqis in Toronto, he was determined to join them. However, as a scientist who had worked in Iraq's nuclear programme, he was barred from leaving the country. He appealed for help from Foreign Minister Muhammad Saeed Sahhaf who aided his escape through the Kurdish area. Able to depart only with possessions he could carry, Imad packed a few clothes and the elegantly carved wooden stem of his pipe.

"It has a story," he said. After graduating from Michigan State University, he returned to Baghdad where his father made him a present of five Iraqi dinars, a fair sum at the time. Since Imad wanted a particular type of water pipe, he went to the souk to consult a master craftsman. "He told me to go to a certain house in the red light district and to ask for the last leg." A puzzled Imad was greeted as a potential customer at the house but when he explained to the madame what he wanted, she produced the leg of a table. "The last leg of Nuri Said's table," an historic piece of furniture. Iraq's final pre-revolution prime minister Nuri Said was slain along with the king when the palace was overrun on July 14th, 1958. When he left Iraq, Imad had been compelled to leave behind the pipe's antique glass bowl and was looking for another.

Beirut, June 10th, 2011

Clad in her party black Ma Radi arrived with a small bowl filled with cream gardenias, their robust perfume competing with the muted scents of bunches of flowers placed on the long dining table, covered in crisp white linen and laid with gleaming knives and forks and sparkling glassware. For the first party in decades, the hotel roof was festooned with lights, the bar stocked with a range of drinks, and the small pergola of latticed wood furnished with couches.

Friends of a dozen nationalities – Lebanese, Syrian, Iraqi, Iranian, Palestinian, Indian, Irish, French, Cypriot, British, German, and US – I had met during the 50 years since I spent my first night at the Mayflower. At that time parties were hosted on the roof but a 15-year war had intervened. Sherif, who had taken over management of the Mayflower from his parents, had been delighted with the idea when I had put it to him earlier in the year. The party was a happy, peaceful moment during the turmoil of the Arab Spring. Most attendees had been touched by one war or another.

Dinner was a mezze of Lebanese specialities served with Lebanese wines. The night was warm, the breeze from the Mediterranean gentle, soft. Before the guests arrived, the wind had picked up briefly while I was setting out place cards, sending several spiralling into the street below. No one fell into the small splash pool or, the next morning, felt the ill effects of too much wine. Ten of us set off in a minibus for the Bekaa Valley to visit the majestic ruins of the Roman temples of Baalbek, transformed in the 12th century into a fortress where the warrior Salah ed-Din had lived as a child. We lunched in a restaurant near the Roman site at Anjar, where Armenians fleeing Ottoman massacres had settled after World War I. War is a constant presence in this region.

Amman, 26 April 2015

Jordan was an island of relative peace and stability in the region's storm-ridden lands. Bordered in the west by the Israeli-occupied Palestinian territories, the north by devastated Syria, the east by sectarian-conflicted Iraq and militarist Saudi Arabia, and the south by troubled Egypt, Jordan weathered the turbulence stirred by the Arab Spring. While facing the scourges of poverty, corruption and paternalism, Jordan muddled through.

Fired by the powerful images of hundreds of thousands of Egyptians demanding "Bread, Freedom and Justice" broadcast from Cairo's Tahrir Square during 2011, thousands of Jordanians poured into the streets. "Jordanians hoped freedom was coming: freedom to end corruption, and a minimum level of social justice," stated veteran journalist Lamis Andoni.

But these demonstrations did not draw millions or take place countrywide, as did those in Egypt. Tunisian, Egyptian, Yemeni and Syrian protesters soon called for their republican rulers to stand down but Jordanians did not ask King Abdullah to abdicate. When he promised reform and an end to corruption, demonstrators left the streets and squares.

Lamis observed, "Today people are just as angry and marginalised [as other Arabs] but they fear that the alternative [to the monarchy] will be *Daesh* or a bloody regime like those of Syria, Iraq, or Egypt. The difference between Jordanians and the rest is that they chose the Jordanian regime. Although there is still a lot of marginalisation, stability is a priority." This had negative consequences. "The regime is using this to silence dissent and impose economic policies that do not solve any problems. It does not feel it needs to address problems."

Analyst Oman Obeidat argued, "All the people – Jordanians and Palestinians – have interests in preventing an explosion. No one wants to divide the country. The regime is not a dictatorship." He differed with Lamis when he said, "People can criticise the government... The Gulf countries, Saudi Arabia, the US and Israel do not want an explosion in Jordan as the [other Arab monarchies] would be threatened. The Gulf countries support Jordan financially and politically."

He did not say these countries, along with Turkey, backed the Syrian opposition and insurgents, promoting and prolonging the war in that country.

Businessman Hasan Wahbeh believed external powers "want Jordan to be stable because it is a dumping ground" for people fleeing conflicts in neighbouring states.

When asked how Jordan had avoided unrest, a senior Jordanian statesman observed, "We are accustomed to survive." He paused and added, "We have never had a balanced budget since the state was founded" thanks to Palestinian, Iraqi, Lebanese, Syrian and other refugees who have sought sanctuary in Jordan and stayed.

Jerusalem, May 6th, 2015

With no end to the Israeli occupation in sight, despairing young Palestinians had begun a "lone wolf intifada" by mounting individual attacks with knives and vehicles on Israeli soldiers and civilians. As always, this violence was more deadly for Palestinians than Israelis.

Sipping red wine in the garden restaurant of the Jerusalem hotel near the old Green Line dividing the eastern and western sides of the city, Israeli peace activist Jeff Halper said there can be no more traditional intifadas involving Palestinian resistance movements or organised groups. Since Israel has divided occupied East Jerusalem, Gaza and Palestinian-administered areas in the West Bank into tightly controlled enclaves, Palestinians are physically and politically fragmented. "The Israeli army is everywhere. Squads posing as Palestinians enter Palestinian town and villages at will and arrest and shoot Palestinians. Israeli and Palestinian Authority intelligence and police forces co-operate as neither wants an explosion.

"Nothing is unknown, thanks to Israeli surveillance by satellites, drones and balloons," stated Halper, a veteran critic of Israeli policy, He said 43 senior Israeli operatives serving in Unit 8200, a key Israeli intelligence gathering agency, had resigned because they objected to the fact their work "intruded into the private lives of Palestinians." He contended Palestinians do not face South African style apartheid but "warehousing." He compared their plight to the situation of inmates in US prisons, locked away and excluded from society.

During a meeting in his office in Ramallah, former Palestinian foreign minister Nabil Shaath said there could be "no progress in talks as long as Benyamin Netanyahu heads the Israeli government. There will be no political peace and no economic peace... Oslo is dead... the talks chaperoned by the Americans are dead. Oslo was a Trojan horse [that enabled the Israeli takeover] of 62 percent of the land in the West Bank, 92 percent of the water, and 100 percent of its minerals. [Israelis] control all access and movement.

"The only option is non-violent resistance modelled on the campaign led by Nelson Mandela [in South Africa]." He disagreed with Halper by characterising the Palestinian struggle as an "anti-apartheid struggle that will put pressure on the Israelis to change their policies and make them think peace is better than occupation."

Speaking to me at his office on campus on the edge of Ramallah, Bir Zeit University vice-president Ghassan al-Khatib said Palestinians have no choice but to focus on "internationalisation" through the UN, the International Criminal Court, international law and the campaign of boycott, divestment and sanctions (BDS). "Israel is dependent on the outside world: governments, parliaments, and public opinion. BDS [which can involve all three] is the choice of the Palestinians. BDS began here, at Bir Zeit... Europe can make changes in policy. The problem is with the US," he stated.

The Palestinian Authority "is bankrupt, the current leadership has no credibility with the public in the territories or the diaspora. We have to dig in our heels and stay put... find a way out of our lack of unity, have new faces in our leadership... Our political system is not healthy at all... and there is no peace camp in Israel." Palestinians like Ghassan once joined Israelis in the peace camp in trying to map out a route to the two-state solution. He and former Israeli peace partners were in despair.

Back in East Jerusalem at a leading Palestinian think tank, Mahdi Abdel Hadi summed up, "There is a crisis of leadership and a crisis of vision. There is no two-state solution and no one-state solution. We live under an apartheid regime. There is no challenge to the Israeli occupation."

Geneva, January 29th, 2016

After a meeting with Syria's UN ambassador Bashar al-Jaafari and his delegation, the UN's third envoy seeking peace in Syria, Staffan de Mistura declared peace talks had "started" in the expectation he would shortly hold discussions with the Riyadh-sponsored opposition team. "The first, immediate objective is to ensure talks are ongoing and everyone is on board."

The Saudi-backed Higher Negotiations Committee (HNC) had delayed the talks by four days by putting forward preconditions for participation. The HNC had insisted on being the sole representative of the opposition and demanded an end to sieges of insurgent held areas, a ceasefire and access for the delivery of humanitarian aid.

De Mistura had initially said no preconditions and argued that invitations would be sent to a broad range of Syrian opposition groups in line with UN Security Council resolution 2254 which had laid down the ground rules for the talks. Although granted the status as "main" opposition group, the HNC had refused to engage. Kurds fighting Islamic State had been excluded at the insistence of Turkey, and civil society and women's groups had been relegated to the status of advisors and consultants. HNC allies Saudi Arabia and Turkey said the team was free to leave Geneva at any time. De Mistura postponed the talks and everyone left.

The war continued. Government forces given air cover by Russia advanced against western, Turkish and Arab-backed insurgents, making the HNC all the more reluctant to talk peace while Damascus was fighting insurgent factions represented in the HNC.

Munich, September 9th-13th, 2015

Unarmed policemen in light blue short-sleeved uniform shirts and summer issue trousers walked a ragged oval of docile refugees through Munich railway station. Among the throng of men were two women, one in jeans and jacket, head uncovered, chatting with a man beside her; the other with a headscarf pushing a pram bearing a small child. At the ticketing office, clean-shaven Syrian men in knee length shorts and t-shirts carrying plastic bags and talking on mobile phones waited their turns to be summoned by clerks. Several were on my train to Regensburg, talking, staring out the windows at the glowing green fields and lush blocks of trees, roofs of pastel painted houses and white barns fitted with solar panels that provide 40 percent of Germany's power, the blue sky, a few clouds riding high. This was not their scene – or mine. In Syria, the landscape between dusty oases is seared brown, the flat roofed houses of cement, stone and raw breezeblocks do not sport solar panels although the sun is year round, and the sky soars to the heavens.

Elise, a doctor at a public health facility near Regensburg, said many of the refugees have injuries to their feet and ankles as well as problems with their legs and backs from walking great distances. Some have untreated or partially treated war wounds others were tortured. Injured and ailing refugees were referred to local hospitals. Since the stream of refugees through the centre moved quickly, Elise expressed frustration over her inability to treat trauma and other psychiatric disorders. She argued, "Germany needs a big emergency plan" to handle the influx.

Back in Munich where I stayed with Liza – the Liza who gave Godfrey the nickname of "Goffey," or "Gof" – refugees flowed through the railway station, busy with usual weekend traffic. Liza and I followed a group of German men and women wheeling trolleys piled with boxes of biscuits and bottles of water. We passed ramps where German trippers with bicycles and backpacks waited for trains to carry them to the mountains for a day in the sun. The volunteers stopped at a shelter where the next train from Salzburg was due to arrive. An elderly man and woman waited on a bench, unperturbed by the thought of the hundreds of Syrians, Iraqis, Afghans and counterfeit Syrians (non-Syrians claiming to be Syrians) pouring from the train the volunteers planned to meet.

Uncertain when the train from Austria was due to arrive, Liza and I went to the area outside the back gate of the station to see if there was any action at the tents where refugees were initially processed and given cursory health exams to make certain they were fit to travel to centres. At these facilities they were registered, tested for AIDS and other ailments, and held until they could be assigned to flats or refurbished army barracks in the provinces. Outside the barricade near the line of buses receiving refugees, stood a clutch of friendly Germans, some simply curious about the arrivals, others who understood they were witnessing a turning point in the history of Germany and Europe. Newcomers from the Middle East, Asia and Africa flowed in with the intention of staying on and by their presence, would transform the composition of the communities and societies where they settled.

The station, primed by the annual tsunami of visitors for Oktoberfest, easily handled the arrival of 14,000 refugees on the 12th. Germany's problem was how to house, feed, employ and educate the hundreds of thousands of desperate, often traumatised people once they arrived in the country. Their liberation came at a high price for Germany and other host countries.

Aleppo, March 12, 2017

World leaders, archaeologists, and historians were outraged over the devastation wrought during Syria's civil war on the Old City, a UNESCO World Heritage Site, which had largely survived since its construction between the 12th and 16th centuries during Arab and Ottoman rule. In July 2014 east Aleppo was seized by anti-government rebels whose advance through the Old City into west Aleppo was halted by the army. The rebels were gradually replaced by radical fundamentalists from various groups, some connected with al-Qaeda, who refused to budge. After heavy bombardment and siege the insurgents had left the ravaged east and the city was reunited under government control.

Inhabited for more than 8,000 years, Aleppo vies with Damascus in claiming to be the oldest continually inhabited city in the world. Aleppo was a key commercial centre on the Silk Road. Silk, horses, spices and technologies flowed along this route from the civilisations of Japan, China and India to Mesopotamia, Persia, Greece and the west. Aleppo was well known even to 16th century English dramatist William Shakespeare who referred to the city in Othello and Macbeth. From the19th century until unrest erupted in March 2011, foreign visitors flocked to Aleppo, drawn by its historic sites and covered markets.

Before the war, the 8th century Omayyad mosque was the spiritual and communal heart of the Old City. Post-war the mosque's distinctive 11th century square minaret was a pile of broken stones near the entrance. The minaret was either brought down by Syrian army tank fire; or rebel explosives during heavy fighting. Soldiers camped just inside the door to guard the vast, dusty compound and charred cloisters. On one wall a sandbagged insurgent firing position. The red carpets spread on the mosque floor were torn and covered in grit. A woman and her granddaughter walked around, site-seeing, without removing their shoes as is the custom when entering mosques, revealing the mosque was no longer regarded by local folk as a place of prayer and peace.

The massive Citadel, perched on a 50-meter mound, loomed over the city, its thick walls repelled shells, mortars and bullets while the Syrian army held firm. The Citadel is one of the world's most ancient castles; the current structure dates to the 13th century, although its foundations may go back to the 3rd millennium. Flight after flight of stone stairs led to the broad top where yellow flowers basked in the sun and spent bullet casings were scattered among stones. The city lay far below, its wounds shrouded in dust haze.

In the Old City's famous souk shops were destroyed or seriously damaged. Their carved wooden doors and panelling were smashed and burned. The market's narrow streets, laid out on a grid by 4th century BC successors of Alexander the Great, were littered with debris. Narrow, shallow shops had sold Aleppo's famous soap, others clothing made with Syria's fine cotton, Iranian carpets and perfumes distilled from rose petals and orange flowers. Elegant bijou hotels established in Ottoman mansions, restaurants, sweet shops, small factories and craft workshops have been obliterated, their owners forced to open elsewhere or find new occupations.

When I returned to Damascus, I went to see my friend, Syria's director of antiquities Maamoun Abdulkarim who said, "The damage in Aleppo is more than in all the other sites in the country. Thirty percent of the Old City is destroyed, catastrophic. Forty percent is good, and 30 percent has medium damage and can be restored." The ancient souk is, however, 60 percent destroyed. The Aga Khan Foundation has agreed to renovate the Citadel, the ancient souk and the Omayyad mosque. This amounts to 20 percent of the Old City. "

In spite of the painful, tragic loss, he adopted an upbeat view, "For me, Aleppo has been liberated from the war."

Amman, December 2010

Elegant in a black trouser-suit, Aysar greeted mourners entering her large flat. Arranged along the walls of the L-shaped salon were chairs for family and friends of Selma, who had died on October 7th, winning freedom from cancer and dementia. At the corner of the L were the chairs and microphones of the shaikh and musicians who would perform the religious service of the "*mawled*."

Selma's husband Qais greeted each newcomer gravely. The five musicians, led by sharp faced Hamed al-Saadi, Iraq's most famous praise singer, and a turbaned Sunni cleric accompanied by three other men, took their places. All were Iraqis. Only Iraqi Muslims hold such observances for their departed; elsewhere in the Arab world *mawleds* are staged only on the birthday of the Prophet

Muhammad or on saints' days. I had attended Nuha's modest *mawled* in Beirut in 2004.

Ma Radi, then 93, arrived in a flurry of hugs. Small and sturdy, curly grey hair, quick stepping behind her stick. Guests were still arriving as we took our seats. Although a dozen men had congregated near the musicians' corner, elsewhere men and women were interspersed rather than separated, the tradition in most Muslim gatherings mourning a lost relative or friend. Only three women wore headscarves. This was a Christian household with foreigners and Muslim and Christian Iraqis attending. Sitting side by side sat two Amals, one Shia, the other a Sunni, school friends whose fathers had rebelled against the British in 1920 and 1941. Iraqi painters, poets, archaeologists, and former diplomats, a husband and wife medical team from the US, a British photographer, and a Canadian war correspondent still based in Baghdad had come to honour Selma. The singers opened with songs of praise, pausing for silent recitation of the first verse of the Quran, the *Fatihah*. An elderly woman wept for Selma, for herself, for Iraq. On the wall opposite me was Nuha's painting depicting a snarl of wires atop an electricity pole in post-war Beirut. It might have been in post-war Baghdad.

The musicians improvised the melodic *maqam*, their voices fluctuating from soft, to harsh, to gentle. Saadi, a Shia, wove in references to the ongoing commemoration of *Muharram* when Shias commemorate the slaying of the Prophet's grandson, Hussein, at a battle in 680 at Karbala in Iraq. He slowly progressed from sorrow to celebration of Selma's life.

The gathering represented the old tolerant Iraq, the cosmopolitan Iraq of the Arab and Ottoman empires, the Iraq of the British colonial era and the republic declared in 1958. The Iraq where no one asked religion or sect. The Iraq that had survived Saddam Hussein's brutal but secular reign but fell apart when the US imposed a policy of divide-and-rule, setting Sunnis against Shias, Kurds against Arabs, and put into power exiled politicians with ethnic and sectarian agendas. Politicians about whom the Amals and Ma said, "Rode into Baghdad on the backs of American tanks."

EPILOGUE

LET US ABIDE A WHILE AND SEE INJUSTICE DONE

I don't. I fret and fume and, eventually, write. They say, "The pen is mightier than the sword," so a multi-tasking computer must be mightier than a brigade of swords. I write because I fight. The truth, perhaps, as I see it I admit, must be told, victims defended, bullies blasted. I have felt this from a very young age, infected by my mother's impotent rage over the way the US has treated its native citizens. Writing is a way to express rage against injustice in the hope of infecting others with rage.

Of course, I like writing. I like the feel of turning a phrase on the wheel of my brain, of placing it in the setting of a sentence and growing the sentence into a paragraph. Like a potter forming a bowl with his hands on a circling wheel.

When I agitated to rush from Lebanon to Cyprus after Turkey's invasion of the island during the summer of seventy-four, an irritated Godfrey quite rightly demanded, "What do you expect to do? You don't have a newspaper." He was right and wrong at the same time. I could have helped the Red Cross cope with the refugee crisis, perhaps. I felt powerless. I felt I had to do something. If only to witness injustice being done. Instead of sailing to Cyprus on the deck of a cargo ship, the only way to reach the island as the airport was closed, I stayed at home and looked after Marya, then four. Godfrey boarded a freighter, became the family witness and wrote about what happened for *The Economist*. He, above all, was driven by Housman's dictum that heads this afterword. Housman was Godfrey's favourite poet.

After I graduated from Mount Holyoke I believed I would escape deadlines. Deadlines for papers, for articles, and for columns in the college newspaper. Instead, I found new deadlines imposed by the Economic Research Institute at the American University of Beirut, deadlines for course papers and, ultimately, for my MA thesis. Once I left academia, more deadlines loomed and, once I was writing regularly for a daily newspaper, I had to confront not only deadlines but also travel for datelines where I witnessed events at first hand. If you have persisted with "*Windows*", you have seen that the book is a mix of datelines from the past, some happy, many deadly, most with insistent, dreaded deadlines of hours or even minutes.

Several years ago I was asked to speak to a crop of young *Deccan Herald* journalists about the job. Although it was unlikely that any would gain the privilege of becoming "foreign correspondents" – which I believe is the best job in the world – I told them to make the most of each and every article they were assigned and ensure the stories were interesting enough to catch the attention of readers. None of us achieves this objective with the majority of stories we suggest, are assigned, or submit. But once in a while one or other of us grabs a grand story, a story that tells us, and our readers something exceptional. Tahrir Square was just such a story. Hopefully, in these instances we write faithfully about the actors, their causes, and their dreams.

In 1962 when I settled in Beirut, the region's prospects were rosy. At the time of writing in 2015-17, the situation could not be worse. Tahrir Square was an aberration. A marvellous aberration. Within the charmed circle, surrounded by tanks and troops, Egyptians were one, unified across economic and social divides and classes: upper class women in elegant shawls carrying folding chairs, taxi drivers who had to scrabble for every penny, students, professors, lawyers and judges, Coptic Christians, ultra-orthodox Salafis, Muslim Brothers, civil servants by the busload, even the occasional army officer, revolutionaries all. But outside, at Talaat Harb, across Qasr al-Nil Bridge, lurked agents of the status quo devoted to counter-revolution. The promise of Tahrir never materialised. Egypt and the rest of the countries celebrating the Arab Spring were caught and crushed by the vice of the past.

Tahrir moments are rare. The Egyptian army crossing the Suez Canal in October 1973. Palestinians proclaiming independence in Algiers in November 1988 and walking down Salah ed-Din Street in East Jerusalem carrying a huge Palestinian flag after the signing of the Oslo accord on the White House lawn. My friend Selma al-Radi accepting the Aga Khan award for rescuing a 16th century palace in Yemen. Tahrir Square moments keep us going.

When I began my career by writing about the 1958 Iraqi revolution for *The Bay City Times* I saw my job as reporting what Iraqis thought about this seminal event in their modern history.

This, too, was a Tahrir moment. The moment Iraq finally shed foreign tutelage. The readers of that modest newspaper may have thought my contributions eccentric for a 17-year-old, but at least, the Iraqis I interviewed had a hearing. I progressed to analysing events with the aim of judging their impact on Middle Eastern countries and their citizens. My fourteen days in Tahrir Square gave me the opportunity to do both. I had access to Egyptians from all classes and walks of life. They were eager to say what they thought about the uprising and describe their post-revolutionary hopes and dreams. The world was riveted by events in Tahrir and Egyptians were able to put their views to peoples round the world thanks to non-stop satellite television and newspaper coverage.

A great deal has also been broadcast and written about the suppression of the revolution by the military with the collusion of the Muslim Brotherhood which had never trusted the majority of Egyptians who flowed into the square day after day. They were mostly secular not Brotherhood. When the Brotherhood's Muhammad Morsi was ousted from the presidency, *al-Jazeera* became the movement's cheerleader; western media complained he had been Egypt's first elected president. They did not examine why millions of Egyptians came to oppose him and the Brotherhood-dominated People's Assembly and *Shura* (consultative) Council.

Reporters covering the unrest in Syria took their cue from what had happened in Tahrir Square although the two cases were not the same at all. There were, of course, genuine Syrian revolutionaries and reformists who took to the streets to demand, "Bread, freedom and justice," as the Egyptians had done. But almost as soon as protests erupted, gunmen, armed groups and external forces sought to exploit the situation. Weapons of war flowed across the border from Lebanon: Syrians died at the barrels of the guns of security forces and rebels.

During Egypt's uprising Tahrir Square was generally safe for journalists but this was not the case for the squares and streets of Syria. Truth became an early casualty of the war waged by partisan media, which did not necessarily reflect the power struggle in Syria's cities, towns, villages and countryside. Since the government granted few visas to foreign journalists, they crossed illegally into Syria from Lebanon or Turkey, embedded with rebel factions and reported from that side. Government-controlled news was broadcast on local television stations while foreign satellite channels put out their own skewed version of events. Anti-regime Arab channels, Qatar's *al-Jazeera*, Saudi Arabia's *al-Arabiya*, and US-funded expatriate opposition *Barada* were prominent in the media campaign.

Political balance and Syrian voices were lost. Correspondents dismissed government coverage and fell captive to the opposition. This made it very difficult to obtain facts and break free of narratives produced by both sides in order to make independent assessments without being accused of being biased toward one or the other. The media claque applauded the rebels, the rest of us tried to keep our distance, our heads, and our ears open to the voices of Syrians crying out for an end to the war. During this conflict, the Israeli wars on Gaza, the West Bank, and Lebanon, and the US wars on Iraq, I have tried to be in watching and listening mode and to report what I saw and heard in an effort to reflect reality and avoid perpetrating the injustice of telling it wrong.

Dramatis Personae in Order of Appearance

Conor McNally, a graphic designer who has travelled the globe. He is the son of Islode Moylan and Tom McNally.

Isolde Moylan, Irish ambassador to Cairo during the 2011 uprising and representative to the Palestinian Authority during Ariel Sharon's invasion of the West Bank in 2002. She retired in 2015 after 40 years in the Irish diplomatic service. Born and raised in the US, Tom McNally, her husband, has had an interesting life travelling the globe with their family.

"Ma", my mother, Dorothy Ellen Kibby born in Salt Lake City in 1910. She married my father Robert Fancher and later Chauncey Wood. She had never left the US until she visited me in Beirut in 1965 when we went to Cairo, Jerusalem and Gaza.

Karin Leukefeld, a German journalist based in Bonn whom I met in Baghdad in 2003. We have often teamed up while covering events in Iraq, Egypt, and Syria.

"Mar", Marya Jansen Gruber, my daughter. Brian, is her husband, Brian Gruber, and Lili, their daughter, Elise Jansen Gruber.

Godfrey Jansen was my husband, partner, and dearest friend. He was a teacher, soldier, diplomat, journalist and author.

Lakhdar Brahimi, served as the Algerian National Liberation Front's representative in Tunis and elsewhere, independent

Algeria's ambassador to Cairo and London and under secretary general of the Arab League for cultural affairs. He was in charge of UN peacekeeping and served in South Africa and Haiti. He was Algeria's foreign minister and ended his career trying to make peace between warring Syrians. We became good friends over the years.

Liza Seymour, the daughter of Ian, highly respected oil expert working for Middle East Economic Survey, and Prue, a talented clothing designer. Liza graduated from Oxford, married Klaus Voegt, another Oxford graduate, and worked as a judge in the European Patent Court until 2016.

John and Peggy Carswell, former Beirutis. He is an artist, former professor of fine art at the American University of Beirut, visiting professor at the School of Oriental and African Studies in London, curator of the Oriental Institute at the University of Chicago, and director of the Islamic and South Asian department at Sotheby's. He and Peggy live in Spain.

Penny Thomas and Eric Bostic, our neighbours in Chemlan. They lived in an old house owned by Nimr Eid, the shopkeeper in the lower village.

Nicole Maillard, a close friend who works with the Canadian embassy in Beirut on development projects. During the civil war she was an anchor on Lebanese television and used to broadcast early morning news on the radio. Her first husband was Georges Corm, who became Lebanon's finance minister; her second ex-husband was Muhammad Mashnouk, who served as director of the national news agency during the civil conflict and eventually became environment minister.

The Radis, an Iraqi family: Suad, known by family and friends as "Ma;" archaeologist Selma trained at Cambridge; ceramist Nuha who studied in London; and architect Abbad, based in the United Arab Emirates.

Neville Thomas, an ex-British army officer who settled with his partner, Rosemary, in a house above Chemlan.

George and Elie Eid, sons of Nimr, who tutored Marya after her school closed. George married Leila in 1976 and joined us in our emigration to Cyprus.

Mr. Hayani, local staff member at the Indian embassy.

Abu Hamzeh, Muhammad Mashnouk's driver.

Khalil Hitti was a Chemlani and librarian at the British Council Library in Beirut.

Sami Said al-Ahmad was a professor of the ancient history of the Middle East. Born in Hillah in 1930,he took his first degree at Baghdad University and doctorate at the University of Chicago. He died in Baghdad in 2006.

Georges Abi Saab, an Egyptian of Lebanese descent who studied law at Harvard and politics and economics at other distinguished universities. He became honorary professor of international law at the Graduate Institute of International and Development Studies at Geneva and is a former ad hoc judge on the International Court of Justice and a former judge of the Appeals Chamber of the International Criminal Tribunal for the Former Yugoslavia and the International Criminal Tribunal for Ruanda.

Genevieve Maxwell, originally from the US, wrote a social column for Beirut's Daily Star newspaper.

Dyala Husseini, a member of one of Jerusalem's oldest families, lives in the city and oversees charitable foundations benefitting Palestinians.

Constantine Vlachopoulos, a Greek national, worked for the public information office of the United Nations Relief and Works Agency for Palestinian Refugees when I met him and later for the Pontifical Mission for Palestine.

Yusif Sayigh, professor of economics at the American University of Beirut and author.

Usama Khalidi, professor of biochemistry at the American University of Beirut, he served as the dean of the medical school at the University of Bahrain and became scientific advisor to Crown Prince Hassan of Jordan. He died in 2010.

Caroline Isber, my roommate for three years at Mount Holyoke, worked in radio in Boston before moving to Washington where she has made a career as a lobbyist for environmental issues.

Rasha Khalidi, the wife of distinguished professor Walid Khalidi, was a Lebanese political activist.

Israel Shahak was a Holocaust survivor, biochemist, dissident Israeli who fought for human rights for both Palestinians and Israelis. Following Israel's 1967 war and conquest of the West Bank, East Jerusalem and Gaza he campaigned against the occupation.

Amin Hafez was a Lebanese politician and member of parliament who briefly served as prime minister. Leila Ossairan Hafez was a writer and political activist.

John Hadidian was a Lebanese Armenian architect and artist; his wife, Aza, a painter of Ossetian origin.

Sulafa Khalidi Salam was a Beiruti lady of Palestinian origin. Our daughter Marya was named after daughter.

Soraya Antonius was a Palestinian activist and author of two novels. Her father George Antonius wrote The Arab Awakening,the classic study of the rise of Arab nationalism during the waning years of the Ottoman Empire. Her mother, Katy, was a socialite who founded an orphanage for Palestinian boys who lost their parents in Israel's 1948-48 war of establishment.

Michael Wall was an editor on The Economist and chief editor of Middle East International.

Willy Lazarus was Middle East correspondent of the Press Trust of India and served as Indira Gandhi's spokesman during the emergency, 1975-77.

Clovis Maksoud was a Lebanese academic, Arab League diplomat, and academic who headed the Centre for the Global South at American University in Washington, DC. He died in 2016. His wife was Hala Salam, a founding member of the American-Arab Anti-Discrimination Committee, who taught at George Mason University and Georgetown. She was recognised as a human rights activist. She died in 2002.

Munir Shamaa was a doctor of internal medicine and professor at the American University of Beirut who was world renown. He died in 2013.

Abdul Wahab Kayyali, "Abed," was an Arab nationalist, member of the Iraqi Baath party, author and publisher.

Zuhair al-Kadiri was the foreign minister of the Iraqi Baath party until the party and government were ousted by the US occupation in 2003.

Lamia al Gailani Werr is a London-based Iraqi archaeologist who has both worked in the field and in institutes and museums.

Suvi Raj Grubb was a producer of classical recordings at EMI studios in London. His wife, Chandra, was a cytologist specialising in cancer.

Mary Galle was a friend from high school in Bay City, Michigan.

Yasmine Mashnouk is the daughter of Nicole Maillard and Muhammad Mashnouk.

Charles Snow was a editor on Middle East Economic Survey.

Diana Markides is an academic, history professor and author; Sophocles Markides is a Cypriot businessman and mukhtar of the village of Fikardou.

Rachel Michaelides is an architect and painter; Andreas is an accountant, banker and genius chef.

Silvi Vreede is a former teacher of English in Nicosia; Joris is a businessman and bon viveur.

Eleni Protopapas was an inspector of schools for home economics and promoter of Cypriot handicrafts; Nicos taught chemistry at the English School in Nicosia. Both have written books about Cyprus.

Patrick Smyth, a former foreign editor of The Irish Times, has served as the paper's correspondent in Washington and Brussels.

Caoinmhe Butterly and Mary Kelly are Irish peace activists.

Adam Shapiro is a US political activist married to Palestinian colleague Huwaida Araf.

Mahdi Abdul Hadi heads the Palestinian Society for the Study of International Affairs (Passia) based in Jerusalem.

McGguire Gibson, “Mac”, is professor of Mesopotamian archaeology at the University of Chicago..

Imad Khadduri is an Iraqi nuclear scientist who attempted to counter US allegations about Iraq’s possession of weapons of mass destruction ahead of the 2003 war.

Aysar Akrawi, An Iraqi based in Jordan, is executive director of the Petra National Trust.

Godfrey, Marya, and Michael
in Cyprus

Beit el-Hindi in Chemlan,
Lebanon

Refugee Hajji in Cyprus,
after restoration

Michael during Hajj, January 1974.
Photo by Muhammad Amin, *Aramco World*

Godfrey and Michael at a meeting with Arafat
in Tunis in 1985

Women Walk Home,
Cyprus 1987

Michael with the Irish Battalion in South Lebanon,
July 2001

Media waiting for the end of the siege of the Church of the Nativity
in Bethlehem, May 2002

Suad "Ma" al-Radi
in Baghdad after 2003

McGuire Gibson and Selma and Nuha al-Radi
in Baghdad, 2003

The second-hand book market in Baghdad, 2003,
with Michael's book in the foreground

Magic Carpet fountain by Mohammad Ghani,
Baghdad 2003

The Amariya, Selma al-Radi's palace
in Yemen, 2005

Irish ambassador, Isolde Moylan in Tahrir Square, Cairo 2011
Photo by Karin Leukefeld

Waiting for Arafat's return for his funeral,
Ramallah, 2014

The street called Straight in the ancient city of Palmyra,
April 2016

The Bel Temple in Palmyra after *Daesh* was first driven from the site in April 2016

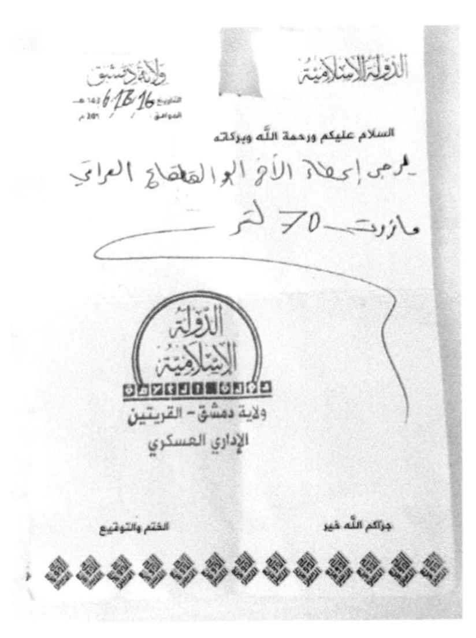

الدولة الإسلامية

ولاية دمشق

التاريخ 6/12/16 143 هـ

الموافق / / 201 م

السلام عليكم ورحمة الله وبركاته

يرجى إعطاء الأخ أبو القعقاع العراقي

مازوت 70 لتر

الدولة الإسلامية

ولاية دمشق - القريتين

الإداري العسكري

جزاكم الله خير

الختم والتوقيع

Receipt for fuel stamped by *Daesh* found at al-Qaryatain monastery, April 2016

Two views of the ancient souq in Homs:
One section cleared of rubble, the other partially restored, March 2017

Michael on the top of Aleppo's Citadel,
March 2017

The new Clock Tower: a symbol of Homs,
March 2017